Gentrification, Displacement
and Neighborhood Revitalization

SUNY SERIES IN URBAN PUBLIC POLICY
Mark Schneider and Richard Rich, Editors

Gentrification, Displacement and Neighborhood Revitalization

Edited by
J. JOHN PALEN *AND* BRUCE LONDON

State University of New York Press
ALBANY

Mulstein

HT

175

·G47

1984

Published by
State University of New York Press, Albany

© 1984 State University of New York

For information, address State University of New York Press, State
University Plaza, Albany, N.Y., 12246

Library of Congress Cataloging in Publication Data
Main entry under title:

Gentrification, displacement, and neighborhood
    revitalization.

    (SUNY series on urban public policy)
    1. Urban renewal—United States—Addresses, essays,
lectures.   2. Neighborhood—United States—Addresses,
essays, lectures.   3. Residential mobility—United
States—Addresses, essays, lectures.   4. Middle
classes—United States—Addresses, essays, lectures.
I. Palen, J. John.   II. London, Bruce.   III. Series.
HT175.G47   1984   307'.342'0973   83-5038
ISBN 0-87395-785-7 (pbk.)
ISBN 0-87395-784-9

Contents

Preface

This volume is divided into four sections: (1) Issues and Perspectives in Neighborhood Renovation, (2) Recent Research Findings on Gentrification, Incumbent Upgrading, and Displacement, (3) Comparative Cross-National Patterns, and (4) Concluding Remarks. The papers comprising part 1 provide an introduction to major issues in urban revitalization and an overview of salient theoretical perspectives. Chapters 2 and 3 elaborate several of the themes developed in the editor's introductory chapter, especially the various theoretical frameworks that are explicitly or implicitly used by researchers in interpreting their data. Irving L. Allen's discussion, "The Ideology of Dense Neighborhood Redevelopment," in chapter 2, is essentially sociocultural in its treatment of the ideologies undergirding neighborhood redevelopment. By contrast, Smith and LeFaivre's "Class Analysis of Gentrification," in chapter 3, provides a Marxian or *political-economic* analysis of aspects of the revitalization movement. It is also instructive to note that each of these chapters contains some information relevant to the proposed *"social movements"* interpretation of gentrification: chapter 1 discusses some of the demographic underpinnings of the movement. Allen focuses on ideologies that motivate the behavior of the cohort involved, and Smith and LeFaivre emphasize both the role of elites with land-based interests in promoting the movement and the conflictive, intergroup power relations involved in competition over the increasingly scarce resource of inner-city space.

Part 2 contains six articles describing empirical research projects in a variety of cities. DeGiovanni (chap. 4) measures some of the costs and benefits of revitalization in twelve neighborhoods in six cities. Baldassare (chap. 5) provides an overview of the extent of neighborhood revitalization in a strangely neglected site: New York City. In a rare panel study, Spain and Laska (chap. 6) re-examine the attitudes of renovators in New Orleans two years after their initial survey, while Palen and Nachmias (chap. 7) compare the attitudes of newcomers and old-time owners and renters in Milwaukee. In a pair of papers that focus on displacement, Lee and Hodge (chap. 8) confront the question of the vulnerability of the urban underclass, while Henig (chap. 9) looks specifically at the impact of gentrification on the elderly.

Part 3 contains three articles providing a cross-cultural perspective, another area too often overlooked. Canadian patterns in Vancouver are discussed by Ley in chapter 10. Patterns in Great Britain and in Europe are analyzed by Williams (chap. 11). In chapter 12, Kendig gives us some insight into comparative gentrification patterns in Australia. Interestingly, a reading of these cross-national studies immediately impresses one with the remarkable overall similarity in the processes attending gentrification and the patterns gentrification yields.

Finally, the concluding chapter by Palen and London briefly re-examines the state of our knowledge about gentrification, discusses the wider implication of the subject of gentrification in light of the evidence presented in this volume, and suggests possible future development and trends.

I

Issues and Perspectives in Neighborhood Renovation

INTRODUCTION

The focus of this section is on the major issues and perspectives in discussion of and debate about current questions of urban renovation, revitalization, and gentrification. Alternative theoretical approaches are detailed and discussed in order to assist the reader in placing the research studies of parts 2 and 3 in perspective.

Chapter 1 has three purposes. First, it provides an introduction to the state of knowledge in the field. It then identifies major current issues and areas of debate. Third, it outlines five alternative theoretical explanations in the literature for the occurrence of urban revitalization. These explanations are not mutually exclusive and, more often than not, have been only implicitly identified in the research literature. The five alternative approaches we identify are (1) demographic-ecological, (2) sociocultural, (3) political-economic, (4) community networks, and (5) social movements. We believe that an understanding of urban revitalization and its consequences can best be fostered by a more explicit acknowledgment and testing of alternative theoretical perspectives.

Since chapter 1 presents some discussion of the demographic-ecological appproach, we have chosen for chapter 2 a paper that typifies a sociocultural approach and, for chapter 3, one that takes a Marxist political-economic point of view. Papers systematically explicating the social networks and social movements theories of urban revitalization are not yet available.

Unlike the demographic-ecological approaches, sociocultural studies of gentrification do not focus on aggregate or structural units of analysis (i.e., populations and their characteristics). Rather, their explanation is derived from a socio-psychologial perspective that emphasizes the importance of value systems in interpreting behavior. Proponents of this point of view suggest that the increased clustering of middle- and upper-middle-class groups in inner-city enclaves can best be understood by looking at the values these people share.

It is frequently noted that those who are deciding to live in the inner city are highly educated young adults. By and large, this cohort was educated during the middle sixties to early seventies. At that time, new values were emerging that included a high regard for community participation, shared living experiences, self-help and cooperative efforts, and an ecological ideology that stressed preservation. In contrast, then, to the widely criticized suburban way of life, the inner city offered at least a portion of this cohort an oportunity to live out an emergent set of values—values that emphasize social participation and responsibility, a greater degree of acceptance of different ethnic and racial groups and of "deviant" lifestyles, or, in sum, an unprecedented degree of prourbanism.

Irving Allen's chapter, "The Ideology of Dense Neighborhood Redevelopment," explores in detail the impact of such value changes. Allen suggests that the back-to-the-city migration has undertones of ideology and utopia. He stresses the role of the prourban values of cultural diversity and pluralism and the search for a transcendent community experience in the middle-class repopulation of the central city.

Analyses falling under the heading of political-economic are clearly divided into traditional and Marxist approaches. The former tend to emphasize that inflation in suburban housing costs and rising transportion costs have created a decreasing supply of, and increasing demand for, middle-income housing. One result has been increased competition for inner-city space. Operating under these circumstances, market forces and the impersonality of the state are said to account for urban revitalization.

Marxist interpretations, on the other hand, rely less upon the "invisible hand" of political and economic forces. Rather, emphasis is placed on the role of economic interest and political power in guiding neighborhood change. A direct focus on intergroup power relationships and the uneven costs and benefits of revitalization often highlights the negative consequences of recent trends, especially the displacement of the poor.

The chapter by Smith and LeFaivre is a prototypical example of the emerging Marxist point of view. As such, it stands in rather sharp contrast to the majority of the more conservative pieces in this volume. This is especially the case in regard to Smith and LeFaivre's analysis of displacement—an analysis which suggests that the extent and severity of this phenomenon is significantly and purposefully underestimated by elites.

CHAPTER ONE

Introduction: Some Theoretical and Practical Issues Regarding Inner-City Revitalization

BRUCE LONDON AND J. JOHN PALEN

During the 1970s, the air was filled with lamentations about the urban crisis and the death of the city. Cities in general, and central-city residential areas in particular, were supposedly destined for inevitable decline. Now a new orthodoxy is appearing, one that hails urban regeneration and neighborhood revitalization. The media that once trumpeted decline and fall now feature stories of gentrification and neighborhood renewal. Such terms as *gentrification* and *revitalization* are now commonly used to refer to alterations in land-use patterns and changes in the composition of the neighborhood populations that are resulting in new social organizational patterns in inner cities throughout the United States and other industrialized Western nations. Our interest, in this volume, is the consequence of the widespread emergence of middle- and upper-middle-class enclaves in formerly deteriorated central-city neighborhoods. We are also concerned with the impact revitalization is having on other city neighborhoods.

Bruce London is Associate Professor of Sociology, Florida Atlantic University. J. John Palen is Professor of Sociology, Virginia Commonwealth University. Portions of this chapter appeared in London's 1980 paper, "Gentrification as Urban Reinvasion," in *Back to the City*, ed. S. B. Laska and D. Spain (New York: Pergamon Press). The material is presented here, in substantially revised form, with the kind permission of Pergamon Press.

Newspaper, magazine, or television features on central-city residential regeneration typically focus on a young, white, middle-class couple. Having purchased a dilapidated dwelling in a deteriorated area, the couple, with limited funds and limitless energy, is now tastefully restoring and rehabilitating the structure to its former glory. Displacement of previous tenants is seen as an inevitable, if lamentable, consequence. To what extent does this picture reflect the reality of the contemporary urban situation? How extensive is rehabilitation? Who is involved in rehabilitation? Does revitalization mean gentrification? Does renovation result in substantial displacement of former residents? What is the effect of neighborhood revitalization on the city as a whole? These questions—and others—beg for answers.

The newness of the phenomenon (most renovation has taken place since 1975) means that most answers must remain tentative. Nonetheless, some patterns are emerging. This volume will attempt to detail these patterns in both the United States and other highly urbanized nations. As such, it is a report on the state of the art as of the 1980s. The focus throughout will be on current empirical work on neighborhood renovation. Therefore, with few exceptions, the research reported in this volume is published here for the first time. Since there is a range of disciplines concerned with analyzing aspects of urban regeneration, and since there is among analysts considerable theoretical and ideological disagreement about the phenomenon, the papers gathered here are not written by members of one discipline alone, or by adherents to any single perspective Thus, the authors include political scientists, sociologists, planners, demographers, geographers, and members of urban affairs departments; further, in terms of theoretical or ideological perspectives, various papers can be characterized as conservative, liberal, or radical in their interpretations. Uniting all, however, is an emphasis on empirically researching the contemporary patterns of change in the urban neighborhood.

DEFINITIONS AND INTERPRETATIONS

The goals of this introduction are both descriptive and analytical. In particular, we first provide the baseline knowledge necessary to an understanding of the unprecedented changes taking place today in inner-city neighborhoods. We then specify the major issues, debates, and disagreements that are current in the analysis of this phenomenon. We can begin to address both of these goals by dealing with some preliminary definitional considerations in order both to specify the matter at hand and to dispel some of the harmful or misleading myths that have developed.

Urban literature uses, often without definition, terms such as *urban regeneration, urban revitalization, gentrification, neighborhood renewal, rehabilitation,* and *renovation* (Clay 1979; Gale 1976, 1977). A cursory search of the literature reveals that the form of neighborhood change we are studying has also been called a "back-to-the-city movement" (Laska and Spain 1980) and "urban reinvasion" (London 1980). The existence of such a welter of terms to describe the very same phenomenon is not simply meaningless terminological entrepreneurship. One of the lessons of the sociology of knowledge is that words are not passive; indeed, they help to shape and create our perceptions of the world around us. The terms we choose to label or describe events must, therefore, convey appropriate connotations or images of the phenomenon under consideration in order to avoid serious misunderstandings. In fact, one source of the existing theoretical and ideological disagreements about current inner-city neighborhood change may well be that the terms used by different scholars reflect different perceptions of the phenomenon and of its significance. Thus, a discussion of definitions and the dissolution of myths go hand in hand.

This point is illustrated by a consideration of the widespread conception that inner-city changes reflect a back-to-the-city movement. Early descriptive accounts of neighborhood changes popularized this term, along with its implication that the renovators were ex-suburbanites returning to the city from the suburbs outside the city. It has become clear, however, that no such significant migration pattern exists. There is currently no support for the back-to-the-city (i.e., suburb-to-city) hypothesis from census and other Federal data sources (Long 1980). Many case studies also confirm that central-city newcomers are not dissatisfied suburbanites throwing off the yoke of suburban dullness for a return to the excitement of city life.

Rather, study after study confirms that renovators represent a stay-in-the-city pattern among some younger, dual wage-earner families. Gale's (1976, 1977, 1980) findings for Washington, D.C., and those of Palen and Nachmias (1982) for Milwaukee, suggest that much neighborhood revitalization is a result of movement from neighborhood to neighborhood *within* the inner city. In other words, a substantial portion of the upgrading of inner-city areas is the result of internal movement, not migration into the city from the suburbs. Indeed, even among younger, upwardly mobile, white-collar families, the major population flow continues to be from, rather than toward, the central city. (Between 1975 and 1978, American central cities underwent a net loss of more than four million people [U.S. Bureau of the Census 1978].) Thus, while the belief that Americans are coming back to the city may be the profound hope of central-city mayors, it is not the message of the most recent census data.

If the term "back-to-the-city" is to have any utility at all, it will come, not from its erroneous suppositions about migration patterns, but from its implication that there is a renewed interest in city living among a limited but influential group of middle-class home buyers (see Spain and Laska, chapter 6).

Another area of confusion stems from the use of the word "gentrification" as a generic description of neighborhood revitalization. In a manner similar to the term "back-to-the-city," "gentrification" yields erroneous perceptions of current changes in inner-city neighborhoods (see Palen and Nachmias, chapter 7). Although it is probably the most widely used concept, gentrification is inappropriate for summarizing the process of upper-status groups replacing lower-status groups in inner-city neighborhoods that had previously experienced "decline." The dictionary defines "gentry" as a person of gentle birth; the condition or rank of a gentleman; upper or ruling class; aristocracy; landed proprietors of noble class. Thus the term "gentrification" suggests the return of some sort of landed aristocracy to the inner city from some place outside the urban area.

The best evidence available to date suggests that this is not what is happening in American cities. The term gentrification was apparently coined by Ruth Glass (1964) to describe changes in London neighborhoods in the late 1950s and 1960s. The term "gentry" is historically more appropriate for describing British stratification patterns than American. However, since a process of the changing social-class composition of neighborhoods is occurring in both societies (as well as in Canada, Europe, and Australia), we need a term that is not culture specific (see chap. 10-12).

A final criticism of the term " gentrification " questions whether those people who are the "actors" in the process are, in fact, "gentry" even in the broad sense of being upper middle class. Especially in the early stages of neighborhood change, the renovators themselves may be only marginally middle class. Newcomers are attracted to revitalizing areas because house prices are moderate compared to other alternatives, and their own economic resources are limited. Rather than money, they provide "sweat equity" with their own do-it-yourself labor. Such renovators hardly fit the classical image of a "gentry" and, in sum, the image of a returning aristocracy conveyed by the term "gentrification" is clearly inappropriate if we are seeking a concept of wide comparative applicability and precision.

Neighborhood revitalization may involve social mobility without spatial mobility. London's (1980) observations in certain areas of East Boston lead to this conclusion. It is not uncommon for second- or third-generation inhabitants of a house, many of whom have been upwardly mobile intergenerationally, to inherit the dwelling from their parents, upgrade the physical structure, and remain as adults in the neighborhood in which they grew up. In the process, whole neighborhoods may change in apearance and, to a degree, in social class without any appreciable migration. This suggests that sentiment and symbolism (Firey 1945) may well be relevant ecological variables for the understanding of certain aspects of the revitalization of inner-city neighborhoods. The "meaning" of neighborhood for upwardly mobile residents of longstanding may contribute to the reversal of patterns of deterioration.

This is not unrelated to Clay's (1978, 1979) suggestion that neighborhood revitalization involves the two distinct processes of "incumbent upgrading" and "gentrification." (See also Baldassare's discussion, in chapter 5, of different types of neighborhood revitalization.) According to Clay, incumbent upgrading tends to occur in solid working-class or blue-collar neighborhoods where settled, older families with dependent children predominate. After upgrading, however, a substantial increase occurs in the number of both young families and lower-middle-class families. Although Clay attributes such changes in social characteristics to "inmigration of a replacement cohort," it is entirely possible that a portion of the change results from the process of local intergenerational upward mobility as young adults take over their childhood homes or "come back to the old neighborhood" after a period of apartment living. As some substantial portion of the change occurring in inner-city neighborhoods today is *not* a function of migration into the city from points outside the city, it is likewise a mistake to identify renovation as being synonymous with "newcomers."

Another concept worthy of note is the term "urban reinvasion" (London 1980). Urban sociologists, especially those who incorporate the insights of human ecology into their work, have had a long tradition of discussing changes in the composition of social class in inner-city neighborhoods in terms of the invasion-succession cycle (Burgess 1925; McKenzie 1926). Invasions are of two types: those that result in changes in land use and those that result in changes in population composition. The present concern is with the latter process of group displacement. If the original occupants of an area are completely displaced because another population has moved in and assumed residence, a succession has occurred.

A very common conception of the implication of the invasion-succession cycle—and one that is crucial in the present context—is that "when one type of residential use is succeeded by another, the area usually becomes less desirable as a place to live"; also, "cases of neighborhood deterioration far outweigh cases of improvement" (Gist and Fava 1964: 173). In other words, the invasion-succession cycle usually results in the replacement of higher-status groups by lower-status groups in particular, and the deterioration of the neighborhood in general.

This is a misconception in some instances of the invasion-succession process. London (1980) contends that the current reversals of the commonly held pattern—that is, the replacement of lower status groups by higher status groups—may be understood as an extension or continuation of the invasion-succession process, one that may legitimately be called reinvasion. This is in no way meant to imply the inevitability of cycles of invasion, succession, and reinvasion. Rather, the suggestion is that change in the composition of a neighborhood's social class may be understood as a movement along a continuum that ranges from high to low status.

Most studies of succession emphasize decline and deterioration. Theoretically, however, movement can occur in either direction along the continuum. McKenzie (1924, 1926) clearly recognized this in his early discussions of the process. He noted that the socioeconomic characteristics of a neighborhood may "rise or fall" as a result of invasion, and that although the displacement of a higher by a lower cultural group is historically the more common process, there are sometimes cases in which "a higher economic group drives out the lower-income inhabitants" (1926, p.31). With reinvasion, we have an unprecedented number of examples of movement from low to high status. This, however, in no way implies that all declining neighborhoods will reverse themselves.

Reinvasion does imply that, in a rather unanticipated reversal of the common pattern, upper-status groups are replacing lower-status groups in inner-city areas and, in so doing, they are (in a sense) reclaiming the territory they once held prior to its deterioration. As they purchase and renovate old "Victorians" and "brownstones," they are reinvading the space that once was theirs and had been taken by other social classes. In the process, other people are displaced. If we view this displacement as a form of involuntary movement imposed upon lower-status groups, then the connotations of "invasion" take on additional relevance.

In a related vein, Weiler (1978) described current urban

reinvestment patterns as being governed by a "beachhead mentality." This yields an image of reinvasion proceeding incrementally, with each building on each block serving as a "foothold" for further advances. The "combative" nature of the process is further highlighted by accounts of tension between newcomers and earlier residents in changing neighborhoods (Cybriwsky 1978a, 1978b). This sort of conflict is, of course, nothing new. As McKenzie noted in 1924, "the early stages [of an invasion] are usually marked by keenness of competition which frequently manifests itself in outward clashes." Also relevant is the formation of block organizations and antispeculation groups (Goldfield 1980) by long-term area residents as reactions to reinvasion-displacement and as attempts to "defend" their neighborhoods (Suttles 1972).

It is clear that the process of reinvasion is often characterized by intergroup conflict. This very conflict calls into question the connotations of still another term widely used to describe the phenomenon: *urban revitalization*. As Hudson (1980) notes, this term seems to suggest that the transformations occurring in these neighborhoods are positive. Such an assumption may reflect the sort of middle-class ethnocentrism that views the replacement of low-status groups by middle-class groups as beneficial by definition. It thus ignores the fact that many of the working-class neighborhoods undergoing reinvasion are indeed already "vital." They possess viable social networks that function to meet the needs of their populations (Hudson 1980; Hunter 1974; Kornblum 1975; Suttles 1968). In fact, much of the conflict that occurs stems from the very vitality of the community undergoing invasion.

Our intention in this discussion of definitions is not to advocate the superiority of one or another of the terms mentioned, but to sensitize ourselves to the descriptive parameters of the phenomenon at hand and to the issues involved in its analysis. To an unprecedented degree, selected inner-city neighborhoods are changing in population composition from low to high status. The migration patterns involved in this change tend to be predominantly intraurban, although both newcomers and incumbents may contribute to the changing appearance of formerly deteriorated areas. Also, intergroup competition and conflict are salient aspects of the phenomenon. In other words, the changes occurring in inner cities today have important—and highly controversial—theoretical and policy implications. Let us turn now to the question of how extensive these changes might be. As will become clear, this too is a matter of debate.

AMOUNT OF GENTRIFICATION

To date, the best evidence on the amount of gentrification in the United States is found in the work of Lipton (1977), Clay (1979), and Black (1975, 1980). Lipton's study of the twenty largest cities in the United States was designed to see if the centers of these cities had experienced an increase in the number of middle- and upper-class neighborhoods during the 1960s. While not all of the cities showed evidence of revival, at least half did show improvement. Significantly, this revival was associated with high levels of white-collar employment and long commuting distances to the suburbs.

In 1977, Clay (1979) conducted a survey of neighborhood change in the 30 largest American cities. He found evidence of change in 105 neighborhoods in these cities. Of these, he considered 48 to be instances of incumbent upgrading and 57 to be gentrification. He described gentrification as a small, but widespread phenomenon, observable in all regions of the country, and found in many smaller cities as well. But he emphasized that "gentrification neighborhoods account for only a tiny fraction of any city's neighborhoods and housing stock" (Clay 1978, p. 17).

Additionally, in 1975, the Urban Land Institute (Black 1975) conducted a mail and telephone survey of the 260 American central cities with populations of 50,000 or more. From the results received, it was estimated that some degree of "private-market nonsubsidized housing renovation in older, deteriorated areas" is occurring in almost half of these cities and, when considering only cities of 500,000 or larger, estimates suggest that almost three-quarters are experiencing this type of renovation activity. (See Baldassare, chap. 5, for data on activities in New York.) In a 1979 survey update, Black (1980) found that renovation had spread to even more cities, with activity being reported in 86 percent of cities with more than 150,000 residents. (See DeGiovanni, chap. 4, for analysis of the costs and benefits of revitalization.)

Certainly it is clear that there is activity in cities in every section of the nation. However, it is also clear that, to date, revitalization has taken place in only a handful of any one city's neighborhoods. Renovating areas, particularly those attracting middle-class inmovers, are usually neighborhoods that were originally built to house the elite of an earlier era. Although the residences are in various states of decline, they were originally constructed with hardwood woodwork, marble mantels, leaded glass, brass fixtures, and other features of high quality. Such overall quality is rarely available in contemporary middle-class structures. Also the neighborhoods are generally situated favorably within the city, having good transporation access to the central business district. Obviously only a limited number of city neighborhoods have these characteristics. Most of the housing in most cities was built to house workers rather than owners or managers. Thus, if neighborhood revitalization is to have impact on city housing stock, renewal will have to spill over beyond former elite areas into the far more numerous "gray areas" of the city. (See chap. 7 for a case study of a revitalizing working-class neighborhood.) The future of the renovation movement, and in fact the ultimate future of the city as a place of residential choice, will depend on the extent to which restoration and renovation become increasingly widespread.

DEGREE OF DISPLACEMENT

In addition to questions about the extent of renovation, perhaps the major unanswered question is whether inner-city revival also means widespread or significant displacement of poor people from the neighborhoods undergoing change. In this context, displacement most frequently refers to the forced involuntary dislocation of needy households (i.e., the poor, blacks, ethnic minorities, the aged). The data on this question are not so much ambiguous as they are contradictory. A 1978 National Urban Coalition survey of urban officials and experts in forty-four cities indicated that displacement was a real problem. This report is frequently misidentified as an empirical study of gentrification and displacement. In reality, however, it is a survey, not of actual displacement, but of the opinions of experts regarding what they believed to be occurring. Clearly, its findings must be interpreted in this light.

A number of case studies conducted in such cities as Washington (Gale 1980), Philadelphia (Cybriwsky 1978a, 1978b), and Boston (Auger 1979) do attempt an empirical documentation of displacement trends. By and large, such studies attest to the significance of displacement, although more emphasis is placed on its disruptive meaning for the people involved than on its quantitative dimensions.

On the other hand, aggregate national data seem to indicate that displacement is not as serious a problem as case studies would portray (Grier and Grier 1980; Sumka 1980). The Griers (1980, pp. 260-61), for example, suggest that the number of people displaced by private-market rehabilitation is quite small—on the order of 100 or 200 people per year in most cities. In some cities, like Washington or San Francisco, displacement is more common. But, even here, the Griers estimate annual displacement to be "in the low thousands at most." These researchers suggest that concern with displacement tends to distract attention from more important policy issues.

The developing consensus—if indeed consensus is the appropriate term—as expressed by U.S. Department of Housing and Urban Development (HUD) reports appears to be that displacement is as yet only a serious problem in selected cities (1981). In most cities, gentrification—and thus potential displacement—has been limited by slow, or in some cases no, growth of white-collar jobs in the central city (Lipton 1977), as well as by the concentration of gentrification in only a few neighborhoods of any one city and the relatively slow pace of gentrification within many of those neighborhoods where it is occurring.

Nationwide patterns of high interest rates during the early 1980s have slowed both central city renovation and new construction in the suburbs. Whether there will be a dramatic expansion of gentrification and concomitant displacement as interest rates decline and construction activity increases is a matter of some dispute. As of the early 1980s, however, high costs for construction and rehabilitation, and high interest rates, were acting as a deterrent to all housing change.

This debate over the nature and extent of displacement is clearly reflected in the chapters of this volume. DeGiovanni (chap. 4) and Lee and Hodge (chap. 8), for example, both suggest that gentrification-induced displacement is only one type of involuntary dislocation. In fact, displacement is not a problem limited solely to either revitalizing neighborhoods or the urban core; it is found in suburbs and nonrevitalizing urban areas as well. This, however, should not be taken to mean than displacement caused by gentrification is limited in scope, impact, or importance.

Indeed, the papers in this volume present strong evidence that members of the urban "underclass" (DeGiovanni, chap. 4; Lee and Hodge, chap. 8)—including lower-income, black female-headed households, and especially the elderly (Henig, chap. 9) living in inner-city neighborhoods—bear a disproportionate share of the costs and burdens of displacement. Smith and LeFaivre's class analysis of gentrification and displacement (chap. 3) argues this point most forcefully by suggesting that the extent of displacement may be deliberately underestimated by official sources in order to encourage gentrification. Thus, it is becoming clear that gentrification-induced displacement may be more extensive than the major studies to date have indicated but that, regardless of the numbers involved, whenever and wherever it does occur, displacement imposes the greatest costs on those people who are least able to bear them.

ALTERNATIVE EXPLANATIONS OF URBAN REINVASION

We have now gathered and assimilated enough baseline information to begin to answer the questions posed earlier about gentrification and displacement and to understand why disputes arise when those questions are asked. But we have yet to move beyond description toward explanation and analysis. This is because, until recently, instances of residential upgrading have been rare; neighborhood deterioration and decline have been the norm. Now the widespread and unprecedented process of urban reinvasion of the last decade has rendered these generalizations invalid.

Like all new phenomena, gentrification has stimulated a variety of reactions, interpretations, and evaluations. Some observers see in this process the coming end of the urban crisis; others stress the increasing impoverishment of the displaced. Some feel the process has primarily economic antecedents; others see it as a function of changing demographic forces. In the following section, we will attempt to organize and summarize this diversity of analysis and to specify the place of each succeeding chapter within this theoretical diversty.

A review of what literature exists reveals the use (at least implicitly) of five alternative "explanations" of urban reinvasion: (1) demographic-ecological, (2) sociocultural, (3) political-economic, (4) community networks, and (5) social movements. Each of these "theories" will be discussed in turn. Before beginning, however, two points must be made. First, these approaches are not mutually exclusive. They point to constellations of factors that tend to be emphasized by given observers, but a satisfactory interpretation of the phenomenon of urban reinvasion should incorporate insights from all perspectives. Second, each theory will be dealt with only in barest outline. The discussion is meant to be suggestive of analytical insights and, perhaps, researchable hypotheses; it does not pretend to be a complete, logically well-developed statement of any given theory or of the potential for synthesis among theories.

Demographic-Ecological

Demographic-ecological approaches emphasize the variables in "the ecological complex": population, social organization, environment, and technology (Duncan 1959). One variation on this theme begins by hypothesizing that recent changes in both population composition and basic demographic processes have, in the aggregate, contributed to reinvasion—itself a form of migration. The coming of age of the baby boom generation is one factor frequently cited in this regard (Bourne 1977; Cades n.d.; Clay 1978,

1979; Kern 197). By the 1980s the growing percentage of the population between the ages of 25 and 35 was placing tremendous demands on the housing supply. This demand will continue throughout the decade as succeeding cohorts enter this stage of the life cycle. This demand is being met, in part, by the "recycling" of inner city neighborhoods.

Several other demographic factors are seen to be important. For example, the rising age at first marriage; improved contraceptive methods and declining fertility rates; later birth of the first child; increasing entry of both single and married women into the labor force; and the rising number of dual wage-earner families are all well documented, recent demographic changes (Cades n.d.). These factors are not only reciprocally related but, in a variety of ways, they may also contribute to reinvasion. Taken together, they may represent a decline of the "familism" that played such an important part in the postwar flight to the suburbs (Bourne 1977; Cades n.d.; Kern 1977).

Relatively affluent, young, child-free couples, who need not worry about the quality of inner-city schools and the shortage of playgrounds, are more likely to choose to live in the city, close to places of work and adult recreation. To the extent that aggregate demographic changes are producing more family units of this type than ever before, we have another partial explanation of urban reinvasion in the 1970s.

A second type of demographic-ecological explanation (perhaps more ecological than demographc) is hinted at in the literature on reinvasion. The starting point for this analysis is Lipton's (1977) finding that "central city revival" is positively correlated with white-collar, administrative activity in the central business district (CBD) and negatively associated with blue-collar or industrial activity. These data might be profitably analyzed using techniques recently developed to test an ecoloical explanation of migration and population redistribution (Frisbie and Poston 1975, 1978; Sly 1972; Sly and Tayman 1977). Building on the work of Gibbs and Martin (1959), this research has found that variations in "sustenance organization" (i.e., the number, mixture, and salience of various primary, secondary, and tertiary sustenance activities) are strongly related to patterns of population change.

It may well be that cities whose sustenance organizations are disproportionately high in white-collar activity and low in blue-collar activity are those most likely to experience reinvasion. These speculations take on added significance (and the ecological explanation seems all the more worthy of empirical testing) in light of the recent trends toward the decentralization of industry and the increasingly corporate nature of the nation's major inner cities.

Sociocultural

A second theoretical thrust in the literature on reinvasion is sociocultural. Here, explanation focuses not on aggregate or structural units of analysis (i.e., populations and their characteristics) but on values, attitudes, ideas, choices, and beliefs as factors determining human behavior. Actually, the distinction between demographic-ecological and sociocultural approaches is in certain respects a false dichotomy. It parallels the debate *within* theoretical human ecology between "materialist/neo-classical" and "non-materialist/sociocultural" ecologists (Bailey and Mulcahy 1972; Sjoberg 1965; Willhelm 1962). The essence of the sociocultural point of view is the suggestion that no ecological phenomenon, including urban reinvasion, can be fully understood if the focus of explanation is solely on structural phenomena to the exclusion of those learned, cultural values that often motivate individual behavior. Firey's (1945) classic study of "sentiment and symbolism as ecological variables" illustrates the salience of "culture" in determining locational choices and land-use patterns.

A wide variety of specific causes of reinvasion fall under the general sociocultural rubric. Some of these emphasize changing values, attitudes, and lifestyles as factors contributing to the new migration of middle-class and upper-middle-class people to the center city. This sort of analysis may present a challenge to the conventional wisdom regarding the pervasiveness of an antiurban ideology or value system in the U.S. (Allen, chap. 2). It has long been stressed that some sort of "rural ideal" (Warner 1962) motivates our location choices. The suburbs, in this view, provide a compromise between the rural lifestyle we seek and our need to be near employment and services in the city. It is possible that greater proportions of our population are now developing a prourban value system, that this may well be reciprocally related to the demographic changes stressed above, and that such changes in values or lifestyle preferences also contribute to the trend toward urban regeneration.

Indeed, some literature does suggest that the degree of antiurbanism of the American value system has been exaggerated and that prourban values are far more salient than usually recognized (Glaab and Brown 1967). For example, in chapter 2, Allen suggests that urban reinvasion has undertones of ideology and utopia. He stresses the role of the prourban values of cultural diversity and pluralism and the search for a transcendent community experience in the middle-class repopulation of the central city.

If such value changes are under way, they may have a tendency to become cumulative. People often do what is in vogue. If enough "urban pioneers" define the inner city as an appropriate place to live and then proceed to demonstrate its viability, many others may follow their lead. The result is "inner city chic" and, ultimately, rapid rates of reinvasion.

Another variation on the sociocultural approach seeks to explain reinvasion in terms of dominant American values rather than changing values. Fusch (1978), for example, focuses on a number of the core cultural values stressed by Williams (1970), for example, economic success, individuality, and so on. He suggests that reinvasion may be understood within this value structure. The restoration of a home in an inner-city (possibly historic) area may be a new way to realize the old values of the expression of self-identity and the symbolization of material success. The need for new means to express such a long-standing goal, however, may itself be an expression of such cultural phenomena as the Bicentennial (with its rediscovery of the American past), the Historic Preservation movement, and the waves of nostalgia sweeping the nation. Regardless of whether we are dealing with core values, value changes, or value conflicts, the fact remains that sociocultural factors must be taken into consideration for a full understanding of reinvasion.

Political-Economic

The third type of explanation of reinvasion might well be called political-economic. Analyses falling under this general heading are clearly divided into traditional and Marxist approaches. The former tends to emphasize competition, supply and demand, market efficiency, the impersonality of the liberal state, while the latter focuses on intergroup power relationships and the uneven costs and benefits of neighborhood change.

As an example of a traditional approach, Cades (n.d.) explains "urban residential reconstruction" at least partly in terms of conventional economic theory and the political and legal changes of the late 1950s and early 1960s. He sees the decreasing availability of suburban land, rampant inflation in suburban housing costs, rising transportation costs, and the relatively low cost of slum "shells" interacting to encourage reinvasion. Political factors complement this trend. For example, Cades argues that civil rights legislation has played an unanticipated role in reinvasion. Antidiscrimination laws in employment and housing and school desegregation laws have contributed to decreasing segregation in suburbs. Increased interracial contacts have led to decreases in prejudice (the contact hypothesis) and, in terms of population redistribution, the suburbs have become open to some blacks while the inner city is no longer automatically rejected by some whites as a place to live.

Marxist approaches rely less on the so-called invisible hand of political and economic forces in their analysis of reinvasion. Smith (1979), for example, suggests that "American gentrification has been actively planned and publicly funded." Emphasis here is placed on the role of economic interests and political power in guiding neighborhood change. The questions of Who decides? Who benefits? and Who pays? are addressed. The implication is that powerful interest groups follow a policy of neglect of the inner city until such time as they become aware that policy changes could yield tremendous profits. Then, policies change accordingly, with little regard for those powerless inner-city residents who will be displaced from their homes. All this is legitimated by reference to the public interest and predictions of the end of the urban crisis.

The image of the city as a growth machine guided by land-based interest groups is potentially appropriate here (Molotch 1976). A loose coalition of business leaders, large developers, and large financial institutions plays a significant role in the development *and* underdevelopment of a city's space. Smith (1979) suggests that such interest groups actually "developed areas as slums" in the 1950s by their refusal to lend money for productive investment. Reversals of such redlining policies are increasingly common today as powerful clients, aware of the profit to be made in inner cities, are persuading lending institutions to finance rehabilitation projects in areas formerly considered too risky. These efforts are often accompanied by the sort of advertising "boosterism" (Molotch 1976) that is designed to encourage the return of the middle class to the city.

Smith and LeFaivre's "A Class Analysis of Gentrification" (chap. 3) is an excellent example of the Marxist approach to the analysis of urban reinvasion. Especially noteworthy are their closely related concepts of "the rent gap" and "the movement of capital." The rent gap refers to "a gap between the ground rent actually capitalized with a given land use at a specific location and the ground rent that could potentially be appropriated under a higher and better land use at that location." The development of such a rent gap is seen to be a basic prerequisite for gentrification. It enables developers to purchase and rehabilitate structures while still generating a profit. In turn, however, a prerequisite for the development of such a rent gap is the movement of capital out of, and then back into, the neighborhood.

According to Smith and LeFaivre, investment capital was

systematically moved out of inner cities and into the suburbs following World War II because profit rates were higher in the suburbs. The subsequent deterioration of inner-city neighborhoods set the stage for development of the rent gap. This, in turn, made it possible for capital to return to the central city in search of emergent potential profits. In elaborating upon this argument, Smith and LeFaivre emphasize that gentrification is the product of decisions made by land-based interest groups ("those most able to control the real estate market"). As a class, these groups benefit financially from their decisions, while the costs of gentrification fall disproportionately on the urban underclass (see Lee and Hodge, chap. 8) in the form of displacement.

A number of additional links between urban political economy, in general, and the analysis of reinvasion, in particular, may be noted in papers compiled by Tabb and Sawers (1978). Gordon's (1978) analysis of the relationship between the stages of capital accumulation and urban form is just one example. In part, Gordon shows that the commercial, industrial, and corporate stage of capital accumulation are each conducive to different distributions of people and functions in space. Industrial accumlation, in particular, encouraged the polarization of cities and suburbs by race and class. The corporate city, on the other hand, is characterized by the decentralization of industry and the dispersal of working-class residential areas, on the one hand, and a proliferation of corporate headquarters and employment opportunities in the tertiary sector, on the other. Remembering the earlier reference to the correlation between central-city revival and administrative activity (Lipton 1977), we would suggest that "the stage of capital accumulation" is another possible factor contributing to reinvasion.

Community Network

The fourth general aproach to studying revitalizing areas is to view the community as an interactive social group. This community approach has a long history in sociological research. Classic case studies, such as those by Wirth (1938), Whyte (1943), and Suttles (1968), have examined neighborhoods as microsocieties. Indeed, some critics charge that "urban sociology has tended to be *neighborhood sociology*" (Wellman and Leighton 1981, p. 80, emphasis in original). The community approach directly confronts the basic sociological question of how groups interact and maintain interpersonal ties within a socioeconomic system stressing division of labor, diversity, and perceived hostility of a larger society. As such, the community approach occupies a crucial juncture between the macrolevel demographic and microlevel sociocultural approaches. Questions relating to the persistence and viability of kinship, community involvement, and social networks are integral to the community approach.

The classical (1920-30) Chicago School's description of community change has been most often popularized and stereotyped by Louis Wirth's (1938) essay, "Urbanism as a Way of Life." Based on the theoretical writings of Weber, Marx, Durkheim, and Simmel (particularly the latter two), the work emphasized the destruction of local attachments and the emergence of mass society. This emphasis on "Eclipse of community" (Stein 1961) has more recently been characterized as the "community lost" perspective (Hunter 1978). Technological changes in transportation and communication were seen as replacing the spatially and temporally bound world of the local community with large-scale political and social organizations (Greer 1962). The role of the neighborhood was perceived as becoming sharply limited and circumscribed (Fischer 1976). Such "residual," "minimalist," or "liberated" neighborhoods are viewed as representing the future (Wellman and Leighton 1981). By contrast, place-based social neighborhoods remain as (overstated by Webber [1968]) "the last viable remnants of pre-industrial societies." In this view, existing close ethnic and other central-city neighborhoods are only remnants of a past age.

Contrasting with the above are theorists of the "community saved" or "emergent" view. Those holding the community-saved prespective (Hunter 1978; Suttles 1972) suggest that, rather than mass society's resulting in a breakdown of community, there may be, today, an increase in community activity, involvement, and commitment. The process of inner-city neighborhood revitalization and local upgrading would be seen as one consequence of these changes. Rather than focusing on the loss of local sentiments, the question is, for whom are local cohesion and neighborhood significant, and under what circumstances? What, for example, is the significance of length of residence, age, sex, race, and social and economic circumstances? The community of limited liability proposed by Janowitz (1952), and elaborated by Greer (1962), emphasized that attachments to communities were limited and variable. This concept has been used traditionally to demonstrate the breakdown of neighborhoods. However, community sentiments and involvement can be voluntarily increased as well as decreased.

A major question is the degree to which networks of kinship, friendship, and ethnicity are significant in the process of neighborhood revitalization and upgrading (Palen and Nachmias, chap. 7). We hypothesize that upgrading neighborhoods evince networks that are relatively extensive, tightly knit, and clustered. If the local community is perceived as an important social unit, then individuals are more likely to become emotionally, socially, and economically involved. This might be manifested through high rates of participation in local community organizations, block clubs, and anticrime activities. It is possible that upgrading fosters new mechanisms for creating networks and a sense of community. Such common concerns as local policing and inadequate local services, housing speculation, and the intrusion of outsiders (whether poor minorities or affluent gentrifiers) tend to unify residents and produce a sense of *gemeinshaft*. City government often serves as a convenient adversary against which an otherwise apolitical populace can be mobilized.

An ideology of community control with its emphasis on the maintenance of local autonomy and values also provides residents with a common cause. Block clubs, antispeculation committees, and neighborhood organizations help convince residents that they can control their own local environment. Shared sentiments and identification with a named and bounded community may facilitate the mobilization of a critical mass of the neighborhood population to meet perceived threats (Nachmias and Palen 1982).

Social Movements

The fifth and final approach to the study of reinvasion is, paradoxically, the least well-developed in the literature, but it may hold the greatest potential for providing a synthesis of the multiple causes of the phenomenon. This is an analysis of urban reinvasion as a social movement. While there is considerable disagreement regarding the definition of a social movement, most analyses suggest that movements are ideologically based, oriented toward change or improvement, and socially organized, often in terms of leader-follower relationships.

There is some precedent in the literature for analyzing other forms of population redistribution as social movements, especially for suburbanization and the development of "new towns" (Allen 1977). Often based on an antiurban ideology, these movements represent a reaction to industrial change and a search for an alternative. They may also be "led" by a coalition of big land developers, real estate interests, and lending institutions acting in concert with the Federal government both to "boost" the rural ideal, and to provide the financial and technological (transportation and communications) means to realize that ideal.

A similar perspective may be applied in a number of ways to the analysis of reinvasion. This may be best illustrated by elaborating the "resource-mobilization" theory of social movements (McCarthy and Zald 1977; Zald and Berger 1978). Here, such analytical dimensions of social movement as ideology, goals, participants, leadership, and tactics are used to evaluate "the struggle over possession of resources." In other words, control over the allocation of resources is often the specific type of change sought by a movement. This assumption clearly links resource-mobilization theory with political sociology and political economy.

These considerations provide a useful framework for the analysis of both reinvasion and displacement. In the process, many of the insights of demographic-ecological, sociocultural, and political-economic theories will be drawn together. To begin with, the resource involved in the struggle is inner-city space. The "combatants" are the middle-class newcomers versus the usually poor and powerless present residents. The behavior of both interest groups in the struggle may be interpreted in terms of the creation of, and participation in, conflicting social movements.

The reinvaders may be motivated by an emergent ideology of prourbanism, or by an effort to realize the old values of individualism and material success in a new, urban land of economic opportunities (Allen, chap. 2). They may be encouraged in their efforts by a variety of leaders. The first successful urban pioneers may have served as a sort of role model, providing evidence that the economic risks of inner-city living were not as high as often assumed. The political-economic elites that decided to end redlining and make investment capital available may also be viewed as assuming a leadership role. This is especially so if, in order to promote their investments, these groups become the boosters of inner-city living. They may be seen as both decision makers and cultural taste makers, opening the slums to reinvestment for profit, on the one hand, and applauding inner-city chic as an attractive new lifestyle for young, affluent couples, on the other.

The opponents of reinvasion—the current residents of deteriorated neighborhoods who are threatened with displacement—have begun to form what might be called *countermovements* in the defense of their neighborhoods. This dialectic is perhaps best understood in terms of intergroup power relationships. The relatively powerless residents attempt to gain power by forming organizations to preserve existing lifestyles and prevent "elite" intrusions into their space (Rubin 1979). Block clubs and antispeculation committees are often motivated by an ideology of community control. They derive their leadership from grassroots organizers—members of the community or, perhaps, political hopefuls appealing to their constituents in an election year.

However, newcomers often dominate neighborhood organizations (Schoenberg and Rosenbaum 1980). The presence of a critical mass of residents who are willing to participate in a neighborhood organization is a political resource that can be mobilized to negotiate with public officials, to apply for historic designation, to enforce norms of housing repair, and, in general, to use collective strength to shape the community in the interests of the gentrifiers.

Many of the chapters in this volume contain some information relevant to the roles of demographic underpinnings, motivating ideologies, and interest groups—each of which is a defining characteristic of a social movement—in the process of gentrification.

REFERENCES

Allen, I. L., ed. 1977 *New towns and the suburban dream*. Port Washington: Kennikat.

———. 1980. The ideology of dense neighborhood redevelopment: Cultural diversity and transcendent community experience. *Urban Affairs Quarterly* 15:409-29.

Auger, D. A. 1979. The politics of revitalization in gentrifying neighborhoods: The case of Boston's South End. *Journal of the American Planning Association* 45, 4 (October): 515-22.

Bailey, K. D., and Mulcahy, P. 1972. Sociocultural versus neoclassical ecology: A contribution to the problem of scope in sociology *Sociological Quarterly* 13:37-41.

Biggar, C. 1979. *The sunning of America: migration to the sunbelt*. Washington, D.C.: Population Reference Bureau.

Black, J. T. 1975. Private-market housing renovation in central cities *Urban Land* 34 (November): 3-9.

———. 1980. Private-market housing renovation in central cities: An urban land institute survey. In *Back to the city*, ed. Laska and Spain. New York: Pergamon Press.

Bourne, L. S. 1977. Perspectives on the inner city: Its changing character, reasons for decline and revival. Toronto: University of Toronto, Centre for Urban and Community Studies, Research Paper No. 94.

Burgess, E. W. 1925 (1967). The growth of the city: An introduction to a research project. In *The City*, ed. R. E. Park, E. W. Burgess, and R. D. McKenzie. Chicago: University of Chicago Press.

Cades, S. n.d. Rebuilding the urban residential core: The end of an American anomaly. Unpublished paper. Chestertown, Md.: Department of Sociology, Washington College.

Clay, P. L. 1978. Neighborhood revitalization: The recent experience in large American cities. Unpublished paper. Cambridge: Department of Urban Studies and Planning, Massachusetts Institute of Technology.

———. 1979. *Neighborhood Renewal: Middle-class resettlement and incumbent upgrading in American neighborhoods*. Lexington, Mass.: Lexington Books.

Cybriwsky, R. 1978a. Social aspects of neighborhood change. *Annals, The Association of American Geographers* 68 (March): 17-33.
_____. 1978b. Benefits and social costs of gentrification in inner city Philadelphia. Paper read at AAG Annual Meeting, New Orleans, La.

Duncan, O. D. 1959. Human ecology and population studies. In *The Study of Population*, ed. P. M. Hauser and O. D. Duncan. Chicago: University of Chicago Press.

Faris, R. E. L. 1967. *Chicago sociology 1920-1932*. Chicago: University of Chicago Press.

Firey, W. 1945. Sentiment and symbolism as ecological variables. *American Sociological Review* 10:140-48.

Fischer, C. S. 1976. *The Urban Experience*. New York: Harcourt Brace Jovanovich.

Frisbie, W. P., and Poston, D. 1975. Components of sustenance organization and non-metropolitan population change: A human ecological investigation. *American Sociological Review* 40:773-84.
_____. 1978. Sustenance differentiation and population redistribution. *Social Forces* 57:42-56.

Fusch, R. 1978. Historic preservation and gentrification: A search for order in the urban core. Paper read at the AAG Annual Meeting, New Orleans, La.

Gale, D. E. 1976. The-back-to-the-city-movement revisited. Washington, D.C.: Department of Urban and Regional Planning, George Washington University.
_____. 1977. The back-to-city movement revisited. Washington, D.C.: Department of Urban Regional Planning, George Washington University.
_____. 1980. Neighborhood Resettlement: Washington, D.C. In *Back to the City*, ed. S. Laska and D. Spain. New York: Pergamon Press.

Gibbs, J. P., and Martin, W. T. 1959. Toward a theoretical system of human ecology. *Pacific Sociological Review* 2:29-36.

Gist, N. P. and Fava, S. F. 1964. *Urban Society*. New York: Crowell.

Glaab, C. N., and Brown, A. T. 1967. *A history of urban America*. New York: Macmillan.

Glass, R. 1964. London: aspects of change. In *London: Aspects of Change*, ed. Centre for Urban Studies. London: MacGibbon and Kee.

Goldfield, D. R. 1980. Private neighborhood redevelopment and displacement in Washington, D.C. *Urban Affairs Quarterly*. New York (June): 453-69.

Gordon, D. M. 1978. Capitalist development and the history of American cities. In *Marxism and the Metropolis*, ed. W. K. Tabb and L. Sawers. New York: Oxford.

Greer, S. 1962. *The emerging city*. New York: Free Press.

Grier, G., and Grier, E. 1980. Urban displacement: A reconnaissance. In *Back to the City*, ed. S. B. Laska and D. Spain. New York: Pergamon Press.

Hoover, E. M., and Vernon, R. 1962. *Anatomy of a metropolis*. Garden City: Doubleday.

Hudson, J. R. 1980. Revitalization of inner city neighborhoods: An ecological approach. *Urban Affairs Quarterly* 15 4:397-408.

Hunter, A. 1974. *Symbolic communities: The persistence and change of Chicago's neighborhoods.* Chicago: University of Chicago Press.

Hunter, A. 1978. Persistence of local sentiments in mass society. *Handbook of contemporary urban life,* ed. David Street et al. San Francisco: Jossey Bass.

Janowitz, M. 1952 *The Community Press in an Urban Setting.* Chicago: University of Chicago Press.

Kern, D.R. 1977. High income neighborhoods in the city: Will the new demography guarantee their future? Paper read at the Annual Meeting of the Regional Science Association, November 1977 in Philadelphia, Pa.

Kornblum, W. 1975. *Blue collar community.* Chicago: University of Chicago Press.

Laska, S.B., and Spain, D. eds. 1980. *Back to the city: Issues in neighborhood renovation.* New York : Pergamon Press.

Lipton, S. G. 1977. Evidence of central city revival. *Journal of the American Institute of Planners* 45 (April): 136-47.

London, B. 1980. Gentrification as urban reinvasion: Some preliminary definitional and theoretical considerations. In *Back to the city,* ed. S. B. Laska and D. Spain. New York: Pergamon Press.

Long, L. 1980. Back to the countryside and back to the city in the same decade. In *Back to the city,* ed. S. B. Laska and D. Spain. New York: Pergamon Press.

McCarthy, J. D., and Zald, M. N. 1977. Resource mobilization and social movements: A partial theory. *American Journal of Sociology* 82 (May): 1212-41.

McKenzie, R. D. 1924. (1968). "The ecological approach to the study of the human community." In *Roderick D. McKenzie: On Human Ecology,* ed. A. H. Hawley. Chicago: University of Chicago Press.

————. 1926. (1968). The scope of human ecology. In *Roderick D. McKenzie: On Human Ecology,* ed. A. H. Hawley. Chicago: University of Chicago Press.

Molotch, H. 1976. The city as a growth machine: Toward a political economy of place. *American Journal of Sociology* 82 (September): 309-332.

Morrison, P. A. 1976. *Rural renaissance in America? The revival of population growth in remote areas.* Washington, D.C.: Population Reference Bureau.

Nachmias, C., and Palen, J. J. 1982. Membership in voluntary neighborhood associations and urban revitalization. *Policy Sciences* 14:179-93.

Palen, J. J., and Nachmias, C. 1982. Newcomers and oldtimers in a revitalizing working-class neighborhood. *Occasional Papers,* vol. 3 (winter): 15-24, University of New Orleans.

Rubin, M. 1979. The transportation factor in neighborhood revitalization: Boston's southwest corridor. Paper read at SSSP Annual Meeting, Boston, Mass.

Shoenberg, S., and Rosenbaum, P. 1980. *Neighborhoods that work.* New Brunswick, N.J.: Rutgers Press.

Sjoberg, G. 1965. Theory and research in urban sociology. In *The Study of*

Urbanization, ed. P. M. Hauser and L. F. Schnore. New York: Wiley.
Sly, D. F. 1972. Migration and the ecological complex. *American Sociological Review* 37:615-28.
Sly, D. F., and Tayman, J. 1977. Ecological approach to migration reexamined. *American Sociological Review* 42:783-95.
Smith, N. 1979. Gentrification and capital: Theory, practice, and ideology in Society Hill. *Antipode* 11:24-35.
Stein, M. 1961. *The eclipse of community*, New York: Harper Torchbooks.
Sumka, H. J. 1980. Federal antidisplacement policy in a context of urban decline. In *Back to the City*, ed. S. B. Laska and D. Spain. New York: Pergamon Press.
Suttles, G. 1968. *The social order of the slum*. Chicago: University of Chicago Press.
―――. 1972. *The social construction of communities*. Chicago: University of Chicago Press.
Tabb, W. K., and Sawers, L. eds. 1978. *Marxism and the metropolis*. New York: Oxford.
U.S. Bureau of the Census. 1978. Geographical mobility: March 1975 to March 1978. *Current Population Reports*, ser. P-20, no. 33. Washington, D.C.: U.S. Government Printing Office.
U.S. Department of Housing and Urban Development. 1981. *Residential displacement: An update report to Congress*. Washington, D.C.: Office of Policy Development and Research.
Vernon, R. 1960. *Metropolis 1985*. New York: Doubleday.
Warner, S. B., Jr. 1962. *Streetcar suburbs: The process of growth in Boston, 1870-1900*. Cambridge: Massachusetts Institute of Technology.
Webber, M. W. 1977. The post city age. In *City Scenes*, ed. J. J. Palen. Boston: Little Brown.
Weiler, C. 1978. Optimizing reinvestment, minimizing displacement. In *Queen Village, the eclipse of community: A case study of gentrification and displacement in a Philadelphia neighborhood*, ed. P. R. Levy. Philadelphia: Institute for the Study of Civic Values.
Wellman, B., and Leighton, B. 1981. Networks, neighborhoods, and communities. In *City Scenes*. 2nd ed., ed. J. J. Palen. Boston: LIttle Brown.
Whyte, W. F. 1943. *Street corner society*, Chicago: University of Chicago Press.
Willhelm, S. M. 1962. *Urban zoning and land-use theory*. New York: Free Press.
Williams, R. M., Jr. 1970. *American society: A sociological interpretation*. New York: Knopf.
Wirth, L. 1938. Urbanism as a way of life. *American Journal of Sociology*, 44 (July): 1-24.
Zald, M. N., and Berger, M. A. 1978. Social movements in organizations: Coup d'etat, insurgency and mass movements. *American Journal of Sociology* 83 (January): 823-61.

CHAPTER TWO

The Ideology of Dense Neighborhood Redevelopment

IRVING L. ALLEN

In a few neighborhoods of many mature North American cities there is a clear resettlement, and sometimes a complete succession, by middle-class people "reclaiming" old city neighborhoods (James 1977; London 1978). This phenomenon of "gentrification" or "reinvasion" (London Forthcoming) is occurring principally in larger, older cities, especially those with a still vital core, many white-collar workers, and long commuting distances to suburbs (Lipton 1977).

This essay is a sociocultural interpretation of emergent ideology and utopian quest for community in the social movement of neighborhood reinvasion. The new settlers are the trend-setters, the tastemakers, and perhaps the harbingers of a wider social movement. They are formulating new definitions of the acceptability and desirability of dense "traditional" city living. I will argue that, for a minority of the participants, the movement represents a change in American community ideology toward the value of social diversity of ethnicity. Similar principles apply to emerging interests in pluralism with respect to other kinds of human variety, such as difference in class and status, age groups, sexual orientations, and

Irving L. Allen is Professor of Sociology, the University of Connecticut, Storrs. Reprinted, with changes, from *Urban Affairs Quarterly*, Vol. 15 (June) 1980: 409-428, © 1980 Sage Publications, Beverly Hills/London, with permission of the publisher.

many other styles of life that are equally part of the heterogeneous city. Hunter (1975) made a comprehensive analysis of the role of ideology in the social construction of community in a stably integrated urban neighborhood that can be compared usefully with gentrifying neighborhoods.

The value implicit here is that complexity, especially the complexity of ethnic diversity, is a desirable quality in the urban environment, more so when the reailty is fully confronted and experienced. The view that there are positive values in the size, density, anonymity, segmentalism, and diversity of city life has endured in social thought even at a time when antiurbanism permeates popular thought and implicitly a great deal of social science thinking about the city (Hadden and Barton 1973). Cox (1966), for example, wrote of the redemptive quality of urban life. Berger (1977), with a similar voice, commented upon the complexity and universalism of the city as a "signal of transcendence" and as a social experience of redemptive power. After a long history of the city's being viewed as a negative value and as a metaphor for everything that is wrong with the society of advanced capitalism, there is a note of promise in this unanticipated, large-scale population redistribution.

The emerging ideology of the reinvasion movement is a popular version of what Greer (1972, pp. 265-79) called the "conservative utopian" thoughtway in the intellectual politics of urban re-development. Greer, as though anticipating the gentrification movement, wrote that conservative utopians

> believe that the concrete good city...is being eroded by various mistakes and evils and [they] believe this should be corrected. At one time they believed the rural life to be the only one fit for man, the city evil. Today, they remain fixated on the past, but it is now the dense, polyethnic, centralized city of the railroad age (1972, p. 274).

The reinvasion movement also has, at once and with some ambivalence, a good measure of what Greer called "liberal utopianism" in the tradition of such visionary thinkers as Lewis Mumford and Paul Goodman.

In a general way, I call the new interest in the diversity of dense city life "ideology" because it is a value-laden organization of cognition and perception concerning the good workings of alternative community forms. It is latently ideology in the Marxian sense of a class-linked social knowledge that serves to maintain existing economic arangements. But it is also utopian in the Mannheimian distinction. While also a distorted image of reality, utopia has the "dynamism" to transform reality into an image of itself (Berger and Luckman 1966, p. 10). In order to grasp the meaning of ideology and utopia in the movement, we need, first, to look briefly at its ecological and demographic context and, second, at the hierarchy of motives that predispose this migration behavior.

MOTIVES AND MOVING

There is much speculation and some data (Gale 1976, 1977; Bradley 1978) on the motives for people staying in, or moving back to, the city and participating in the redevelopment of an old neighborhood. Essentially, there are three types of motives: (1) *practical*, mainly economic, incentives; (2) people's *preferences* for certain neighborhood and housing types—really matters of taste and style of life; and (3) *ideological* factors. Practical incentives and preferences (which mainly indicate the direction and desiderata of the movement) interact with ideology more than is appreciated in most formal migration models, even in those that emphasize the mediating variables of preferences and levels of community satisfaction (Speare 1974; Bach and Smith 1977).

We hear mostly about the so-called practical reasons why people find the central city increasingly attractive compared with the suburbs. Many reasons, in fact, have to do with the narrowing of residential alternatives now that the suburbs are "maturing" or coming to resemble the cities and to have similar problems for similar reasons. The suburbs around the older industrial cities, all things considered, are no longer always bargains. Suburban housing costs and taxes have risen to the extent that, in some old city neighborhoods, structurally sound, turn-of-the-century houses can be purchased *and renovated* for substantially less that the cost of a new house and lot in the suburbs. Of course, as such neighborhoods are reinvaded and complete succession nears, prices do rise to meet those in the most expensive neighborhoods of either city or suburb. In spite of this, however, the practicality of inner-city living tends to be further enhanced by energy shortages, poor public transportation between cities and suburbs, and the convenience of extant public transportation within cities.

Some people (and their numbers may be growing) have tastes and preferences for dense neighborhood styles of life. These follow from and are related to practical motives, especially strategic factors of centrality and proximity, such as wanting to spend less time commuting and more time with families. Other examples of taste are liking the architectual or historical character of a neighborhood, preferring to live in a restored old house than in a new one, and in the case of big cities a preference for apartment or condominium living. Many gentrified neighborhoods, moreover, offer a participatory style of life, often through a neighborhood voluntary association (Hunter 1975). The cities afford simple pleasures, such as taking walks, that many suburbs paradoxically have lost in the scatter through growing dependence on the automobile.

Inextricably involved with matters of practicality and preferences are many ideological undertones of commitment to a dense, redeveloped city neighborhood (Hunter 1975; Gale 1976, 1977; Bradley 1978; Fusch 1978; London Forthcoming). Gale (1976), 1977) emphasizes intergenerational differences in social values. Some young people in the 1960s, now in their home-buying phase of life, were inculcated and remained concerned with the urban social problems they were exposed to in college and the mass media. The commitment to a gamey city neighborhood amounts to a personal affirmation of belief in the future of cities, as well as that they yield the gratifications of involvement and participation in a social movement. Among the great variety of other prourban values that could be mentioned, the motif of social and cultural diversity is of most interest here. The wish to live in an integrated neighborhood (Hunter 1975; Gale 1977) or, more generally, "among a mixture of social types" (Bradley 1978) is a value expressed to survey interviewers, though it is never the most important reason given. Probably only a few people actually seek out racially integrated neighborhoods; but perhaps more like to have *within perceptual range* a variety of styles of life, particularly those of ethnic communities.

More than anything else, then, reinvasion is motivated by practical considerations, particularly economic incentives and strategic factors. Moreover, there is the commanding argument that the phenomenon should be understood basically as a requisite response to the needs of advanced capitalism or postindustrial society. Smith (1979), for example, writes that "cultural desires and demands are of primary importance only in determining the final form and character of a revitalized neighborhood" (also see Smith Forthcoming). Yet it is also likely that sociocultural factors, such as new roles for women, and the exigencies of the real estate market interact from the beginning and reinforce one another. Ideological factors, in particular, generate and reflect an emerging consumer taste for dense city neighborhoods and possibly a desire for a better community experience as an alternative to what the suburbs have come to represent to some people over the past thirty years (Hunter 1975). Thus, while preferences and ideology do not "cause" intrametropolitan migrations, they nonetheless mediate and actually trip consumer decisions when economic advantage is marginal.

Collectively, these individual decisions result in a migration. Migrations usually take on certain features of collective-behavioral phenomena. As social movements, they develop informal leaders or trend-setters, the diffusion of innovative ideas, and imitative behavior. Interpreters stimulate public debate and articulate the goals of the movement. Finally, there emerges a consensually shared set of social definitions or an ideology that rationalizes and celebrates the goals of the movement. This was true of the migration to the suburbs in this century (Hadden and Barton 1973) and of the here-and-there resettlement of "rural" nonmetropolitan areas in the 1970s, such as the "back to the land" movement of the counterculture (Berger 1979). The emergence of ideology also seems true of the recent reinvasion of dense, city neighborhoods. In the suburban emigration, ideology was more important earlier than later in the movement, and its role is sometimes exaggerated. Suburbs are not just an ephiphenomenon of ideology, and neither is the reinvasion movement. Nonetheless, the idea of "urban neighborhood" as an alternative community form is burgeoning in the gentrification movement. "Neighborhoods are back in fashion," says the promotional rhetoric.

THE AMBIVALENT VALUE
OF CULTURAL DIVERSITY

Large, heterogeneous cities attract and then engender ethnic subcultures much as they attract and sustain other subcultural ways of life (Fischer 1975). The ethnic-cultural diversity of many large cities is one of their most visible and enduring features. Indeed, one of the most popular images of the city is that of a mosaic of ethnic neighborhoods, which symbolizes differences between central cities and certain homogeneous suburbs as much as the contrasting images of density, anonymity, pace, and tempo.

Sociocultural diversity is a leitmotif in the new tastes for central-city housing and neighborhood. One of the great amenities of dense city living, it is said, is exposure to such social and cultural diversity as ethnicity. A composite statement of the idea made up from many fragments is as follows: A milieu of diversity represents a child-rearing advantage over "homogeneous" suburbs, because children are exposed to social "reality" and to the give and take of social and cultural accommodation with those who are different. For adults, the urban ambience of diversity is a continual source of stimulation and renewal and a reminder of the cultural relativity of one's own style of life. It is said to be a relief from the subcultural sameness and "boredom" of many suburban communities. If these rather thoughtful goals are not enough, then ethnic diversity in particular is said to offer local color, a wide selection of ethnic restaurants and food shops, and generally a satisfying air of cosmopolitan community.

There is some irony in people's looking to the centers for diversity, including ethnic variety, that they feel is not present in the suburbs. Actually, the suburbs around a large city are nearly as ethnically diverse as the central cities. Many white immigrant groups settled initially in the centers but pursued the suburban housing ideal as soon as they could afford it, especially after the first generation. The suburbs today are a thoroughly diverse entity and are an ethnic mirror image of the white city; the differences between city and suburb are mostly economic and, of course, as yet racial. This is but another lesson on the point that the failure of the suburbs as a physical arrangement lies in their low densities. The suburbs create the illusion of homogeneity because one seldom sees or has much face-to-face contact with different kinds of people in distant and in quite different suburbs. The high density and high visibility of many groups at the center of the city allows one to see the diversity. The real ingredient that is missed in the suburbs is density. In this sense, the *proximity* of variety is another amenity of density and is another pull of the center.

Moreover, the old ethnic neighborhoods of the dense, core city remain the *symbol* of ethnic community, and some have become tourist centers for that reason. They are also service centers for suburban ethnic populations, provisioning the accoutrements of ethnic styles of life and providing a historically appropriate place for community integrative activities, such as street festivals. The old city neighborhoods are, so to speak, the "old country" for many children and grandchildren of immigrants.

There has always been a small minority of cosmopolitan city dwellers that has valued the ambience of community diversity and the stimulation of cultural variety. Some would say they are only those few intellectuals who write the books about, and otherwise celebrate, the charms of city life. But perhaps the intellectuals have influenced the tastes of some of the middle-class people who now seek community alternatives. It is not clear, in any event, whether many residents initially seek out such subcultural diversity or whether they choose the neighborhood for other reasons and *then* find things to like about it. The latter interpretation, of course, is compatible with the view that economic factors lead such social movements and the associated ideology. But even if it is an *ex post facto* rationalization, the fact that the ambience of diversity is being defined as a *positive* feature of the social environment is remarkable in that it follows upon a generation or more of rejection of the city and its way of life.

The value of social diversity in city life is regularly proclaimed by the planning professionals, by trend-spotters in the redevelopment industry, and by monitors of neighborhoods' interests from the Federal Department of Housing and Urban Development. The ideal of diversity received its most lyrical enunciation by Jacobs (1961), and her work marks a boundary between two generations of popular planning thought. A younger generation of planners and developers has recanted the antiurban sins of urban renewal, which in the 1950s and 1960s resulted in the destruction of so much variegation of land use and diversity of ethnic communities. Now that so much has gone, the values of ethnic diversity and pluralism are axioms in the rhetoric of city and suburban development and redevelopment.

These themes are congenial with those of the restoration or preservation movements and with the sentiments of "links to the past" and "continuity." Generally, the idea is to preserve what is old, fragile, and integral to an area—especially solid and distinctive housing—rather than sweepingly replacing it with what is new, big, and undifferentiated. But it is not all a concern with historical continuity and community identity. When an old house is not simply viewed as an "investment-quality antique," the historical preservation movement also represents looking to the past rather than to the future of the city. One of the national moods is a loss of faith in the value of economic growth and modernity. Ley (1978) argues that gentrification is a postindustrial, self-serving elitism representing the ascendency of the values of consumerism and amenity over the values of production and growth. Some people, moreover, are seeking warmth and order in tradition by preserving selected aspects of the physical city of the past.

With regard to the human community in the city, the received wisdom of many planners is to regard ethnic differentiation of neighborhoods as a resource to be cherished and preserved. The preservation of ethnic neighborhoods is not only to value the communities themselves but also to serve the edification of others in the plural community, including the gentrifier/consumers of the city scene. The hard question, of course, is to what extent the spirit of preservation is simply to keep some of the symbols of ethnic community, while the vital community has since expired or, more likely, moved to the suburbs. To what extent is the value of ethnic diversity in city life simply a search for a wax museum of colorful ethnic types? There is a distinct possibility that the ethnic neighborhoods of the city are being romanticized by some as survivals of an earlier, better age, as quaint "urban villages," as so many colorful "ethnics" living in warm neighborhoods of a "human scale" in the midst of the "cold, impersonal" city.

The diversity that is so much valued does not, however, include all of the variety of city life. Wilson (1975, pp. 27-28) believes that the few urbanites who value diversity usually mean "safe" diversity, by which they mean "a harmless variety of specialty stores, esoteric bookshops, 'ethnic' restaurants, and highbrow cultural enterprises." The ethnic diversity that is valued, when it is valued, is that of communities whose residents are not so socially different or hostile as to threaten peace in the street. The ethnicity of the lower classes, perennially viewed as the "dangerous classes," usually is not part of the diversity sought by the new settlers. Some of those seeking a new community ambience are hoping to find Old World, European cafe charm, while the reality also includes (and increasingly so) transplanted settlements of third world poverty and, sometimes, threatening street life.

PLUS ÇA CHANGE, PLUS C'EST LA MEME CHOSE

This familiar French cynicism catches the venerable sociological observation that culture and society do not change as rapidly as fashion seems to indicate. In this regard, the urban-neighborhood movement, in its deepest sentiments, could have something in common with the earlier suburban trend. The suburban trend of a generation ago had clear overtones of a social movement with an ideology (Wood 1958, pp. 4-19; Dobriner 1963, pp. 61-80; Donaldson 1969, pp. 32-44). Others have written of the anti-pluralism of the movement (Gans 1967, pp. 408-32; Fogelson 1967, ch. 15; Sennett 1970a, pp. 214-17). This was a flight from the cultural, class, and ethnic diversity of the city and a seeking of an ordered, homogeneous community in the suburbs.

Suburbanization was in part a reaction to the apparent disorder of "citification." Americans may never have valued cities for their citification, but instead may have come to them solely for economic advantage (Elazar 1966). They left for suburbs as soon as technology and income permitted. Thus, they shared certain values and aspirations to a style of life and, by self-selecting themselves into suburbs, they proceeded to act out their values (Fava 1959; Gans 1962).

The trend toward city neighborhood redevelopment does *not* signal a reversal of this traditional antiurban bias that informed the decentralization of the American city. Nor does it indicate that the bias is less pervasive than we thought. It certainly does not indicate that older cities will cease losing their middle-class residents in the foreseeable future. Public opinion polls still show that most Americans, regardless of present residence, express a preference for suburban, small-town, and country residential environments.

At most, the new interest in staying in, and sometimes coming to, the city centers may signal the emergence of a minor duality of community tastes, perhaps bifurcating along generational lines. Alternatively, the trend may be more a matter of economics buttressed by fashion than of people seeking a genuine alternative to the class-exclusive and legally defended community that suburbs represent in the American metropolis. The chic row houses and Victorian frames may be but one of this generation's collective representations of personal success, status, conformity, and order in parallel with the symbols of suburban convention in the 1950s and 1960s.

Fusch (1978) analyzed the preservation and gentrification movements as latter-day expressions of the traditional values that guided past migration behavior. These are (1) "the high value placed on economic success"—the meaning of house ownership; (2) the importance of individuality and personal identity—the status symbolism of an old, architecturally distinguished house in a prestigious neighborhood; (3) the "need" for conformity and community homogeneity; and (4) the search for small-town and "rural" values and the quest for community. Finally, as a reaction to social change in American life, the movement is driven by a wave of nostalgia and seeking a sense of place.

What the new ilk of urbanites are seeking in the city is perhaps not that different from what their parents sought in the suburbs. If the older generation looked to the suburbs for romantic middle-class communities that represented a new way of life, some members of the younger generation may well be looking to the cities for romantic middle-class communities that represent an alternative to the suburbs. But is the alternative that different? Insofar as they are searching for "urbanity," over and above the housing bargains and proximity to work, it is safe to assume that many of the new settlers are seeking a selective, buffered, and entertaining encounter with the social diversity of city life. Their parents sought a selective, buffered, and entertaining encounter with small-town and "rural" life.

When the early suburban settlers had the money and leisure to indulge their fantasies, some affluent suburbs became nostalgic semblances of small-town and rural communities of a past that never was. These romantic suburbs were also an effort at "restoration," in the sense of trying to establish a link to, and to recapture the best of, a fictive past. The affluent new urbanites similarly are socially constructing an urban past with the paraphernalia of town houses and other Victoriana of the gaslight era and railroad age of the American city. Both movements have a nostalgic element of preserving symbols of the past while eschewing the substance. And both movements have an element of the never-ending search for "community," if only its symbols. Nevertheless, the new urban romantics are more realistic than were their suburban forebears, and their quest holds more potential for redemptive community experience.

DISENCHANTMENT AND
THE SEARCH FOR MAGIC

There may be an altogether new element in the attraction to the dense city centers. The new interest in downtown has an implicit element of flight from the sameness, order, and rationality of the suburbs. There is a novel and engaging view, only superficially contrary to the traditional interpretations of urban sociology, that magic rather than rationality is the stuff of city life (Raban 1974, pp. 157-83). The element of surprise is undeservedly one of the least appreciated amenities of city life. Berger (1977) writes of the magical and surreal experience of big-city life. "The magic of the city can be summed up in a sentence that points to a recurring experience: anything can happen here—and it could happen right now." Some of the new settlers, I suspect, are hoping that the dense, heterogeneous city will infuse their lives with magic, novelty, and excitement. And well it may.

Complexity of social environment affords interest, and the psychological principles are not unlike those of the physical environment of architecture. Rapoport and Hawkes (1970) write that environmental complexity "is a function of violated expectations." These gentle "violations" provide much in the making of interest and novelty in the social environment of dense city life and they directly reflect sociocultural diversity. Rapoport and Hawkes propose that "the greater the difference among elements, the greater the complexity of the set, suggesting that complexity and variety are closely related." Great cultural variety thus becomes a source of violated expectation or surprise. The centers of great cities offer plenty of this.

However, search for magic, novelty, and excitement is distressingly close to a passive use of the city as an entertainment commodity—or, as some like to put it, the "tourist view." There seems to be a boundless contempt for (or amusement at) people who visit the city with the voyeuristic attitude of "going to a circus." Tourists in the city (and some would add the gentrifiers as "resident tourists") do tend to see the "natives" as actors against a romantic scenery in a kind of theatre-in-the-round. The actors sometimes come forth and interact with the spectators, surprising, delighting, and sometimes embarrassing them, but always leaving them with a feeling that they have "participated."

This kind of relationship with the city, if and when it becomes predominant, eventually changes the very character of the city that is most valued. The tourist effect is all too often to change the observed to meet the expectations of the observers. Or more likely, the juxtaposition of diverse cultures loosens and scatters before the new economic pressures. Central-city redevelopment has the latent potential of driving out cultural diversity, and its economics often predispose development toward homogeneity of class and ways of life. Yet this new interest in diversity, magic, and even entertainment is nonetheless closer to the actualities of metropolitan life than the fantasies of one-dimensional community that marked the suburban quest.

THE AMBIVALENT VALUE OF PLURALISM

The ideal of great diversity in local community is in some part a legacy of the 1960s and of the counterculture, which rejected the smugness and parochialism that seemed to the young to characterize so much of American life. While diversity is simply a demographic description of the ethnic composition of the population, pluralism is the norm that all groups should nurture their ethnic heritages and identities, rather than assimilating and surrendering their cultural distinctiveness. The plural community rests upon the ideal of a mutual respect among all communities, with no group dominant or culturally superior. The beneficence of the idea gives it wide appeal, especially perhaps to the members of an age group who were in their teens and twenties in the 1960s.

The ideal lost some of its moral force as it was popularized. It emerged in the articulation of tastes for central-city living as a valuation of ethnic diversity for its own sake. For some, the ideal of pluralism has degenerated simply to "ethnic chic." It is understandable that the new interest in redeveloping central-city neighborhoods should merge with the intellectually fashionable ideas of

ethnic diversity and pluralism. It is only in the dense central city
that a variety of groups and their community symbols are within
the perceptual range of most observers. Central cities are being
seen anew as lively and attractive mosaics of social worlds, many of
them ethnic settlements. But there are yet more reservations
about this apparent new interest in diversity.

The ethnic diversity that many of the new urbanites value, as
mentioned earlier, is "safe" diversity around, rather than within,
their neighborhoods. Many prefer that irritating aspects of other
styles of life be softened by the haze of a certain distance, though
still within view and accessible in ways and at times of one's own
choosing. This is forgivable to a degree. Segmental relations among
individuals in their public aspects and roles is essential to the social
organization of everyday life in a complex society. Similarly,
segmental relations among communities in their various public
aspects, and in ways and to degrees of their own choosing, is part of
the arrangement that makes pluralism workable. Indeed, responsible and positive uses of segmental relationships in the community
of strangers is the core of civility and discloses the character of
what Sennett (1977) called "the public man."

Much experience in urban and suburban redevelopment indicates
that most consumers of housing and neighborhood prefer style-of-
life enclave living over random, house-by-house, scatter patterns of
ethnic integration. And the economics of neighborhood redevelopment militate toward homogeneous blocks. This is not always an
unmitigated moral failing of the economics of redevelopment. In the
long run, a mosaic of distinct enclaves, insofar as the pattern is
voluntary, may prove to be the most stable and workable. Multiple
enclaves are compatible with the ideal of plural community.
Moreover, when enclaves have a "critical mass" of size and density,
they sustain the subcultures (Fischer, 1975) that compose the
diversity.

The willingness of the new urbanites to live cheek by jowl with
low-status communities may testify to the apartness that some feel
from those communities and, at worst, suggests something of the
spirit of slumming. Perhaps the most important social meaning of
space is that of social distance. Voluntary neighborhood segregation and exclusion (the involuntary segregation of others) often
express social distance. The most graphic expression of social
distance, at least in the past, has been far removal to the suburbs.
But sentiment sometimes excepts ecological principle. When social
distance is great and status is held securely, physical distance is of
less symbolic importance. A famous and striking example is the
alleged willingness before the Second World War of high-status

Southern whites to live in cities and towns interspersed, salt-and-pepper fashion, with black households, mostly those of domestics and menials. The utter security of their status may be one reason the new urbanites are willing to settle in such close proximity to poor neighborhoods. Paradoxically, the proximity in fact may be valued for its implicit assertion of social distance. The symbolism of spatial ordering based on sheer distance, such as far removal to the suburbs, is normative for most middle-class people. For those who would stay ahead, it is declasse. A chic new neighborhood at the heart of an interesting city is for many the newest status symbol.

CONCLUSIONS

There is some reason to believe that the new tastes that mediate and accommodate the resettlement of dense city neighborhoods are a latter-day version, *mutatis mutandis*, of the same conservative-utopian values that guided the early suburban exodus. But at the same time there is much that is positive and promising to be found in the liberal-utopian aspects of the movement. The direction of the movement, if not all of its ideological content, at least flirts with the social realities of metropolitan life.

Sennett (1970b) describes the seeking of an "adolescent" or "purified" identity that motivated the early flight to the suburbs. He proposed planning for anarchistic "survival communities" in which middle-class people (who would somehow return to, or stay in, the city) would confront and find accommodation with the class, age, and ethnic diversity of the metropolitan community. The immediate reaction of many readers was that the anarchism was unworkable and that the establishment of "survival communities" was politically unfeasible. This utopian scheme would require, among other things, sizable numbers of middle-class people *voluntarily* staying in the city or moving in from the suburbs. A decade ago, few readers could imagine many middle-class people willing to settle near lower-status neighborhoods. For the first time, the redevelopment trend gives some basis at least for imagining a voluntary commitment to the plural community.

It is more imaginable that some of the old city centers simply may be reclaimed by middle-class people who seek an alternative to the low-density suburbs and their emerging social problems. Such a mass movement would not "solve the urban problem," however. Specious expectations that it might could seriously detract from the issue of greater Federal and state aid to the cities. The idea that a gradual "return to the city" in and of itself will revitalize the old central cities is, of course, but another example of what Fava (1973) calls the "pop sociology" of urban development issues. These are the oversimplified ideas that offer instant analysis and easy answers to complex social problems and phenomena and, moreover, that may mask a "conservative-ideological" (Greer 1972) view of the problem. The "pop sociology" of the reinvasion movement implies the idea of waiting for a reclamation of the centers through unfettered, "natural" market processes as an acceptable alternative to addressing the national social problems of inequality and social justice that weigh so heavily upon the old city centers.

Yet the new sociocultural interest in the centers and a substantial movement back to the cities could mean a new *vested* interest by middle-class people in the welfare of the centers. This could result in a limited political realignment by reducing the class polarization between the separate political entities of city and suburb. Political fragmentation in metropolitan areas is the chief administrative instrument that expresses the root economic conflict between city and suburb or, more to the point, between the classes that the spatial entities represent. A renegotiation of their differences could lessen this tension. Alternatively, there could emerge new devices to maintain the status quo. At worst, reinvasion could drive low-income people into declining inner suburbs, further isolating them and, this time around, making them less visible and thus less effective politically. Both scenarios probably will be played out side by side. But which one we allow to be most influential for the future of the cities is an open question for public policy.

REFERENCES

Bach, R. L. Smith, J. 1977. Community satisfaction, expectations of moving, and migration. *Demography* 14: 147-67.

Berger, B. M. 1979. American pastorialism, suburbia, and the commune movement. In *On the making of Americans: Essays in honor of David Reisman*, ed. H. J. Gans, N. Glazer, J. R. Gusfield, and C. Jencks. Philadelphia: Univ. of Pennsylvania Press.

Berger, P. L. 1977. In praise of New York: a semi-secular homily. *Commentary* 63 (February): 59-62.

Berger, P. L. and Luckman, T. 1966. *The social construction of reality:* A treatise on the sociology of knowledge. Garden City, NY: Doubleday.

Bradley, D. S. 1978. Back to the city? *Atlantic Economic Rev.* (March-April): 15-20.

Cox, H. 1966. *The secular city.* New York: Macmillan.

Dobriner, W. 1963. *Class in suburbia.* Englewood Cliffs, NJ: Prentice Hall.

Donaldson, S. 1969. *The suburban myth.* New York: Columbia Univ. Press.

Elazar, D. J. 1966. Are we a nation of cities? In *A nation of cities*, ed. R. A. Goldwin, pp. 89-114. Chicago: Rand McNally.

Fava, S. F. 1959. Contrasts in neighboring: New York City and a suburban county. In *The suburban community,* ed. W. M. Dobriner, pp. 122-130. New York: Putnam.

———. 1973. The pop sociology of suburbs and new towns. *American Studies* 14 (Spring): 121-133.

———. 1975. Beyond suburbia. *Annals, AAPS* 422: 10-24.

Fischer, C. S. 1975. Toward a subcultural theory of urbanism. *Amer. J. of Sociology* 80: 1319-41.

Fogelson, R. M. 1967. *The fragmented metropolis: Los Angeles, 1850-1930.* Cambridge: Harvard Univ. Press.

Fusch, R. 1978. Historic preservation and gentrification: A search for order in the urban core. Presented at the annual meetings of the Association of American Geographers, April, 1978, New Orleans.

Gale, D. E. 1977. The back-to-the-city movement revisited. Washington, D.C.: Dept. of Urban and Regional Planning, George Washngton University. (mimeo)

———. 1976. "Back-to-the-city movement...or is it?" (Mimeograph). Washington, D.C.: Dept. of Urban and Regional Planning, George Washington University.

Gans, H. J. 1962. Urbanism and suburbanism as ways of life: A re-evaluation of definitions. In *Human behavior and social processes,* ed. A. M. Rose, pp. 625-48. Boston: Houghton Mifflin.

———. 1967. *The Levittowners.* New York: Random House.

Greer, S. 1972. *The urbane view. New York: Oxford Univ. Press.*

Hadden, J. K., and Barton, J. J. 1973. *An image that will not die: thoughts on the history of anti-urban ideology.* In *The urbanization of the suburbs,* ed. L. H. Masotti and J. K. Hadden, pp. 79-116. Beverly Hills, Ca.: Sage.

Hunter, A. 1975. The loss of community: An empirical test through replication. *Amer. Soc. Rev.* 40 (October): 537-52.

Jacobs, J. 1961. *The death and life of great American cities.* New York: Random House.

James, F. 1977. *Back to the city: An appraisal of housing reinvestment and population change in urban America.* Washington, D.C.: The Urban Institute.

Ley, D. 1978. Inner city resurgence in its societal context. Presented at the annual meetings of the Association of American Geographers, April, 1978, New Orleans.

Lipton, S. G. 1977. Evidence of central city revival. *J. of the Amer. Institute of Planners* 43 (April): 136-47.

London, B. Forthcoming. Gentrification as urban reinvasion: some preliminary definitional and theoretical considerations. In *Back to the city: The making of a movement?,* ed. S. Laska and D. Spain. Elmsford, NY: Pergamon.

———. 1978. *The revitalization of Inner-City Neighborhoods: A Preliminary Bibliography.* Monticello, Il.: Vance Bibliographies.

Raban, J. 1974. *Soft city.* New York: Dutton.

Rapoport, A., and Hawkes, R. 1970. The perception of urban complexity. *J. of the Amer. Institute of Planners* 36 (March): 106-111.

Sennett, R. 1970b. *The uses of disorder: Personal identity and city life.* New York: Alfred A. Knopf.

———. 1970a. *Families Against the City: Middle Class Homes of Industrial Chicago, 1872-1890.* Cambridge: Harvard Univ. Press.

———. 1977. *The Fall of Public Man.* New York: Alfred A. Knopf.

Smith, N. Forthcoming. Gentrification and capital: theory, practice and ideology in Society Hill. *Antipode.*

———. 1979. Toward a theory of gentrification: a back to the city movement by capital not people. *J. of the Amer. Planning Assoc.* 45 (October).

Speare, A. J. 1974. Residential satisfaction as an intervening variable in residential mobility. *Demography* 11: 173-88.

Wilson, J. Q. 1975. *Thinking about crime.* New York: Basic Books.

Wood, R. C. 1958. *Suburbia: Its people and their politics.* Boston: Houghton Mifflin.

CHAPTER THREE

A Class Analysis of Gentrification

NEIL SMITH AND MICHELE LEFAIVRE

Traditional treatments of gentrification (defined as the rehabilitation of working-class inner-city neighborhoods for upper-middle class consumption) have been concerned more with simply describing the process than with explaining it. Where explanations are made, they tend to be impressionistic and eclectic; they invoke a list of likely factors rather than a theoretically rooted understanding of how urban areas grow and develop, decay and redevelop. Precisely this broader theory *is* available, albeit in rudimentary form, to Marxists focusing on urban political economy (Harvey 1978; Forthcoming). This has spawned an initial attempt to explain gentrification in terms of the broader economic development of cities in a capitalist economy (Smith 1979; 1981). While these explanations capture much of the central economic dynamic behind gentrification, they leave unexamined some of the forces invoked (as "factors") by more traditional explanations. In fact, these so-called factors are closely interrelated—population, changing job structure, energy crisis, rising house prices, and so forth. To achieve a richer explanation of gentrification it will be necessary to take a step back and demonstrate the way in which they are logically and

Neil Smith is Assistant Professor of Geography, Columbia University. Michele LeFaivre is a graduate student in the Department of Geography and Environmental Engineering, Johns Hopkins University.

historically related before using their relationships to explain gentrification. Gentrification is not just a physical process, it is a social one, involving the movement of people and the movement of capital, and, as a social process, it embodies many of the characteristics of the larger society in which it occurs. In particular, it is a process involving a clear conflict of class interests. It is not simply a process involving "inmovers and outmovers," different "urban actors," or collective fits of consumer sovereignty; it is a process involving fundamentally opposed class interests.

In order to understand the class character of gentrification it is necessary to begin by placing the process in its broader economic and social context. This will allow us to identify the specific social relationships and historical developments that set the stage for gentrification. The first section will examine the function of community and neighborhood in a capitalist economy, emphasizing the role of community in the reproduction of labor power. The second section will look more closely at the economic function of the neighborhood, attempting to integrate the production, consumption, and reproduction of neighborhoods into the broader process of capital accumulation. The third section will use the preceding analyses to demonstrate the class character of gentrification.

COMMUNITY AND NEIGHBORHOOD

The performance of labor is what produces wealth in any society and capitalist society is no exception. To ensure the continued production of wealth, therefore, requires the continual reproduction of a working class, and this is achieved through a variety of social relationships and institutions. In the first place, and most directly, there is the family. Under capitalism the ideal family is nuclear and privatized—a working husband, a wife, and several children. The family is responsible for biological reproduction and the physical upbringing of children (workers-to-be), as well as for many aspects of their socialization into capitalist society. Women as wives bear the major responsibility for reproduction through the family (J. Smith 1977). In addition, there are social institutions controlled by the state that have as their main function the reproduction of continuous generations of workers. These include schools, churches, and the media, which provide workers with the requisite skills for work as well as an ideological self-understanding of capitalist society and their position in it. The state also intervenes in the family, particularly through legal institutions (marriage, divorce, inheritance laws, abortion legislation, etc.) and social services.

Third, and lying somewhere between the family and the state, is the community. Community is one of the most nebulous and mystified of sociological concepts. As a result, the very clear functions performed by the community tend to be obscured.

First, the community acts as a conduit for the state institutions involved in the reproduction of labor power. Schools, churches, and newspapers may have originated in a few exceptional cases as the organic products of local communities, but today they are provided and governed on a broader regional, national, and even international scale. They therefore provide a conduit into the community for ideas, values, skills, and customs originated elsewhere. Second, the community is a collection of families, but it is more than that, because, in fact, the ideal privatized nuclear family accounts for only 11 percent of households in the U.S. today (J. Smith 1981). In the first place, the majority of women work. In addition there are families with single heads of households, gay and lesbian families, households with several generations of a family, and households in which family members are not married. The importance of this is that, far from being a simple agglomeration of families, the community is a more complex mixture of different kinds of "family" relations. Along with the state institutions, and often, indeed, in conflict with them, these grass-roots social relationships help mold values, lifestyles, and skills, and provide a network of social support at the community level that lies beyond the immediate control of state-imposed institutions. In this way, the crucial role of the community, for capital, is to assist in the reproduction of labor power.

It is important to differentiate between community and neighborhood. While the community is both a social and material entity, the neighborhood is a purely material (spatial) product of the land and housing markets (Harvey and Chatterjee 1974). The neighborhood is a collection of houses and other physical structures in an area defined by the land and housing market. As such it is certainly closely related to the community, particularly in the case of working-class communities. Working-class communities tend to be spatially defined according to neighborhoods; the social relationships and state institutions that create a community are more spatially concentrated at the neighborhood level than they are with the more spatially mobile middle class. This is particularly true when the land and housing market excludes or directs racial, ethnic, and sexual minorities into certain neighborhoods—in the past by exclusionary covenants in land titles, and more recently by denying mortgages or by refusing to rent to these groups.

The nexus of the relationship between community and neighborhood is the house—ideally, for capital, the "single family home." For the family unit (nuclear and privatized or otherwise)—the focus of biological and social reproduction—is based in the house; and the house is the fundamental unit of construction within the neighborhood. The house is therefore simultaneously a center of consumption geared toward the reproduction of labor power and a commodity produced and used as a source of profit for capital. This dual function gives housing a somewhat contradictory role under capitalism, a contradiction that has surfaced during the current economic crisis in which the gentrification of working-class neighborhoods is taking place in the time of an acute housing shortage.

So far, the emphasis has been on the community and the neighborhood as products of capital. This is correct, but it is not the whole story. In order to assist in the reproduction of labor power, the community must have sufficiently tight-knit social relationships and networks of relationships to enable it to provide active support and services. But there is no guarantee that this community solidarity will be used solely to assist the reproduction process. The contradiction here is that communities best organized to facilitate reproduction are also the strongest resistors when they perceive an attack from outside. The very solidarity required by capital can be turned into a weapon against capital. This potential weapon of resistance is even stronger when the working-class community has a clear spatial definition as a neighborhood (Harvey 1977).

Thus we can see already the potential complexity of gentrification as a social process. Far from being a conspiracy by the capitalist class as a whole, gentrification involves opposed interests even within the capitalist class. The class as a whole is interested in the smooth reproduction of labor power, and this requires the maintenance of stable communities, but a number of groups within the class can make substantial profits precisely by destroying certain working-class communities and moving in middle-class homeowners.

Gentrification is an international phenomenon occurring simultaneously in many cities—and at a specific period in the history of capitalism. In other words, after a long period when their dominant function was to assist in the reproduction of labor power, many neighborhoods are now being used for their alternative function—as commodities or groups of commodities, the production, consumption, and reproduction of which are a source of profit for certain members of the capitalist class. At least for the moment, the economic function of neighborhood has superceded the broader social function. How are we to explain this?

HISTORICAL TENDENCIES OF CAPITAL ACCUMULATION

In his analysis of capitalism, Marx demonstrated that the central dynamic behind this mode of production is the necessity of *capital accumulation*. Whereas the worker is dependent for his or her survival on the ability to sell labor power for a wage, the capitalist is entirely dependent on the profits produced by the workers he employs. But the capitalist produces for sale on a market in which he is in competition with other capitalists producing comparable goods. In order to survive in the market, therefore, individual capitalists are forced to invest more and more capital in the more efficient production of more and more goods. Each capital investment must grow in order just to stand still, making capital accumulation a necessity of the capitalist system.

But capitalism does not develop in a linear fashion. A number of orthodox economists have compiled an impressive battery of statistics charting the cyclical character of capital accumulation. Put most simply, there are successive phases of accumulation, overaccumulation, crisis, recovery, then another period of accumulation, etc. Most notable among these researchers has been Simon Kuznets (1961), after whom these cycles are often called "Kuznets cycles." For at least the last 100 years, these cycles of economic development have occurred in the advanced capitalist economies. From depression to depression, each cycle has taken between twenty and thirty years. Orthodox explanations of this cyclical character of capitalist development tend to fasten on one or two "factors," such as changes in the demand for labor, population changes, or variations in consumption levels (e.g., Easterlin 1968). Marxists, however, trace the periodicity of expansion to the basic structure of capitalism itself. According to Marx (1967, vol. 3, chaps. 13-15), there is an inherent tendency in capitalism toward a falling rate of profit. This occurs for the following reason. Profit derives from surplus value produced by workers, that is, from the value produced over and above the value of the labor power itself. But in order to accumulate, under conditions of competition, capitalists are forced to reinvest greater and greater quantities of capital in raw materials and machinery compared to living labor power (i.e., make their operations more capital intensive). But this inherent necessity leads to a systematic diminution of the proportion of capital devoted to the purchase of labor power, yet it is only the performance of labor power that produces profit. This leads eventually to a fall in the rate of profit, and economic crisis ensues (for elaboration of this, see Fine [1975]; Harman [1981]).

This basic picture of capitalist development is important for an understanding of gentrification because urban residential construction is one of the sectors most sensitive to this business cycle. This has been documented by a number of researchers (see, for example, Burns [1935]; Abramovitz [1968]). During periods of rapid accumulation, entire neighborhoods tend to be produced, whereas, with the onset of crisis, *new* residential construction drops precipitously. One can see this clearly by looking, for example, at Baltimore, where Olson (1979, p. 550) has matched peak residential construction with periods immediately preceding major economic crises. Peak construction occurred in Baltimore in 1870-72, 1885-7, 1905-07, 1925, and 1953. In fact, there is a pattern of investment in the built environment as a whole that is related to the cyclical pattern of accumulation and the falling rate of profit. When the major industrial sectors become afflicted with falling profit rates, large quantities of capital are transferred to other sectors, most notably toward construction in the built environment where profit rates remain high and may even be inflated by speculation (Harvey 1978). This includes commercial, recreational, and industrial construction as well as residential. The flow of capital into the built environment is regulated by financial institutions that allocate capital to different sectors according to their potentiality for future profits. Different interest rates between sectors is the precise mechanism employed (Harvey, Forthcoming, chaps. 12, 13).

With investment in the built environment, however, there is a further mechanism for allocating capital investment. If the interest rate helps funnel capital into the built environment during specific periods, the ground rent structure determines which locations will provide the highest return from investment. As will become clear below, the ground rent structure is the most central economic relationship in the analysis of gentrification.

THE RENT GAP

Behind the cyclical periodicity of neighborhood change is a systematic combination of economic processes which, while cyclical, simultaneously determine the secular direction of neighborhood change. It has been suggested elsewhere that neighborhoods experiencing gentrification first underwent what can be called the *devalorization cycle*, leading ultimately to a *rent gap* (Smith 1979). It is this devalorization cycle and the resulting rent gap that prepares the ground for gentrification. Not every neighborhood experiences this devalorization cycle, which depends on specific patterns of capital investment in the area, but empirical observation suggests that, almost without exception, neighborhoods that become targets for gentrification have to a greater or lesser degree experienced this devalorization cycle.

Gentrification begins in neighborhoods that are physically deteriorated, run down, and of low economic value. They arrive in this state by having gone through the devalorization cycle. This cycle is the "rational" outcome of the logic of the land and housing markets but should in no way be viewed as "natural." It is, in fact, the product of myriad decisions by those most able to control the real estate market—financial institutions, developers, landlords, real estate agents. For the sake of analytical convenience, we can divide the devalorization cycle into five separate stages; this helps explain the actual dynamic of devalorization. The first stage is new construction and the first cycle of use; the second is a transition to landlord control; the third is blockbusting; the fourth, redlining, and the fifth, abandonment. The transition from one stage to the next tends to be correlated with phases in the larger accumulation cycle, as suggested in the previous section, and as illustrated below in a case study of Reservoir Hill, in Baltimore. The progressive movement of a neighborhood through the cycle is guided by quite specific decisions and has very clear effects on the value of the properties in an area, their physical state, and the amount of ground rent able to be capitalized for property, either in a sale or through house rent. Thus, the transition from home ownership to landlord control, where it does in fact occur, tends to happen at a period when the housing stock in an area is sufficiently old to begin to need major structural repairs, and when the homeowners decide to move elsewhere rather than incur the cost of these repairs. All of this, of course, depends on the availability of mortgage financing; if the interest rate is high, moving may be costly, and homeowners may decide to make repairs rather than incur a high interest rate on a new mortgage. Under landlord control, the neighborhood's housing stock is used for a completely different purpose. No longer is it owned for direct use as a domicile; rather, it is owned simply as a means of producing a certain percentage of profit. And, since the landlord normally receives his or her profit not so much from the sale of a property as from the house rent on it, the pattern of maintenance tends to be quite different for landlords than for owner occupiers. Landlords may well maintain their properties adequately and thereby keep up the level of ground rent capitalized in an area, but particularly where the market is declining or even just falling behind the market elsewhere, there is an inherently "rational" reason for undermaintaining a property. This leads in turn to the physical deterioration of the neighborhood, and to frequent changes of ownership. Ultimately, this downward spiral of physical deterioration and devalorization leads financial institutions to stop investing in an area, and redlining ensues. The final stage is reached when the landlord can no longer collect enough house rents to cover basic costs, and the structure is abandoned or torched for the insurance payoff.

Now clearly, this is a schematic presentation. A somewhat more elaborate account of the devalorization cycle can be found in Smith (1979). Equally clearly, not every neighborhood undergoes this cycle. Many middle-class residential enclaves remain owner occupied and never begin the downward spiral, since the owners have clearly decided to invest money in the necessary structural repairs. But the, these areas need not be gentrified; they were "gentrified" from the start and stayed that way. Similarly, some of the working-class areas that have become targets for gentrification either missed some of the stages hypothesized in the devalorization cycle or else only partially completed it. Particularly as the process gains momentum, it is not uncommon for neighborhoods of owner-occupied working-class residents to be gentrified. In this case, the neighborhood may never have experienced landlord control or blockbusting, but may well have been redlined by many financial institutions, preventing substantial repairs. The devalorization cycle does convey two things: first, that neighborhoods are "prepared" for gentrification by a basic economic process that is rational by the standards of the capitalist free market; second, that the basic prerequisite for gentrification is a rent gap, namely a gap between the ground rent actually capitalized with a given land use at a specific location and the ground rent that could potentially be appropriated under a higher and better land use at that location. What the devalorization cycle accomplishes is a systematic decrease in the capitalized ground rent, reflected in lower house rents in an area and a relatively lower selling price for structures. When this rent gap becomes sufficiently wide to enable a developer to purchase the old structure, rehabilitate it, make mortgage and interest payments, and still make a satisfactory return on the sale or rental of the renovated building, then a neighborhood is ripe for gentrification.

It is important to emphasize at this point that this process takes place not at the level of individual structures but at the level of neighborhoods. The reason for this is not simply that a neighbor-hood will tend to be fairly homogeneous in terms of the age, condition, and type of tenure of structures, and that therefore what is rational for one structure is likely to be rational for many others. However true this may be, it is of secondary importance. More important is the fact that the potential ground rent to be capitalized as a result of gentrification cannot in fact be capitalized if only a single dwelling is rehabilitated. A renovated mansion in the heart of a slum will not attract a high price unless the entire neighborhood is prime for rehabilitation. This is the celebrated neighborhood effect. It explains why the primary actors behind gentrification are not the romantic exsuburban couple returning for a taste of the urban high-life, but are in fact such major social institutions as the state or the larger financial institutions, or else some other agent with control over substantial proportions of the neighborhood (e.g., a developer who owns a large number of structures in an area). Only when the process has taken root do individuals have any role in spearheading its advance, but even then, they are totally dependent on the state and financial institutions for sources of finance (Smith 1979b).

This historical process is presently being researched in Reservoir Hill, one of Baltimore's "conspicuous consumption" neighborhoods. During the building boom years of the early 1890s, a small group of real estate speculators acquired and consolidated several large parcels of land in the outlying city. These speculators then leased their holdings (the land tenure system in Baltimore permits separate ownership of land and housing) to builders who then constructed hundreds of eclectic style and Richardsonian Romanesque dwellings for Baltimore's bourgeoning capitalist and "professional" families. By the 1920s, the rapid escalation of ground rent levels forced the remaining undeveloped land into its highest and best use—high-rise, luxury apartment buildings. In the middle of the 1930s depression, the foreclosure of owner-occupant mortgages led to the conversion of many houses into landlord control—three- and four-unit apartments that were then further subdivided during the 1940s to accommodate the large numbers of war workers arriving in Baltimore to work in the defense industries.

As a neighborhood, Reservoir Hill had a physical coherence resulting from the history of its construction, but is also received a social coherence from the pattern of capital investment in the Baltimore housing market. The most prestigious garden suburbs of Roland Park were constructed at the turn of the century by mainly British capital, but these suburbs contained restrictive covenants against Jews, blacks and Chinese. The rising Jewish middle class was forced elsewhere, particularly into Reservoir Hill.

Devaluation of the local housing stock in the 1930s made the neighborhood accessible to middle-class blacks living in less salubrious neighborhoods to the west of Reservoir Hill. Some could now afford to take over foreclosed mortgages in Reservoir Hill, prompting existing residents to covenant against property transfers to blacks. Just after the 1935 local building boom, the ability of blacks (middle-class at first) to live in Reservoir Hill became a reality. The old inhabitants moved north, assisted by federally subsidized mortgages (Veterans Administration [V.A.] and Federal Housing Authority [F.H.A.] mortgages were seldom obtained for housing within central cities, especially for rehabilitation), and those who did not sell their houses became absentee landlords. By 1960, most of the owner-occupant families were black. The area was effectively redlined now. House values in 1970 had drastically declined, and absentee landlordism became the dominant mode of tenure; the tenants were for the most part black, working class, and unemployed. In 1972, speculation in this neighborhood began in earnest, due to the development of a rent gap as the housing stock was devalued, and the now real possibility that the area would be redeveloped. Many absentee landlords had either switched their investments into other sectors of the economy (tax-free municipal bonds, for example) or were diverting their capital to other neighborhoods. Today the gentrification of Reservoir Hill is coordinated by the local planning and housing departments who are using state-assisted mortgages and an intense ideological campaign to steer middle-class people into the neighborhood.

The development of the rent gap, which we have identified as the prerequisite for gentrification, came about in the central cities as a result of this movement of capital from one location to another. It was not simply a matter of capital moving out of one neighborhood and into another, but a systematic movement of capital out of the nineteenth-century urban cores and into the suburbs. The reason for this move, obviously, was that profit rates were higher in the suburbs. New industrial facilities, new roads, new suburban residential communities, and eventually new commercial facilities were being constructed in the suburbs beginning initially after the economic crisis of the 1890s and continuing in earnest after the Second World War. Profit rates were higher in the suburbs for a number of reasons. First, land was easily available and ground rent levels were low. Second, the capitalist state, particularly at the Federal level, subsidized new suburban development with such programs as the Interstate Highway System, the FHA subsidies to new home ownership, and so forth. Third, the alternative of *in situ* expansion in the already existing city would have been prohibitively expensive. Both land and buildings would still have had very high acquisition costs since structures were relatively young and had not yet returned their value to their owners; they had not been amortized. Not only because of its size, therefore, but because of the cost, a Sparrows Point Steel Works could not be located in Baltimore, nor a Gary Steel Works in Chicago. The same argument applies to suburban residential development. The development of the suburbs cannot be explained by citing an absolute lack of space in existing urban areas, but rather by understanding the way in which this society produces a differentiated space and the way in which differential costs of development then attach to different spaces.

The Marxist argument about gentrification, therefore, begins from the idea that urban space (as well as space at other scales) is the specific effect of the kind of society in which this urban space is developed; the feudal city is not the capitalist city, although the latter may contain survivals from the former. And the capitalist city, we suggest, is developed according to a logic that is internal to capital itself. Gentrification is therefore the product not simply of a capitalist organization of space but of the specific needs of capital at a given time, and it is here that we must broaden our focus and look not at the rehabilitation of residential structures alone, but at the entire transformation of central cities. Since the late 1950s there has been a systematic movement of capital back into the inner cities. At first, this capital was usually employed to construct large-scale office and commercial structures. These early schemes were typically urban renewal projects with heavy state subsidies. Thus, with the original urban renewal legislation (1949, 1954) followed later by the Community Development Block Grant Program (CDBG) and the Urban Development Action Grants (UDAG), the emphasis of state subsidies has shifted resolutely toward the city and away from the suburbs. Private capital has made a similar spatial reversal, aptly symbolized by the career of James Rouse, the nationally known developer. In the 1960s, his capital was committed to the suburban and exurban fringe; he built Columbia New Town, in Maryland, and was a pioneer of suburban shopping malls and plazas. Now, in the late 1970s and 1980s, he has moved his capital back to the city with such projects as the Inner Harbor and Cross Keys Village, in Baltimore, Gallery I and II, in Philadelphia, Faneuil Hall, in Boston, and many more.

Of this larger movement of capital back toward the city, gentrification is only a small part, but it fulfills the same function. The gentrification and redevelopment of central cities began when the rate of profit in the industrial sector was declining and substantial quantities of capital were moved into real estate in search of higher profits. Clearly, not all of it returned to the city to take advantage of the rent gap, but increasing proportions of capital did. By 1973, the broader capitalist economy was in severe crisis and the function of inner-city redevelopment and rehabilitation—as a means to help prevent a falling rate of profit—became clearer. And as the process proceeds, this function becomes even clearer with the movement of middle-level construction and development corporations into the lucrative gentrification market. Gentrification is therefore not a unique phenomenon. It is, rather, the latest phase in a movement of capital back to the city. It differs from the earlier phase in that it entails generally smaller-scale capital involved in residential properties. These are properties that survived the first wave of urban renewal and, although usually structurally sound, are too small an investment for the largest-scale construction capital to become directly involved.

GENTRIFICATION AND CLASS

If we now conduct an analysis of the benefits and costs of gentrification, it will become clear that the effects of this process are sharply delineated along class lines. Looking first at benefits, the major benefit is financial in the form of profit. The main beneficiaries here, we hypothesize, are the financial institutions that have large quantities of capital tied up in land ownership and in individual mortages. Their profit comes in the form of interest. Developers also appropriate a portion of the profit, and this applies not only to professional developers and construction companies but also to individual landlords and owner occupiers who employ a professional developer to rehabilitate one or more structures. A final portion of the direct profit accrues to the capitalist state (usually at the local level) in the form of property taxes. But benefits appear in forms other than the economic. It is necessary to consider also the acquisition of new living spaces, and in this case, the evidence is overwhelming that the so-called inmovers are white, middle-class professionals, aged usually between 25 and 40 (LeGates and Hartman 1980). Thus the benefits of gentrification appear to accrue to the capitalist class, defined as those who own and control capital for the purpose of investing it for profit or interest, as well as to the middle class in general, who are the beneficiaries not only of new living space but also of profitable, if comparatively small, investments.

The costs of gentrification fall for the most part on an entirely different sector of the population. The major cost of gentrification is the displacement of individuals, families, and entire communities from neighborhoods undergoing gentrification. According to the U.S. Department of Housing and Urban Development, in their *Displacement Report* (1979a), displacement affected between 520,000 and 540,000 households annually between 1974 and 1976. By this estimate, about 1.5 million people would be displaced annually, but compared with other estimates, this figure may be conservative. LeGates and Hartman (1980), for example, put the figure at 2.5 million. The HUD report continues to emphasize that gentrification accounts for only a small proportion of the total occurrences of displacement, and this is used to justify the government's policy of benign neglect toward displacees. The government line is that gentrification is relatively insignificant, that abandonment is a greater threat, that in any case data are impossible to find, that large scale antidisplacement programs may slow down "revitalization," that the problem is in any case a product of the private market where the Federal government should not tamper, and that, at the very most it is a problem for local governments (Sumka 1980; Cicin-Sain 1980; U.S. Department of Housing and Urban Development 1979a).

We would argue that the HUD report and related publications underestimate the extent of displacement as part of a deliberate attempt to encourage gentrification. In the first place, they define displacement in such a way that "gentrification-caused displacement" is seen as quite separate from gentrification caused by abandonment. The latter is somehow dismissed as a "natural" effect of the free market and comparatively more important than the former, which is lamented as somehow unnatural but of little numerical significance. In fact, if there is any truth to the idea of the devalorization cycle, it is clear that displacement due to abandonment has exactly the same cause as so-called gentrification-caused displacement. It is simply displacement one stage earlier; in an area to be gentrified, the residents are displaced before gentrification begins rather than directly by the gentrifiers. Even where abandonment is not followed by gentrification, displacement results from the same cycle of economic events that produces gentrification and has the same effect on the displaced population.

Second, HUD cites the lack of reliable data as a reason for inaction around the issue of displacement, but in fact they have made little effort to compile the necessary data. The 1979 report, the first and, so far, the last of its kind, was hurriedly prepared in response to political pressure, and its authors undertook no original research. Several small, local studies have been funded by HUD, but these have been so unsatisfactory that even HUD has not advertised their results. In Baltimore, for example, HUD commissioned a token study of South Baltimore which, when it finally came out in 1979, reported that this rapidly gentrifying area was experiencing only 2 percent annual displacement (Goodman and Weissbrod 1979). In response to strong local pressure by a community group (Coalition of Peninsular Organizations—COPO), the study was withdrawn by HUD and the data re-evaluated. When the revisions were finally released, the figure had been raised to 8 percent, but during the controversy, a local developer, who was also involved in the execution of the study, estimated privately that the level of displacement in the most active areas of South Baltimore was about 25 percent annually.

The reason for the lack of data, then, has less to do with the inherent complexity of the process or the difficulty of gathering data—the excuses used by HUD and other apologists for gentrification. It has more to do with the fact that HUD wants to minimize the apparent extent of the process in order to justify its minimal support for displacees and its substantial subsidy of the rehabilitation and redevelopment process. HUD is quite explicit about its support for gentrification, arguing that, since disinvestment is still more widespread than reinvestment—the outward middle-class migration, more prominent than any movement back to the city—reinvestment should not in any way be jeopardized. Indeed, in the words of Howard Sumka, one of the principal authors of the HUD *Displacement Report*, "the general federal thrust of federal assistance toward encouraging revitalization should be maintained" since "the overall impact of revitalization is a positive one....To maximize the economic efficiency of the urban system, revitalization should be encouraged to the greatest possible degree" (Sumka 1980, p. 280). The report never states directly for whom revitalization is positive and for whom the urban system is meant to be efficient, but if one reads beneath the seemingly reasonable rhetoric, the discriminatory intent, both racial and class, of this policy is clear; the urban system is made efficient by attracting the middle class and displacing the poor and the working class. Thus, in an analysis of the costs and benefits of gentrification, Sumka lists as a potential cost to gentrifiers the possibility of "physical danger due to conflict with remaining residents" (p. 276). Yet nowhere does he list the reverse: the possibility of physical danger to community residents at the hands of gentrifiers. The assumption is clear: the working class (and particularly the black working class?) is naturally prone to violence, the middle class is the victim. This attitude, we would contend, accurately reflects the ideology upon which Federal displacement policy is based.

The real victims of gentrification are almost entirely low-income members of the working class and the unemployed. Goodman and Weissbrod, for example, in their HUD study of South Baltimore (1979), found that 54 percent of the displacees had an income of under $9,000. Contrary to the stereotype, however, it seems that the majority of displaced working-class tenants and owners are white and not black (LeGates and Hartman, 1980). The percentage of displaced whites compared to displaced blacks varies remarkably from city to city, but there are two likely explanations for this preponderance of whites in absolute, if not in relative, terms. First, gentrification seems to have been introduced in white neighborhoods more often than in black ones, perhaps because white middle-class gentrifiers perceived the white neighborhoods as safer and less threatening than black neighborhoods. But more significantly, many of the black inner-city neighborhoods closest to the Central business district (CBD), and therefore more prone to early gentrification,were destroyed in the first round of urban renewal during the sixties, particularly for highway and office developments. It is likely that a greater proportion of the total number of blacks are still affected, however, and as the process burgeons, the proportion of blacks displaced will increase. Other minorities are also disproportionately affected—elderly tenants, and female-headed households, particularly.

What happens to the displacees is a crucial problem. While Federal officials again call for more research, there is substantial evidence concerning their fate. As early as 1964, Hartman examined the housing conditions of relocated families and, from a review of thirty-four case studies, concluded that as many as 86 percent of relocatees were placed in substandard housing. The median figure was 35 percent (Hartman 1964; see also Hartman [1974] for a later study). As Hartman (1979) emphasizes, there is no reason to assume that displacement has a fundamentally different effect today. Thus there is no real problem with data unless, of course, the problem is self-imposed. In Philadelphia, for example, the Housing Authority published it first report on relocation in 1958, concluding that 72 percent of those displaced were relocated into substandard housing (Philadelphia Housing Authority, 1958). This was also the last such report published by the Authority; they simply refused to keep the data.

This picture of the fate of displacees is consistent with the pervasive if rarely documented experience of displacees from today's gentrifying neighborhoods. As regards the location of displacees, it seems that there is a marked tendency to cluster around the old neighborhood (LeGates and Hartman 1980). In fact, a fairly common sequence seems to involve families being displaced once or twice within the same neighborhood, before moving out to a neighboring area. There, too, they may be displaced as gentrification proceeds, and it is at this stage that a move to the suburbs seems most likely. On this aspect of gentrification—the location of displacees—there is a genuine lack of data. There is some evidence, although of an impressionistic and so far undocumented nature, that a substantial number of displacees eventually moves to the suburbs. This is particularly true of black displacees, who are steered into certain of the older suburbs. This increased suburbanization of blacks (U.S. Department of Housing and Urban Development 1979b) is occasionally seen as a sign that blacks are finally winning access to the suburbs, but the reality is quite different. In fact, the carrot of the suburban dream is often used both to encourage and to give a liberal gloss to the displacement of blacks from the inner city; a forced move can be made to appear voluntary. One need not spend much time in a gentrifying neighborhood to hear about families for whom the suburban dream has become a nightmare, because they either could only afford or were steered to suburban neighborhoods where the housing was as bad or worse than what they had left in the inner city.

Displacement is only the most severe effect of gentrification. Others include the destruction of community, the increased squeeze on housing availability, higher rents. In Baltimore, for example, the vacancy rate remained at about 2 percent throughout much of 1980, making it both difficult and expensive to find new accommodations. For the working class, gentrification is only part of a larger attack on living conditions—displacement from the neighborhood is paralleled by displacement from work (unemployment) and rising rents are paralleled with relatively lower wages, while all around, cutbacks are being made in vital services. Further, the increased unemployment and the reduction of wages relative to inflation has meant that, more than ever, the increased female participation in the labor force is out of necessity not out of choice. Two wages are necessary to make up the family wage. Gentrification threatens the ability of many families to make the family wage in so far as many of the second jobs taken on by a family emanate from the margins and interstices of the "official" economy. Access to this marginal work depends very much on household location since work is generally sporadic and arranged on the spot. By destroying working-class communities and by forcibly displacing families from established locations, gentrification deprives many families of the means with which to deal with economic crisis. In general, the various supportive social networks and links that assist many working-class families in handling crisis are destroyed, along with the destruction of community. This is most costly for women heads of household, who are severely affected by gentrification. A woman's wage is only 61 percent of a man's, by the latest government figures, and the central city contains twice as many female-headed, single-parent households as the suburbs (Freeman 1980, p. 6). These women are especially dependent on community support systems, and of all the victims of gentrification, they are probably the most adversely affected.

Here we confront a basic contradiction. The removal of informal support networks means that some working-class families depend more than ever on achieving a full family wage in order to purchase the things they once obtained informally. This means either an increase in wages—very unlikely during a crisis and a concomitant attack on wages—or else the continued squeezing of the working-class standard of living, and with it the heightened threat of uprising.

Gentrification was certainly well under way before the outbreak of the current economic crisis in 1973. Hence, the falsehood of explanations that narrowly attribute the process to changes in commuting costs consequent upon higher petrol prices. But we suggest—and it is only a hypothesis based on personal observation, given a paucity of data—that the onset of economic crisis has hastened the process of gentrification relative to new suburban house construction. This is what we would expect, but it remains to be substantiated. A further myth about gentrification is that it is a process unique to the late twentieth century. The following quote from a rather well known nineteenth-century figure should suffice to dispel that notion: The Parisian solution consists of turning "the city into a luxury city pure and simple...of making breaches in the working class quarters of our big cities, particularly in those that are centrally situated, irrespective of whether this practice is occasioned by considerations of public health and beautification or by the demand for big centrally located business premises or by traffic requirements, such as the laying down of railways, streets, etc. No matter how different the reasons may be, the result is everywhere the same: the most scandalous alleys and lanes disappear to the accompaniment of lavish self-glorification by the bourgeoisie on account of this tremendous success" (Engels 1975, p. 71).

All that is new about the process is the rehabilitation of old dwellings at the present scale, but that is only a part of the larger restructuring of urban space: "No matter how different the reasons may be, the result is everywhere the same." What makes the process today different from what Engels described—a process, incidentally, which he named "Haussman" after Napoleon III's famous architect and planner—is not a difference in the actual activities taking place but simply a difference of scale and, ultimately, of significance. The restructuring of urban space now taking place is likely to produce nothing short of a bourgeois playground in the downtowns of the largest North American and European cities. This is significant not only for the sake of the product itself or for its disastrous effect on the working class, but also for the function it fulfills for the capitalist class. This time around, we are witnessing the start of what is likely to be a wholesale restructuring of urban space with the deliberate effect of revitalizing not so much inner city neighborhoods as the profit rate. More than ever before, capitalism is appropriating space and using it as a means to survive.

A further myth is that displacement is an accidental byproduct of the gentrification process alone. In fact it is a far more general process affecting the working class. Writing of the broader housing problem, Engels concluded that "in reality the bourgeoisie has only one method of settling the housing question after *its* fashion.... The breeding places of disease, the infamous holes and cellars in which the capitalist mode of production confines our workers night after night, are not abolished; they are merely *shifted elsewhere*" (1975, p. 71-74). And so it is with the displacement of the working class to the suburbs. But this is only one aspect of displacement. Today, millions of workers in all continents are forced to migrate to find work and are effectively displaced from their homes for much of the year. The Irish famine displaced several million agricultural workers—those it did not kill. Indeed, capitalism was born out of the displacement of peasants from the land, forcing them into the city to form the earliest urban proletariat. Thus, capitalism is based precisely on its ability to displace the working class in all sorts of situations. Workers are required to cluster in places of production in order to get jobs, but when runaway shops leave and the jobs go with them, workers are displaced. In order to bring about the reproduction of labor power, workers are required to live in spatially fixed communities, but when these communities become too organized or when the location can be employed by capital for a more profitable economic use, the working class is displaced. Gentrification-caused displacement is only a small part of this process.

CONCLUSION

Gentrification is often referred to as "revitalization," and it is possible now to see a deeper and truer meaning for this term. To be sure, many abandoned and slum neighborhoods are gentrified and thereby revitalized, after a fashion. But particularly as the process gathers momentum in one section of a city, gentrification begins to spread to areas that have not undergone a complete devalorization cycle and in which the neighborhoods are often stable and very vital. In Baltimore, for example, gentrification has spread from its original cores into sections of South and East Baltimore that, prior to gentrification were stable, lively working-class communities. Likewise, in Philadelphia, the success of Society Hill led to a voracious attack on the previously tight communities of Queen Village and Pennsport. In these cases what has taken place is not a revitalization but a devitalization. Summer chairs on the sidewalk, televisions out on the stoop, and children's street games are replaced with herringbone pavements, fake gas lamps, wrought iron window railings, and a deathly hush on the street. The only meaningful use of the term "revitalization" comes from the recognition that what is revitalized is not necessarily the existing community, which is actually quite incidental to the process, but the profitability of capital investment.

Compared with the other processes involved in the restructuring of inner urban space, the specific boosterism that surrounds gentrification is out of proportion. Comapratively little capital is involved in gentrification as such, as against the redevelopment of commercial, office, recreational, and new residential land uses. As a symbol of "revitalization," however, gentrification is ideal and this probably accounts for the boosterism. The larger redevelopment projects are obviously the result of corporate capital and the state, making them easy targets of working-class opposition. Gentrification, on the other hand, can be portrayed with very little effort as almost a public service. The classic image comes in the Sunday newspaper magazine section: eclectic, interesting, renaissance individuals are braving a very risky real estate market, and even— heaven forbid—expending some of their own labor, to rehabilitate a house and do their bit toward rejuvenating a dying neighborhood. In this way, the image of gentrification is used to sell the larger package of revitalization; Baltimore is no longer the "armpit of America" but, if one believes the advertisements prepared by the Mayor's Office, it is "Charm City."

The state has no solution to the problems caused by gentrification. As an active force encouraging the process, the state is part of the problem, not the solution, as far as working-class communities threatened with invasion are concerned. The state not only encourages the process but it systematically covers up the plight of the displacees. Even where the negative effects are admitted, state officials usually concur that higher property taxes accruing from gentrification will be redistributed, resulting in a net gain for everyone. In the face of today's drastic cuts in local and

Federal budgets for much-needed services, together with tax cuts for corporate capital, this justification no longer sounds plausible. Equally implausible is the sentiment expressed in the HUD displacement report, that gentrification "offers a unique opportunity to encourage the development of neighborhoods that are integrated both racially and economically" (1979, p. i). Viewed in the light of the real experience of working-class communities facing the threat of gentrification, this statement is less naive than it is cynical. For working-class communities, it is not a question of how to integrate the white upper middle class, but rather of how to organize to prevent the systematic theft and destruction of their community.

REFERENCES

Abramovitz, M. 1968. *Evidence of long swings in aggregate construction since the Civil War.* New York: National Bureau of Economic Research.

Burns, A. 1935. Long cycles in residential construction. In *Economic essays in honor of Wesley Clair Mitchell.* New York: Columbia University.

Cicin-Sain, B. 1980. The costs and benefits of neighborhood revitalization. In *Urban revitalization,* ed. D. Rosenthal, vol. 18. Beverly Hills: Sage Urban Affairs Annual Review.

Easterlin, R. 1968. *Population, labor force and long swings in economic growth.* New York: National Bureau of Economic Research .

Engels, F. 1975 ed. *The housing question.* Moscow: Progress Publishers.

Fine, B. 1975. *Marx's Capital.* London: Macmillan.

Freeman, J. 1980. Women and urban policy. *Signs,* vol. 5, sup., p. 6.

Goodman, A., and Weissbrod, R. 1979. *Housing market activity in South Baltimore: Immigration, speculation and displacement.* Baltimore: The Johns Hopkins University Center for Metropolitan Planning and Research.

Harman, C. 1981. Marx's theory of crisis and its critics. *International Socialism* 2 (11): 30-71.

Hartman, C. 1964. The housing of relocated families. *Journal of the American Institute of Planners* 30: 266-86.

———. 1971. Relocation: Illusory promises and no relief. *Virginia Law Review* 57: 745-817.

———. 1979. Comment on "Neighborhood revitalization and displacement: A review of the evidence." *Journal of the American Planning Association* 45: 488-91.

Harvey, D. 1977. Labour, capital and class struggle around the built environment in advanced capitalist societies. *Politics and Society* 6: 265-95.

———. 1978. The urban process under capitalism: A framework for analysis. *International Journal of Urban and Regional Research* 2(1): 101-31.

———. Forthcoming. *The Limits of capital.* London: Basil Blackwell.

_____, and Chatterjee, L. 1974. Absolute rent and the structuring of space by governmental and financial institutions. *Antipode* 6(1): 22-36.

Kuznets, S. 1961. *Capital in the American economy: Its formation and financing.* New York: National Bureau of Economic Research.

Le Gates, R., and Hartman, C. 1980. Gentrification-caused displacement. Paper presented at the conference on New Perspectives in Urban Political Economy,May 1980, at American University, Washington, D.C.

Marx, K. 1967 ed. *Capital,* 3 vols. New York: International Publishers.

Olson, S. 1979. Baltimore imitates the spider. *Annals of the Association of American Geographers,* 69(4): 557-74.

Philadelphia Housing Authority. 1958. *Relocation in Philadelphia.*

Smith, J. 1977. Women and the family, 2 pts. *International Socialism,* vols. 100, 104.

_____. 1981. Women, work, the family and economic recessoin. Paper presented at the symposium on Feminism and the Critique of Capitalism, 24-25 April 1981, at John Hopkins University, Baltimore.

Smith, N. 1979a. Toward a theory of gentrification: A back to the city movement by capital not people. *Journal for the American Planning Association* 45: 538-48.

_____. 1979b. Gentrification and capital: Theory, practice and ideology in Society Hill. *Antipode* 11(3): 24-35.

_____. 1981. Gentrification as a process of uneven development. Paper presented at the conference on New Perspectives in Urban Political Economy, May 22-24 1981, at American University, Washington, D.C.

Sumka, H. 1980. Federal Antidisplacement policy in a context of urban decline. In *Back in the city,* ed. S. B. Laska and D. Spain. New York: Pergamon.

U. S. Department of Housing and Urban Development, 1979a. *Displacement report.* Washington, D.C.: Office of Policy Development and Research.

U. S. Department of Housing and Urban Development, 1979b. *Recent suburbanization of blacks: how much, who, and where?* Washington, D.C.: Office of Policy Development and Research.

II

Recent Researching Findings on Gentrification, Incumbent Upgrading, and Displacement

INTRODUCTION

Part II includes six chapters describing empirical research projects in a variety of cities. Five of the six papers have not previously been published. DeGiovanni (chap. 4) presents some general findings on the costs and benefits of revitalization in twelve neighborhoods in six cities. Chapters 5, 6, and 7 use a variety of techniques—some quite innovative—both to document the extent of neighborhood revitalization and to analyze the varying attitudes of such groups as newcomers to neighborhoods, renovators who have lived in gentrified areas for a number of years, longtime owners of homes in changing neighborhoods, and renters.

Next come two chapters that focus on the empirical study of displacement. Lee and Hodge (chap. 8) document the vulnerability of the urban underclass—comprised of the poor, blacks, female-headed households, and the elderly—to displacement, while Henig (chap. 9) looks exclusively at the impact of gentrification on the elderly. In conjunction with DeGiovanni's discussion of displacement, these chapters present a number of complementary findings. For example, both Henig and Lee and Hodge find the elderly poor to be particularly susceptible to involuntary displacement, and both DeGiovanni and Lee and Hodge make the point that displacement does not appear to be generated solely by neighborhood revitalization in the urban core. The focus of these chapters on the displacement of an urban underclass is reminiscent of issues raised by Smith and LeFaivre's class analysis of gentrification in chapter 3.

CHAPTER FOUR

An Examination of Selected Consequences of Revitalization in Six U.S. Cities

FRANK F. DEGIOVANNI

Much of the interest in, and the controversy surrounding, neighborhood revitalization is focused on the presumed costs and benefits thought to be produced by reinvestment. The most publicly contested issue is whether or not revitalization is causing widespread displacement of residents living in the neighborhoods prior to the start of reinvestment.[1] A number of other changes, both positive and negative,[2] may also be generated by reinvestment in previously deteriorated neighborhoods. For example, the improvement in housing quality during revitalization is believed to result in increased property values and, ultimately, increased property tax revenues for the city. Although these changes represent benefits for cities, they may impose costs on original residents who cannot afford increases in the cost of housing.

Frank F. DeGiovanni is Assistant Professor of City and Regional Planning, Pratt Institute.

The research reported here was funded by the Office of Policy Development and Research, U.S. Department of Housing and Urban Development, under Contract No. H-2985. The findings and conclusions presented are those of the author and do not necessarily reflect the views or policies of the Department of Housing and Urban Development or the U.S. Government.

The following individuals made important contributions to the study on which this article is based: Michael Connelly, Barrett Joyner, Nancy Ann Paulson, James Chromy, Jack Shirey, Eva Silber, and Judy Rhew. This paper first appeared in *Urban Studies*. It is reprinted with the permission of the publisher.

This chapter represents a first attempt to measure some of the important costs and benefits thought to be produced by revitalization in twelve neighborhoods, in six cities. Four specific changes in neighborhoods commonly attributed to reinvestment are examined.[3] An attempt is made to determine whether these changes should be viewed as unique consequences of revitalization or as representative of changes occurring throughout the cities during the period.

Conceptual Framework

Any attempt to identify the consequences of revitalization must first classify the changes likely to be observed in revitalizing neighborhoods into three categories: (1) changes that are the distinguishing features of revitalization; (2) changes that may accompany revitalization but which are not essential components of the process; and (3) changes that are probably consequences of revitalization.

Identification of the central, distinguishing feature of revitalization depends upon what the viewer perceives as the most important change in revitalizing neighborhoods. The approach adopted in this study is to consider renovation of properties as the central feature of revitalization. This decision is largely based on Clay's distinction between incumbent upgrading and gentrification, which suggests that actual improvement in the quality of housing is the one change shared by all revitalizing neighborhoods (Clay 1979).[4]

A number of other changes either have been observed, or are claimed to occur, in revitalizing neighborhoods.[5] Differentiating the characteristics of the process from the consequences of reinvestment is largely arbitrary. The approach taken here is to view three specific changes in housing market activity—increase in sales prices, increase in sales volume, and prevalence of apparently speculative sales—as characteristics of the process.

Neighborhood changes supposedly generated by inmigration of higher-income groups, property renovation, or the changed nature of market transactions are viewed as consequences of revitalization. Four outcomes were anticipated as outcomes of revitalization.[6] Two of these are viewed as benefits for the city as a whole: (l) encouragement of neighborhood long-term owners to reinvest in their properties as a result of renovation performed by newcomers to the neighborhood and (2) an increase in the appraised value of properties in revitalizing neighborhoods as a result of the renovation.

The remaining two hypothesiszed outcomes are considered to be costs incurred by residents who lived in the neighborhoods prior to the beginning of revitalization: (1) an increase in the property tax burden of owners who have not sold or improved their properties during revitalization; and (2) widespread conversion of neighborhood properties from renter- to owner-occupied. An analysis of the data on conversion from renter- to owner-occupancy will provide an estimate of the amount of potential displacement occurring.[7] However, since this is a rough indicator of only one source of displacement, it underestimates the total amount of displacement that may have occurred.

METHODOLOGY

The present study was funded by the Department of Housing and Urban Development to document the magnitude and the extent of revitalization initiated by the private market and to identify, where possible, the effects of investment on the housing stock and on residents of the neighborhoods prior to the start of reinvestment. Six cities—San Francisco, Denver, Atlanta, Cincinnati, Hartford, Philadelphia—were chosen for study on the basis of two criteria:

1. The existence of at least two neighborhoods that, at the time of selection, had undergone at least a moderate amount of private market-initiated reinvestment and in which displacement was believed to be a problem[8]
2. The availability of the data required for analysis

The study design specified the selection of three study neighborhoods in each city—two revitalizing neighborhoods and a third neighborhood, similar in important respects, in 1970, to at least one of the revitalizing neighborhoods, but not undergoing reinvestment.[9] This latter neighborhood, which was assumed to be representative of the trends occurring in similar nonrevitalizing neighborhoods throughout the city, was chosen to provide a baseline against which to compare changes in the revitalizing neighborhoods. It would have been preferable to use the entire city as the comparison group, but the cost of collecting city-wide data made this approach unfeasible.

Revitalizing neighborhoods in each city were identified through review of previous studies, telephone interviews, and field visits to the cities. Two additional criteria were used to make the final selection of neighborhoods:

1. That the set of twelve revitalizing neighborhoods recommended for study represents as wide a cross-section as possible with respect to both the amount of revitalization that had occurred and the type of predominant housing stock (single-family vs. multifamily)
2. That the cities selected be located in different geographical regions to take into account potential regional differences in growth rates, economic conditions, age of the housing stock, and other factors that might affect reinvestment

The target population in each neighborhood consisted of residential properties located within the boundaries of the neighborhood, from which were excluded properties receiving any type of public funding. A stratified random sample of 400 residential properties in each of the two revitalizing neighborhoods and 250 properties in the comparison neighborhood was selected from each city's master property assessment file. The sample of properties was stratified by number of housing units and geographic location within the neighborhood to insure that a representative sample of single-family and multifamily properties located in all parts of the neighborhood was selected. Estimates of the beginning date of reinvestment were obtained from local officials. Data on property characteristics, property value, sales activity, property improvements, housing code violations, and tenure were collected for every sample property for a time series beginning prior to the estimated starting date of reinvestment and ending in September-December 1979. These data were merged to create a historical file for each of the 1,050 properties for which data were collected in each city.

Two types of analysis, each using difference of means tests, are employed to determine whether the expected outcomes of revitalization were realized. Three of the four anticipated outcomes—increase in assessed values, stimulation of renovation by persons who owned property in the neighborhood prior to revitalization, and potential displacement—must be investigated by comparing the magnitude of these changes in the revitalizing and comparison neighborhoods. If the changes are significantly greater in the revitalizing than in the comparison neighborhood, one can conclude that reinvestment produced outcomes that did not occur (at least at the same level) in neighborhoods not undergoing reinvestment.

The remaining anticipated outcome is investigated by determining whether the increase in property assessments is significantly different for properties involved in revitalization than for properties not involved in the reinvestment (referred to as "inactive" properties).

One limitation of the analysis should be noted. The property assessment practices of six cities may not be representative of these practices in all cities.[10] At a minimum, we can draw sound conclusions regarding the costs and benefits produced by revitalization in these six cities. To the degree that other cities have similar assessment practices, these results are suggestive of the consequences likely to be produced by reinvestment in other cities.

BACKGROUND ON RENOVATION AND HOUSING MARKET ACTIVITY

More than 20 percent of the properties were rehabilitated after the start of reinvestment in 9 of the 12 revitalizing neighborhoods; more than 30 percent of the properties were renovated in 6 of these neighborhoods (see table 4.1).[11] This is an impressive amount of rehabilitation. Furthermore, the percentage of properties improved is significantly greater in the revitalizing neighborhoods than in the comparison neighborhood in 8 of 12 cases.[12]

A large proportion of properties changed hands during revitalization. More than 40 percent of all properties were sold after the onset of reinvestment in 8 of 12 neighborhoods, with the percentage of properties sold per year ranging from 2.5 percent to 8.2 percent. Sales prices increased dramatically after the start of reinvestment, with the cost of single-family and multifamily housing increasing more than twice as much as the Standard Metropolitan Statistical Area (SMSA) Consumer Price Index for Housing in 8 of the 12 neighborhoods.

Property renovation is the only change that consistently distinguished revitalizing neighborhoods from the comparison neighborhoods.[13] Revitalizing neighborhoods with significantly greater rehabilitation activity than the comparison neighborhood did not always have a significantly greater number of property transactions or substantially greater gains in sales prices. Although sales transactions and prices did rise in these neighborhoods, the amount of increase in not substantially different from increases that occurred in comparison neighborhoods with significantly less rehabilitation.

The unexpectedly large changes observed in the comparison neighborhoods are interpreted as reflections of the influence of macroeconomic factors—inflation, rising interest rates, increased demand for housing—on local housing markets. In most of the neighborhoods, even those in which reinvestment began prior to

Table Chapter 4, g-5

Table 4.1. Rehabilitation and Sales Activity Following Revitalization: Differences Between Revitalizing and Comparison Neighborhoods

City/Neighborhood[a]	Revitalization Period	% Increase CPI All Housing[b]	% Rehabilitated Properties Mean	't' Ratio[c]	% Properties Sold Mean	't' Ratio[c]	% Increase in Single Family Sales Prices[d]
Atlanta							
Midtown	1971-79	73.2	31.1	5.55	67.6	1.57	155.1
Inman Park	1971-79		29.5	5.12	74.0	3.32	298.0
Poncey Highlands	1971-79		14.0	--	6.20	--	48.9
Cincinnati		NA					
Mt. Adams	1967-79		45.5	.89	53.8	5.73	465.4
Walnut Hills	1977-79		12.3	-.08	10.7	.09	-28.3
Avondale[e]	1977-79		41.9	--	32.1	--	62.8
	1977-79		12.5	--	10.4	--	26.0
Denver							
Baker	1973-79	68.6	33.2	-.94	53.1	1.14	182.8
CPW/Whittier/FP	1973-79		45.3	2.21	44.3	-1.03	220.0
Jefferson Park	1973-79		36.7	--	48.4	--	170.3
Hartford		36.5					
Asylum Hill	1975-79		30.4	5.83	30.7	1.81	59.3
West End	1975-79		20.1	2.43	31.9	2.17	16.1
Parkville	1975-79		13.2	--	24.0	--	323.1
Philadelphia[e]		71.0					
Spring Garden	1971-79		16.3	5.26	60.6	4.45	-91.0
Fairmount	1971-79		5.9	.91	46.5	.92	242.2
Kensington	1971-79		4.4	--	42.8	--	33.3
San Francisco		71.1					
Hayes Valley	1972-79		40.0	5.37	47.9	2.74	120.0
Dolores Heights[f]	1972-79		28.8	2.38	39.3	.53	441.1
Mission District	1972-79		20.8	--	37.2	--	172.2

[a] The third neighborhood listed for each city is the comparison neighborhood.
[b] Latest year for Consumer Price Index for Housing is 1978.
[c] 'T' ratios greater than or equal to 1.96 are significant at the .05 level. The 't' ratio is a test of the significance of the difference between the means for the revitalizing neighborhoods and the mean for the comparison neighborhood. Positive 't' ratios indicate that the mean for the revitalizing neighborhood is greater than the comparison neighborhood mean.
[d] Tests of statistical significance could not be performed for differences in mean sales prices because of the sampling design employed in the study.
[e] Earliest year for sales price data is 1968.
[f] Latest year for sales price data is 1978.

the start of the housing recession of the mid-1970s, changes in each of the indicators were greater after, rather than before, the end of the housing recession.

EVIDENCE OF BENEFITS FOR CITIES

Rehabilitation by Continuing Owners of Properties

Most of the discussion of property renovation in revitalizing neighborhoods focuses on the improvement of properties by recent inmovers to the neighborhoods. However, as Clay (1979) has recognized, renovation of properties by inmovers may encourage owners in the neighborhoods prior to the start of revitalizion to maintain or improve their properties. This expectation is based on the assumption that the failure of these original owners[14] to maintain their properties prior to the start of reinvestment stems from a lack of confidence in the neighborhood, not a lack of income. This assumption is not shared by many individuals or groups concerned about the adverse effects of revitalization on long-term renters and owners. Increased property maintenance by owners who purchased in the neighborhoods prior to the start of reinvestment would benefit the city, not only by improving the quality of housing but also by increasing the confidence of original owners in their neighborhood as a viable place in which to live.

A moderately high proportion of properties that were not sold during the period studied were rehabilitated by their owners. The number of unsold properties renovated ranges from 2.7 percent (Fairmont) to 40.6 percent (City Park West) in the revitalizing neighborhoods; the figure exceeds 30 percent in three of the twelve revitalizing neighborhoods. Although owners of unsold properties performed an impressive amount of renovation, inmovers performed most of the renovation in revitalizing neighborhooods (but not in the comparison neighborhoods).[15]

Comparison of the amount of rehabilitation carried out by original owners in the revitalizing and comparison neighborhoods reveals whether revitalization encourages original owners to rehabilitate their properties. The amount of property improvement performed by original owners is significantly greater in the revitalizing neighborhood than in the comparison neighborhood in four of the twelve cases (see table 4.2). Furthermore, an examination of the renovation activity within these neighborhoods—Asylum Hill and West End, in Hartford, Hayes Valley and Dolores Heights, in San Francisco—reveals that most of the rehabilitation performed by original owners occurred after the start of revitalization, not in the period prior to the onset of reinvestment. This same pattern did not exist in the matched comparison neighborhoods.

This analysis provides some—though not overwhelming—support for the hypothesis that reinvestment encourages original owners to rehabilitate their properties. The majority of the renovation, though, has been performed by residents purchasing properties in the neighborhoods after the start of reinvestment.

Table 4.2. Unsold Properties Rehabilitation and Assessed Property Value Revitalization

City/Neighborhood[a]	Revitalization Period	% Unsold Properties		% Increased in Assessed	
		Mean	't' Ratio[b]	Mean	't' Ratio[b]
Atlanta					
Midtown	1971-79	18.4	1.16	109.5	2.16
Inman Park	1971-79	12.7	- .08	100.3	1.68
Poncey Highlands	1971-79	13.1	--	85.6	--
Cincinnati[c]					
Mt. Adams	1967-79	36.8	-1.03	NA	
Walnut Hills	1977-79	11.6	.30	NA	
Avondale	1967-79	41.9	--	NA	
	1977-79	10.7	--	NA	
Denver					
Baker	1973-79	29.6	- .61	12.8	-1.32
CPW/Whittier/FP	1973-79	40.6	1.60	11.4	-1.62
Jefferson Park	1973-79	32.6	--	16.8	--
Hartford					
Asylum Hill	1975-79	22.4	2.61	24.3	-6.54
West End	1975-79	21.1	2.09	125.4	4.78
Parkville	1975-79	14.0	--	76.6	--
Philadelphia					
Spring Garden	1971-79	5.4	.85	55.1	12.0
Fairmount	1971-79	2.7	- .38	108.3	24.0
Kensington	1971-79	3.4	--	10.7	--
San Francisco					
Hayes Valley	1972-79	33.2	4.17	126.2	1.82
Dolores Heights	1972-79	25.3	2.63	113.4	.83
Mission District	1972-79	14.8	--	104.6	--

[a]The third neighborhood listed for each city is the comparison neighborhood.
[b]T ratios greater than or equal to 1.96 are significant at the .05 level. The 't' ratio is a test of the significance of the difference between the means for the revitalizing neighborhoods and the mean for the comparison neighborhood. Positive 't' ratios indicate that the mean for the revitalizing neighborhood is greater than the comparison neighborhood mean.
[c]Assessment data were collected for Cincinnati properties but are not reported here because it was not possible to identify whether the data represented appraised or assessed value.

Increase in Property Assessments

The final potential benefit for the city investigated is the increase in assessed property values and, ultimately, property tax revenue expected to result from renovation in the revitalizing neighborhoods. Findings presented earlier indicate that the market value of properties increased substantially in all revitalizing and comparison neighborhoods, with the rate of increase in most neighborhoods outpacing increases in the Consumer Price Index for Housing. It is reasonable to expect that these increases in market value would bring about corresponding increases in the assessed value of the properties.

At least three different procedures are employed by municipal property appraisal departments in re-evaluating properties. The simplest, and least inclusive in terms of impact, involves reassessing those properties whose market values had increased substantially because of rehabilitation.[16] Implementation of this procedure normally should restrict the tax increases to properties actually renovated.

A second method of reappraising properties is to conduct sales-ratio studies of selected neighborhoods in which noticeable changes (positive or negative) in the market value of properties have occurred. It is very likely that unimproved properties in neighborhoods reappraised through this technique will experience increases in assessed value.[17]

Finally, a re-evaluation of all properties in the jurisdiction may be undertaken at periodic intervals, or when it is obvious that the assessed value of properties in the entire jurisdiction has lagged too far behind changes in market value. The system-wide reappraisal may involve merely increasing the value of all properties by a uniform percentage, or it may involve carrying out a sales-ratio study for the entire municipality. In the latter situation, properties undergoing no change in ownership or physical condition, but located in the most rapidly changing neighborhoods, may receive sizable increases in assessed value.

Although it is recommended that properties be reappraised when it appears that the current assessment does not reflect the changed market value of the properties, such reappraisals may not occur, for a variety of reasons.[18] Consequently, whether or not municipalities obtain increased tax revenues from the reinvestment is largely determined by the appraisal practices of each municipality.

Analysis of table 4.2 indicated that average property assessment increases following reinvestment range from 11.4 percent in City Park West/Whittier/Five Points to 126.2 percent in Hayes Valley, with six of the ten revitalizing neighborhoods for which data are available having average assessment increases greater than 100 percent.[19] Property assessments also increased in the comparison neighborhoods during the same time period. Although the average increase in assessed property values is generally greater in the revitalizing neighborhoods than in the comparison neighborhoods, the differences are statistically significant in ony four of the ten revitalizing neighborhoods for which data are reported (see table 4.2).

Three of the four reinvestment neighborhoods with a significantly greater increase in property assessments also had a significantly greater percentage of properties rehabilitated than the respective comparison neighborhood. However, five of the eight neighborhoods with significantly greater renovation activity than their matched comparison neighborhood had no significantly greater increases in assessed property values.[20] Consequently, it appears that large increases in assesed values were neither an inevitable nor unique outcome of revitalization in the cities.

In general, the results provide modest suppport for the expectation that revitalization benefits cities through generation of increased property tax revenues. In most of the neighborhoods, however, the percentage of increase in assessed property values did not keep pace with the percentage of increase in the market value of the housing. This suggests that the cities are benefiting less than they might from the investment in the neighborhoods.[21]

EVIDENCE FOR NEGATIVE CONSEQUENCES OF REVITALIZATION

Increased Taxes for Continuing Owners of Properties

If assessed values are increased for all properties in revitalizing neighborhoods, including those not sold or renovated, the cost of housing for original owners will increase. The National Urban Coalition (1978) has reported that increases in property taxes for original owner-occupants threatens the ability of these owners to continue owning their homes. The increased cost may not affect original landlords adversely if they can offset the tax increases with rent increases. In this situation, however, renters would be affected adversely. Consequently, increased assessed property values, although beneficial for the city, may represent a substantial burden for owners or renters living in revitalizing neighborhoods prior to the start of reinvestment.

The nature of the tax burden imposed on owners of inactive properties can be investigated by comparing changes in assessed value for four groups of properties: (1) inactive; (2) sold but not renovated; (3) renovated but not sold; and (4) sold and renovated.[22] A significantly smaller increase in assessed values for inactive properties than for properties that have been sold or rehabilitated would indicate that renovation of some neighborhood properties does not necessarily impose serious costs on owners of properties not involved in the revitalization.

Table 4.3. Test of the Hypothesis That Properties not Involved in Reinvestment Activity Have a Smaller Percentage Increase in Assessed Value Than Properties Involved in Reinvestment After the Start of Revitalization

City/Neighborhood[a]	Time Period	Type of Activity	't' Ratio for All Properties[b]
Atlanta			
Midtown	1971-79	None	
Inman Park	1971-79	Rehab. & sold	-2.04
Poncey Highlands	1971-79	None	
Cincinnati			
Not available			
Denver			
Baker	1973-79	None	
CPW/Whittier/FP	1973-79	Sold & not rehab.	2.27
		Rehab. & sold	2.26
Jefferson Park	1973-79	None	
Hartford			
Asylum Hill	1975-79	Sold & not rehab.	NS
		Rehab. & sold	NS
West End	1975-79	None	
Parkville	1975-79	Sold & not rehab.	-2.08
		Rehab. & sold	NS
Philadelphia			
Spring Garden	1971-79	None	
Fairmount	1971-79	Sold & not rehab.	2.14
		Rehab. & sold	2.00
Kensington	1971-79	Rehab. & not sold	NS
		Rehab. & sold	4.49
San Francisco			
Hayes Valley	1972-79	Sold & not rehab.	8.11
		Rehab. & not sold	2.17
		Rehab. & sold	7.88
Dolores Heights	1972-79	Sold & not rehab.	7.82
		Rehab. & sold	6.99
Mission District	1972-79	Sold & not rehab.	5.16
		Rehab. & not sold	2.01
		Rehab. & sold	5.39

NOTES: Rather than reporting the 't' ratios for each of the three comparisons for the period after the start of reinvestment, the 't' ratios are reported only when the change in assessed value for inactive properties is significantly different from the change observed for one of the three other groups of properties.

[a]The third neighborhood listed for each city is the comparison neighborhood.

[b]All 't' ratios listed here are significant. Negative 't' ratios indicate that inactive properties experienced a greater percentage increase in assessed value than active properties.

Table 4.3 reveals that, with few exceptions, properties that remained untouched by the reinvestment were not reassessed at a significantly lower rate than properties that were sold or rehabilitated. This pattern can be observed in neighborhoods where the assessed value did not increase substantially for any group of properties and in places where the assessed value overall increased substantially. For example, the average increase in assessed value for inactive properties in Baker after 1975 is 12.9 percent, compared to 11 percent for properties that were both rehabilitated and sold. In Inman Park, the average increase in assessed value since the start of reinvestment in 1971 for inactive properties is 108 percent, compared to 89 percent for properties that were both sold and repaired during this time.

The major exception to this general pattern is found in San Francisco, where the increase in assessed value of inactive properties is significantly less than the increase in value of properties that were sold or rehabilitated. The provisions of Proposition Thirteen prevent increases in property tax assessments greater than 2 percent annually unless a property is sold or substantially renovated.

The dominant pattern of similar increases in assessed property values for all properties is observed in both the revitalizing and comparison neighborhoods. This similarity, however, does not alter the conclusion that reinvestment disproportionately increases the tax burden of owners who have not sold or improved their property.[23] Although this outcome does not appear to be a unique outcome of reinvestment, a greater tax burden is imposed on owners of inactive properties in revitalizing neighborhoods than in comparison neighborhoods, since the percentage of increase in the appraised value of properties is generally greater in the revitalizing neighborhoods.

The claim that the tax burden of original owners is increased is supported, since revitalization of neighborhood properties creates spillover costs for owners who have not participated in the renovation activity. Some increase in the assessed value of inactive properties seems reasonable, since improvement in the quality of some properties increases the quality of the neighborhood as a whole and, by implication, the value of unimproved neighborhood properties. To be equitable, however, the assessed value of properties actually renovated should increase significantly more than the value of unrepaired properties, since the physical quality of renovated properties, but not that of inactive properties, has been improved. In addition, the market value of improved properties probably has increased substantially more than the value of unimproved properties. It appears that the cities are deriving less property tax revenue from the substantial rise in the market value of properties in revitalizing neighborhoods than they could if they reassessed rehabilitated properties more than unimproved properties.

Dislocation of Residents

The final consequence to be examined is the possible displacement of renters by conversion of renter-occupied properties to owner-occupancy. As defined by the Griers,

> displacement occurs when any household is forced to move from its residence by conditions which affect the dwelling or its immediate surroundings, and which:
> 1. are beyond the household's reasonable ability to control or prevent;
> 2. occur despite the household's having met all previously-imposed conditions of occupancy; and
> 3. make continued occupancy by that household impossible, hazardous, or unaffordable (Grier and Grier 1978, p. 8).

Households in revitalizing neighborhoods may be forced to relocate for a number of reasons, some because their residence is sold or repaired, others because of neighborhood-wide changes caused by revitalization. A renter may be forced to move from her/his residence if the property is sold and converted to owner-occupancy, rehabilitated for higher-income renters, or converted to condominiums or cooperatives. Renters in properties that are not sold or rehabilitated may be displaced if their rent is raised as a result of reinvestment in other neighborhood properties.

Households that moved for any of these reasons could be regarded as having been displaced. However, the only potential cause of displacement that can be measured with available data is the conversion of rental properties to owner-occupancy.[24] Data describing increases in rent levels or the conversion of properties to condominiums or cooperatives were not available. Conversion of rental properties to owner-occupied is a better indicator of potential displacement than the net reduction in rental properties, because dislocation of households could occur in the absence of a net reduction in rental properties. It must be emphasized that this analysis indicates the *potential* for displacement. Knowledge of the specific circumstances surrounding each move is necessary to classify the move as actual displacement.

A substantial percentage of rental properties has been converted to owner-occupancy in most of the study neighborhoods for which tenure data are available (see table 4.4). More than 30 percent of all rental (or vacant) properties were subsequently purchased and occupied by owners in five of the eight revitalizing neighborhoods after the start of reinvestment, and in three of the four comparison neighborhoods. The absolute volume of renter households potentially displaced obviously depends on the number of rental properties in the neighborhood at the start of reinvestment and the total number of dwelling units contained on the properties. For example, an estimated seventy renter-occuppied multifamily

Table 4.4. Rental Properties Converted to Owner-Occupancy Following Revitalization in Revitalizing and Comparison Neighborhoods

City/Neighborhood[a]	Revitalization Period	All Properites	
		Mean	't' Ratio[b]
Atlanta			
Midtown	1971-79		- .23
Inman Park	1971-79	49.3	4.57
Poncey Highlands	1971-79	26.7	--
Cincinnati			
Mt. Adams	1967-79	25.0	-2.30
Walnut Hills	1977-79	6.0	-1.03
Avondale	1967-79	41.0	--
	1977-79	10.0	--
Denver			
Baker	1973-79	32.5	- .18
CPW/Whittier/FP	1973-79	34.7	.06
Jefferson Park	1973-79	34.1	--
Hartford			
Asylum Hill	1975-79	NA	
West End	1975-79	NA	
Parkville	1975-79	NA	
Philadelphia			
Spring Garden	1971-79	43.3	.61
Fairmount	1971-79	41.5	.34
Kensington	1971-79	39.9	--
San Francisco[c]			
Hayes Valley	1972-79	NA	
Dolores Heights	1972-79	NA	
Mission District	1972-79	NA	

[a]The third neighborhood listed for each city is the comparison neighborhood.
[b]T ratios greater than or equal to 1.96 are significant at the .05 level. The 't' ratio is a test of the significance of the difference between the means for the revitalizing neighborhoods and the mean for the comparison neighborhood. Positive 't' ratios indicate that the mean for the revitalizing neighborhood is greater than the comparison neighborhood mean.
[c]Tenure data for San Francisco neighborhoods prior to 1974 are not available.

properties in Inman Park became owner-occupied some time after the start of reinvestment. Obviously, far more than seventy renter households were possibly displaced from these seventy properties. Even without data identifying the number of rental units converted to owner-occupied, these findings provide graphic evidence that many renters may have been displaced by revitalization.

Further evidence that displacement may have occurred in the revitalizing neighborhoods is provided by the results of the household survey administered to current residents of Inman Park and Spring Garden. Approximately one-half of the inmover owners surveyed in each neighborhood stated that renters had resided in their homes before they purchased them (56.2 percent in Spring Garden and 51.6 percent in Inman Park). These current owners replaced renters in an estimated 20.7 percent of all rental units in Inman Park and in an estimated 14 percent of the rental units in Spring Garden.[25]

The threat of displacement apparently was not restricted to the early period of reinvestment. Nearly one-half of the home purchases by current owner-occupants moving to these two neighborhoods six years after the start of reinvestment[26] resulted in the relocation—possibly forced—of the tenants of the properties.

A new loss in rental units also occurred in most of the revitalizing neighborhoods as a result of the conversion of properties to owner-occupancy. In absolute terms, four neighborhoods—Midtown, Inman Park, City Park West/Whittier/Five Points, and Spring Garden—underwent a net gain of more than 10 percent in owner-occupied single-family properties (see table 4-5). Three neighborhoods—Inman Park, Baker, and Spring Garden—underwent a net increase of 10 percent or more in the percentage of owner-occupied multifamily properties. These appear to be major changes when compared to the disinvestment and decline in housing quality and home ownership that characterized many inner cities in the 1960s. Since a number of rental units were contained in the multifamily properties, the supply of rental units appears to have been reduced considerably in Inman Park, Spring Garden, Baker, Midtown, and City Park West/Whittier/Five Points.

Although the absolute reduction in the supply of rental housing is not very high in every revitalizing neighborhood, the conversion of a large portion of rental properties to owner-occupancy seems to be an integral aspect of revitalization. However, the finding that the percentage of rental properties involved in conversions is significantly greater in the revitalizing than in the comparison neighborhood in only one case (Inman Park) indicates that the threat of displacement was not unique to the revitalizing

Table 4.5. Percentage By Type of Owner-Occupied Neighborhood Properties

City/Neighborhood[a]	Owner-Occupied		Owner-Occupied		Percent Change	
	Single Family	Multi-family	Single-Family	Multi-family	Single-Family	Multi-family
Atlanta	1970		1979			
Midtown	61.9	32.4	68.1	37.2	10.0	14.8
Inman Park	51.5	32.4	77.3	51.1	50.1	57.7
Poncey Highlands	65.3	32.4	68.4	38.3	4.8	18.2
Cincinnati	1965		1978			
Mt. Adams	57.2	38.6	53.7	26.6	-6.1	-31.1
Walnut Hills	56.3	26.9	52.2	24.4	-7.3	- 9.3
Avondale	85.6	46.8	77.6	46.5	-9.4	- 0.6
Denver[b]	1972		1979			
Baker	60.8	46.9	63.3	56.9	4.1	21.3
CPW/Whittier/FP	50.0	34.0	72.0	36.8	44.0	8.2
Jefferson Park	67.7	36.7	64.0	36.6	-5.5	0.3
Hartford						
Asylum Hill	NA	NA	NA	NA	NA	NA
West End	NA	NA	NA	NA	NA	NA
Parkville	NA	NA	NA	NA	NA	NA
Philadelphia[c]	1970		1979			
Spring Garden	51.5	55.9	64.5	67.7	25.2	21.1
Fairmount	79.8	77.4	83.3	80.0	4.4	3.4
Kensington	82.4	72.7	85.2	81.8	3.6	12.5
San Francisco[b]	1974		1979			
Hayes Valley	50.7	24.9	52.2	28.2	3.0	13.3
Dolores Heights	76.6	37.9	69.2	37.6	-9.7	- 0.8
Mission District	71.8	37.1	76.9	41.2	7.1	11.1

[a]The third neighborhood listed for each city is the comparison neighborhood.
[b]Tenure data were not available in some cities for the entire study period.
[c]Housing categories for Philadelphia are 1-2 stories and 3-4 stories.

neighborhoods. Rather, it seems to have been a relatively frequent occurrence in at least some comparison neighborhoods as well. Pressure for home ownership appears to have been common to all of these neighborhoods. This finding provides graphic evidence of the significant shift toward home ownership that occurred throughout the country in the 1970s.

CONCLUSION

The analysis reveals quite clearly that these cities have derived some benefits from revitalization. The physical quality of properties has been improved significantly and property assessments have increased substantially. However, the significant improvement in housing quality in revitalizing neighborhoods does not necessarily produce increases in assessed values that are significantly greater than those occurring in comparison neighborhoods in which relatively few properties have been improved. Furthermore, the cities do not appear to be benefiting as much as they could, since increases in assessed property values have lagged far behind increases in the market value of properties in the majority of the revitalizing neighborhoods examined.

The cities appear to be receiving modest indirect benefits as well. The investment in the physical quality of properties by newcomers to the neighborhoods apparently encouraged original owners to improve their properties in approximately 33 percent of the revitalizing neighborhoods. These findings provide limited support for the claims that revitalization encourages original owners to renovate their properties and generates significantly increased property tax revenues for cities. However, these changes are not necessarily the unique (or inevitable) outcome of revitalization, since changes in more than half of the revitalization neighborhoods are not significantly different from changes that occurred during the same time in the comparison neighborhood.

Reinvestment also appears to have generated a number of negative consequences. First, many of the renters living in the neighborhoods prior to the start of revitalization, many of whom had a low socioeconomic status, may have been displaced. It is unlikely that many of these renters could afford the rent increases that inevitably accompanied the increased market value and assessed value of properties. In addition, a substantial proportion of rental properties in both the revitalizing and comparison neighborhoods were converted to owner-occupancy, possibly forcing renters to move elsewhere. This conversion activity also substantially reduced the supply of rental housing in many of the neighborhoods studied. The displacement that may have resulted from the conversion of rental properties to owner-occupancy does not apear unique to revitalizing neighborhoods, but seems to reflect overall pressures for home ownership in central-city housing markets.

The second adverse effect of reinvestment was experienced by individuals owning properties in the neighborhoods prior to the start of reinvestment. The assessed value of properties that were neither sold nor rehabilitated after the start of revitalization increased as a result of the changes in the neighborhood. The percentage increase in assessed value for these inactive properties was *not* significantly less than the percentage increase in value for properties that were improved.

It appears that these cities are underassessing improved

properties relative to their increase in value, since the percentage of increase in the assessed value of improved properties lags far behind the percentage of increase in the market value of the properties in the majority of the revitalizing neighborhoods. The cities could derive additional benefits from reinvestment if the reassessment of improved properties in revitalizing neighborhoods more closely reflected their increased market value.

The cities may also be overassessing inactive properties, although it is not obvious how large an increase in the assessment of these properties is reasonable. In the neighborhoods studied, however, the increase in the tax burden of original owners, if not offset by exemptions for elderly households or other types of "circuit-breakers," could impose a cost burden on households that might threaten their ability to maintain their properties.

Finally, it must be emphasized that many of the important social and sociopsychological consequences of revitalization could not be examined in this analysis. These consequences might be especially serious for the original residents of the neighborhoods who no longer reside there. In addition, possible economic benefits for the city, such as increased demand for certain kinds of goods and services, have not been examined. Despite the restricted number of potential costs and benefits examined, however, the analysis documents quite clearly that reinvestment has produced some benefits for the cities but also has adversely affected the households living in the neighborhoods prior to the beginning of reinvestment.

NOTES

1. See National Urban Coalition (1978, 1980), Sumka and Cincin-Sain (1979), Hartman (1979a, 1979b), Kotler (1980), and Sumka (1980).

2. See Sumka and Cincin-Sain (1979), Urban Consortium (1977), and James (1977).

3. A fifth change—whether an increase occurred in the enforcement of the housing code on properties owned by long-term residents—was examined in the original study.

4. In upgrading neighborhoods, current residents improve their own housing. In the initial stages of this activity, at least, it is believed that there is no marked increase in the volume of property transactions, the price of housing, or the inmigration of higher-income households. In gentrifying neighborhoods, on the other hand, the improvements are made primarily by newly arrived residents of higher socioeconomic status. A further difference between these two types of neighborhoods is that the improvements are thought to be accompanied by a marked increase in the volume of property transactions and the price of housing in revitalizing neighborhoods.

5. Previous studies have employed at least five different indicators to measure the extent of neighborhood revitalization: (1) change in the

socioeconomic composition of the neighborhood (Spain [1980a, 1980b], Spain, Reid, and Long [1980], Long and Dahmann [1980], Lipton [1980], Zeitz [1979], Henig [1980]); (2) change in purchasing prices (Cybriwsky and Myers [1977], James [1977b], Zeitz [1979], Bixhorn [1979]); (3) change in sales volume (Cybriwsky and Meyer [1977], James [1977b], Zeitz [1979], Bixhorn [1979]); (4) percentage of sales accounted for by multiple sales of the same property (James [1979b], Office of Policy Planning Seattle [1979]); and (5) change in the percentage of properties that are owner-occupied (James [1977a], Zeitz [1979]).

6. Much of the evidence describing these consequences prior to this study has been derived from the perceptions of local or national officials. See Urban Consortium (1977), National Urban Coalition (1978).

7. Attempts were made to collect as much information as was available from local, secondary data sources on the total amount of displacement that may have occurred. However, since the focus of this study was to document the extent of private-sector revitalization, not to prepare the most accurate estimates of the total volume of displacement, data identifying the amount of displacement occurring for other reasons were not collected if they were not readily accessible.

8. Selection for study of neighborhoods that were thought to be undergoing moderate to substantial revitalization offered the best opportunity to learn as much as possible about the nature and effects of reinvestment. Furthermore, given the debate about the relative costs and benefits created by revitalization, it was important to choose neighborhoods in which the costs or negative consequences, if present, were most likely to be revealed. In Clay's terminology, neighborhoods supposedly undergoing at least moderate gentrification were chosen for study.

9. The comparison neighborhood chosen in each city was as similar as possible to at least one of the revitalizing neighborhoods in 1970 on five dimensions: (1) age of housing; (2) income level of residents; (3) tenure of residents; (4) amount of residential mobility; and (5) percent of single-family housing. In some instances, it was not possible to identify a nonrevitalizing neighborhood in 1970 on all five dimensions. The comparison neighborhood selected in each city, however, was similar to at least one revitalizing neighborhood on many of the dimensions. Most important, conversations with local officials and visits to the neighborhoods revealed no indication that these neighborhoods were revitalizing.

10. This is primarily the case in San Francisco and Denver. Proposition Thirteen in California limits increases in assessed property values after 1975 to a maximum of 2 percent per year, unless, among other things, the property is sold or competely renovated. A somewhat similar restriction exists in Denver, where Colorado House Bill 1452 (passed in 1977) set the base level for assessments of properties at the 1973 assessed value. Increases in assessments after January 1, 1977, are supposedly restricted only to properties that have been rehabilitated and must be based on the 1973 assessed value. Similar restrictions do not exist in the other four cities.

11. The volume of renovation was measured by identifying the number

of residential properties for which municipal alteration or repair permits with an estimated cost or value greater than or equal to $500 were issued. It is well known that building permits are not a totally reliable indicator of property rehabilitation. Since it is believed that permit data underestimate the amount of property renovation, the estimates of the amount of rehabilitation that has occurred should be viewed as the minimum estimate of the level of property improvements undertaken in the neighborhoods. For a more detailed discussion of this point, see Frank F. DeGiovanni, et al. (1981).

12. The analysis reported in this chapter was performed for all properties and separately for single-family and multifamily properties. Only the results from the analysis of all properties is reported to avoid an excessively detailed presentation. While some of the specific findings differ in the three sets of analyses, the general conclusions are similar.

13. Increases in the rapid turnover of properties already sold once, and in apparently speculative sales, also appear to be central characteristics of revitalization, although the proportion of all sales that were speculative exceeded 10 percent in only four neighborhoods.

14. The phrase "original owner," as used in this report, includes both owner-occupants and investor-owners who purchased their homes before the start of reinvestment.

15. Household surveys conducted in two of the revitalizing neighborhoods—Inman Park, Atlanta, and Spring Garden, Philadelphia—further substantiate this finding. The survey results indicate that the majority of the repairs in each neighborhood were performed by owners moving to the neighborhood after the start of reinvestment.

16. Most property assessment offices receive a copy of each building permit issued for every property. If the value added by the renovation is more than minimal, these properties are then reappraised prior to the computation of the following year's property taxes.

17. Although attempts are usually made to identify homogeneous neighborhoods for these studies and to base changes in assessed value for properties that were not sold or renovated on the changes in value for similar properties of "comparables," the change in assessed value for a given property may not necessarily reflect actual changes in its market value.

18. The appraisal office may be understaffed; the appraisers may not perceive the changes in the neighborhood for a long period of time; the reappraisal of property may be limited by statute or constitutional amendment (as in Denver and San Francisco); the city government may adopt a policy to delay or avoid reappraisal because of likely opposition to tax increases or for fear of inhibiting reinvestment in the early stages; etc.

19. The two revitalizing neighborhoods in Cincinnati are not included in this analysis because of ambiguities involving the data that could not be resolved.

20. The greater volume of improved properties did not lead to significantly greater increases in property assessments in Inman Park, Asylum Hill, Hayes Valley, Dolores Heights, and City Park West/Whittier/-Five Points.

21. It is possible that some unknown proportion of the increase in assessed values attributable to revitalization has not yet occurred because of lags between changes in the neighborhoods and the reappraisal of the properties. This possibility cannot be dismissed entirely. However, the specific situation in each city suggests that underestimation of the increase in assessed values as a result of reinvestment because of lags in the reappraisal of properties is likely to be minimal in these six cities. Most of the cities studied had at least one jurisdiction-wide reappraisal after the start of reinvestment in the neighborhoods. In addition, officials in the assessor's office in each city indicated that the 1979 assessed values include any changes that were made to reflect sales or renovation activity occurring through November or December 1978, in some cities, and February and March 1979, in others. This does not indicate that they made changes, only that whatever changes were made as a result of 1978 activity appear in the 1979 assessed value. Furthermore, officials also stated that changes made in appraised value to reflect property improvement are usually reflected in the appraised value for the year following the improvement of the property. Thus, only sales or renovation activity occurring in all of 1979 or the latter months of 1979—the last year for which data were collected—would not be reflected in increases in property assessments.

22. As indicated in note 21, the 1979 assessed value reflects changes in properties that occurred before a specific date in late 1978 or early 1979. Sales or rehabilitation that occurred after that date would not be taken into account until the 1980 appraisal. To avoid biasing the analysis by including sales or rehabilitation that could not be reflected in increased property assessments within the data collection period, sales or rehabilitation which occurred after the cutoff date for the 1979 reappraisal in each city were excluded in classifying the properties into one of the four types.

23. This assumes, of course, that the increase in assessed value is reflected in increased taxes. This would not occur if the increase in assessments were offset by a reduction in the tax rate or if owners of inactive properties received some type of property tax exemption.

24. As used in this study, however, this indicator of potential displacement has one limitation. The data collected from every city except Cincinnati indicate whether or not the property was owner-occupied in each year. If the property was not owner-occupied, it was not possible to identify whether the property was renter-occupied or vacant. We have assumed that any property not owner-occupied was occupied by a renter. If many of these properties were vacant, the analysis will overestimate the amount of displacement that might have occurred because of conversion of properties from renter- to owner-occupancy. However, since only one potential cause of displacement is investigated here, the analysis underestimates the actual volume of displacement that occurred. Displacement due to rent increases seems especially likely in many of these neighborhoods because of the substantial increase in the market value and appraised value of properties.

25. These estimates are lower than those reported in the secondary data because these data indicate the percentage of current owners who

purchased previously rented properties. As a result of the high turnover of properties in each neighborhood, it is likely that many previous owners also replaced renters.

26. That is, current owners moving to Spring Garden after 1975 and to Inman Park after 1976.

REFERENCES

Bixhorn, H. 1979. A stage model of neighborhood change. Paper presented at American Statistical Association Conference, Government of the District of Columbia, Office of Planning and Development, Statistics and Data Management Division.

Clay, P. L. 1979. *Neighborhood renewal, middle class resettlement, and incumbent upgrading in American neighborhoods.* Lexington, Mass.: Lexington Books.

Cybriwsky, R. A., and Meyer, J. T. 1977. Geographical aspects of the housing market in a rejuvenating neighborhood. *Papers in Geography,* no. 16, December 1977. University Park: Pennsylvania State University.

DeGiovanni, F. F., Connelly, M. D., Joyner, B. R., and Paulson, N. A. 1981. *Private market revitalization: its characteristics and consequences.* Draft report. Prepared by Research Triangle Institute for the Office of Policy Development and Research. Washington, D.C.: U.S. Department of Housing and Urban Development.

Hartman, C. 1979a. Displacement: A not so new problem. *Social Policy* 9(5):22-27.

——————. 1979b. Comment on "Neighborhood revitalization and displacement: A review of the evidence." *Journal of the American Planning Association,* 45(4): 488-90.

Henig, J. R. 1980. Gentrification and displacement within cities: A comparative analysis. *Social Science Quarterly* 61(3, 4): 638-53.

James, F. J. 1977a. Private reinvestment in older housing and older neighborhoods: Recent trands and forces. Statement before the Committee on Banking, Housing and Urban Affairs of the United States Senate.

——————. 1977b. Back to the city: Case studies of private neighborhood revitalization in eight major metropolitan areas. Working paper 0241-02. Washington, D.C.: The Urban Institute.

Kotler, M. 1980. Is residential displacement a critical urban problem? Pro. *Urban Concerns* (February/March): 31-54.

Lipton, G. Evidence of central city renewal. In *Back to the city: issues in neighborhood renovation,* ed. S. Laska and D. Spain. New York: Pergamon Press, 1980.

Long, L. H., and Dahmann, D. C. 1980. The city suburb income gap: Is it being narrowed by a back-to-the-city movement? Special Demographic Analyses, CDS-80-1, March 1980, Bureau of the Census. Washington, D.C.: U.S. Department of Commerce.

Grier, G. 1978. *Urban Displacement: A Reconnaissance.*Washington, D.C.: Memo report prepared for the United States Department of Housing and Urban Development.

National Urban Coalition. 1978. *Displacement: City neighborhoods in transition.* Washington, D.C.: National Urban Coalition.

————. 1980. *Neighborhood transition with displacement: Citizen's handbook.* Washington, D.C.: National Urban Coalition.

Seattle Office of Policy Planning. 1979. *Seattle displacement study.* Physical Planning Division, Office of Policy Planning, Seattle, Washington.

Spain, D. 1980a. Black-to-white successions in central-city housing: Limited evidence of urban revitalization. *Urban Affairs Quarterly* 15(4): 381-96.

————. 1980b. Reasons for intrametropolitan mobility: Are schools a key issue? *Review of Public Data Use* 8(1): 59-68.

Spain, D., Reid, J., and Long, L. 1980. Housing successions among blacks and whites in cities and suburbs. *Current Population Reports*, January 1980, series P-23, no. 101, Bureau of the Census. Washington, D.C.: U.S. Department of Commerce.

Sumka, H. 1980. Is residential displacement a critical urban problem? Con. *Urban Concerns* (February/March): 31-54.

Sumka, H. J., and Cincin-sain, B. 1979. Displacement in revitalizing neighborhoods: A review and research strategy. *Occasional Papers in Housing and Community Affairs*, vol. 2. Washington, D.C.: Office of Policy Development and Research, U.S. Department of Housing and Urban Development.

Urban Consortium. 1977. The displacement problem in revitalized urban neighborhoods. Draft paper of the Community and Economic Development Task Force. Washington, D.C., Urban Consortium.

Zeitz, E. 1979. *Private urban renewal: A different residential trend.* Lexington, Mass.: Lexington Books.

CHAPTER FIVE

Evidence for Neighborhood Revitalization: Manhattan

MARK BALDASSARE

INTRODUCTION

Much has been written about the "turnaround" in central-city neighborhoods, but systematic evidence of microlevel changes in the 1970s is rare. This paper examines revitalization in Manhattan, the inner city of the largest metropolitan area in the U.S., by using profiles developed for each of its thirty-six neighborhoods. These data were compiled by the New York City Planning Department and included 1970 census information, agency statistics, and updates on key indicators from the mid-1970s. These descriptive statistics allow us to ascertain the extent of neighborhood improvement in the inner city and, through analyses of neighborhood rankings over time, provide evidence of unique types of revitalization. The study offers new methods with which to examine the process and potential outcomes of neighborhood change.

Mark Baldassare is Associate Professor in the Program in Social Ecology, University of California-Irvine.

This project was partially supported by grants from the National Institute of Mental Health (MH34412) and the Council for Research in the Social Sciences, Columbia University. Students in the New York Area Undergraduate Research Seminar prepared the neighborhood profiles data, and the computer work was conducted by William Protash. I thank the Population Division of the New York City Department of City Planning for their assistance. Valuable suggestions for revisions received from the editions of this journal and anonymous reviewers are incorporated in this version of the paper.

Little is actually known about the existence, causes, and consequences of inner-city revitalization. Much of what has been reported is found in the media (for example, Alpern [1979]; Allman [1978]) as evidenced by London's (1978) review. Information about neighborhood revitalization in New York, for example, is based on anecdotal accounts of the renovation of housing or the return of the middle class to certain neighborhoods (Bordewich 1979; Brown 1979; Fleetwood 1979; Sullivan 1978).

Systematic attempts to measure neighborhood revitalization have various problems. Examples include inappropriate units of analysis, case studies without comparison areas, a lack of longitudinal data from an appropriate time period, inattention to relative changes in neighborhood rankings, the use of the unsubstantiated reports of local officials and researchers, and unidimensional or highly limited descriptions of local areas in the inner city.

This paper presents an approach to studying inner-city revitalization in response to some of the literature's shortcomings in theory and research. One important need of researchers and planners is to define precisely and then empirically distinguish among different types of neighborhood revitalization. Information about marketing behavior or perceptions is the predominant or favored measure of neighborhood change. Though obviously an important factor, it does not in itself speak to the context, nor always the location, in which improvements are occurring. Neither does any other single measure of local change. In order to meet the challenge of devising more valid and specific data on revitalization, multiple objective indicators of neighborhood change must thus be systematically examined across carefully delineated local areas within the inner city. At this writing, the work of the R. Polk Company meets some of these specifications: they have devised a method for the relative ranking of census tracts through multiple factors, and, separately, one for indexing absolute (i.e., positive or negative) change within any given census tract (cited in Goetze [1979, pp. 32-41]). The approach reported in this paper combines and extends some of these important contributions. A method that directly takes into account the more current and baseline conditions of the neighborhood, and various local changes over time relative to other areas, is proposed for examining the extent and character of neighborhood revitalization within a given city.

THEORY AND HYPOTHESES

A number of predictions guide this study of neighborhood change in Manhattan. Since inner cities have continued to decline in population size and economic significance, overall improvement is not expected. The continuing problems of housing abandonment, the loss of jobs, and declining revenues constrain the recovery of the total inner city (Baldassare 1981). Thus, neighborhood revitalization is found at most in only a few areas.

The literature review indicates certain basic characteristics of neighborhood revitalization. There is a rising level of affluence among residents of the area, usually because of an inmigration of middle-income professionals. A marked improvement in housing quality also occurs as capital for renovation and rehabilitation is invested. The area's perceived attractiveness results in a greater desire by existing residents to remain in, and new residents to move into, the area, resulting in a net increase in population size. Finally, investors' confidence in real estate appreciation leads to a high level of sales activity. Of all these, rising income seems to be the most dependable indicator of revitalization, primarily because it represents the most fundamental change. Problems exist with other measures. Real estate sales, for example, may also be numerous in areas where disinvestment is present. Population size may decline in some revitalizing neighborhoods if large families are replaced by childless couples and single-person households. Despite real improvements, complaints about housing quality may actually increase as individuals with higher standards, paying higher rents, comprise the local population.

While increasing affluence is a primary indicator of revitalization, it must occur along with other basic neighborhood improvements. In addition, given a negligible or nonexistent net migration to central-city areas, these neighborhood changes must be viewed in terms of gains in some areas at the expense of other districts. Neighborhood revitalization thus involves relative gains in particular areas and not for the city as a whole, while the definition of revitalizing neighborhoods includes multiple rather than single measures of local change.

Three possible types of neighborhood revitalization are considered in the analysis: upper-strata revitalization, upgrading, and lower-strata revitalization. In order to conceptualize different forms of positive change, one must rank all neighborhoods hierarchically on the basis of population and housing character-isitics. Lower-strata revitalization takes place when neighborhoods that received among the lowest rankings in 1970 have so improved that they are now closer to the median. Neighborhoods that were just above a median point in 1970, and have improved to the extent that they are now among the few best areas, offer examples of upper-strata revitalization. Upgrading describes neighborhoods that have clearly moved from below to above the median-ranked area. Lower-strata revitalization is perhaps rare, since it requires the social mobility of the poor, or massive government subsidies at the local level. There may be a strong representation of upper-strata revitalization today because of the growth of high-level professional employment in central cities. Thus, though it is the most widely publicized form of revitalization, we are not certain of the proportion actually accounted for by upgrading.

METHODS AND RESULTS

The empirical information for this study was provided by the "Neighborhood Profiles" prepared by the New York City Department of City Planning (1978). Manhattan was divided into thirty-six groups of census tracts, which were defined as neighborhoods (fig. 5.1), and the neighborhood boundaries were determined by considering census data, historical information, and staff perceptions of the areas. Neighborhoods containing few dwellings and residents in 1970 (i.e., Battery Park, Lower Manhattan, and Roosevelt Island) were excluded from the analysis, resulting in a sample size of thirty-three.

Each profile included 1960 and 1970 aggregated census tract statistics concerning population and housing characteristics. Additional 1970 information and the post-1970 statistics were derived from local government agencies: personal income from the New York State Department of Taxation; public assistance cases from the New York City Human Resources Administration; real estate sales and tax arrears from the New York City Department of Finance; housing violations from the New York City Department of Housing Preservation and Development; updates on housing vacancies from a survey by the Sanborn Company; and recent population estimates from the New York City Department of City Planning.

Several variables that capture important dimensions of neighborhood change, previously mentioned, were chosen. "Basic" changes in population and housing characteristics, viewed as the most direct measures of neighborhood revitalization, included: per capita income, 1970 and 1974; violations per dwelling unit (in buildings with violations), 1972 and 1976; population size, 1974 and 1976. "Secondary" measures of socioeconomic changes are modifications that are not primary signs of neighborhood revitalization, but rather important events (or byproducts) presumably correlated with this phenomenon, such as: public assistance cases, 1970 and 1976; tax lots in arrears, 1972 and 1975;

1. Marble Hill
2. Inwood
3. Polo Grounds
4. Hamilton Heights
5. Harlem River Houses
6. Manhattanville
7. St. Nicholas
8. Harlem River Drive
9. Morningside Heights
10. West Harlem
11. Millbank-Frawley
12. Upper West Side
13. West Side
14. Lincoln Square
15. Clinton
16. Chelsea
17. Midtown
18. Union-Herald

19. Turtle Bay
20. Murray Hill
21. Gramercy
22. East Village
23. West Village
24. Soho-Noho-Tribeca
25. Battery Park
26. Lower Manhattan
27. Chinatown-Little Italy
28. Lower East Side
29. Two Bridges
30. East Side
31. Roosevelt Island
32. Yorkville
33. Lower East Harlem
34. Upper East Harlem
35. North Washington Heights
36. South Washington Heights

Figure 5.1. *MANHATTAN NEIGHBORHOODS*

and percentage of occupied dwellings, 1970 and 1975. Descriptive statistics for each of these factors are used to determine the extent to which the sample of neighborhoods has improved or deteriorated.

The neighborhoods that have revitalized are specified by examing "basic" improvements in neighborhoods relative to changes occuring in other areas by using quartile rankings. Then, a scale scoring each neighborhood in terms of relative change in the four basic housing and population factors provides a listing of neighborhoods that have revitalized. Finally, an analysis of 1970 and mid-1970 characteristics of these areas offers evidence of the character of neighborhood revitalization.

Table 5.1 provides little evidence that, overall, inner city neighborhoods have improved since 1970. Per capita income has risen somewhat, but the average change across all neighborhoods has not kept pace with the inflation rate of 27 percent for the metropolitan area between 1970 and 1974, cited by the U.S. Bureau of Labor Statistics. As a result, fewer than half of the districts could be categorized as having improved along this dimension. Our measure of housing quality, housing code violations per dwelling, did not decline in any neighborhood, and average and percentage changes reflect startling increases. Only six neighborhoods gained more residents than were lost, and the outmigration rate was about 6 percent. Changes in real estate sales could not be computed. Public assistance cases, and especially tax lots in arrears, grew at alarming rates in most neighborhoods, providing negative support for revitalization. Changes in occupancy rates were rather small and also not indicative of a turnaround in the inner city. In sum, if there are neighborhoods that are revitalizing, they are improving in the midst of a continuing decline for the inner city as a whole.

Table 5.1. Neighborhood Change: Data From 33 Manhattan Residential Districts

	Circa 1970	Circa 1976	Gross Change	% Change	% of Improved Neighborhoods
Basic Factors					
Per capita income	4,810	5,348	538	11.2	14
Violations per dwelling	13.3	24.7	11.4	85.7	0
Population size	46,420	43.754	-2,666	- 5.7	6
Real estate sales	--	70	--	--	--
Secondary Factors					
Public assistance cases	1,691	1,806	115	6.8	11
Tax lots in arrears	237	351	114	48.1	1
Percentage of occupied dwellings	96.4	95.9	-0.5	2	2

A method that emphasizes relative improvements in housing and population is necessary for selecting inner-city areas that have revitalized. In the case of housing quality, for example, one must delineate the neighborhoods that have had a slower growth in code violations and thus become improved relative to others. Similarly, changes over time in per capita income are important if they allow the neighborhood to rise substantially above other areas. Thus each neighborhood was ranked in quartiles, based on their income and housing scores for 1970 and for post 1970. As table 5.2 displays, within the overall climate of decline there is actually a large degree of stability in rankings. Few neighborhoods indicated relative changes for better or worse, and 25 neighborhoods for income (76%) and 24 neighborhoods for housing violations (73%) maintained the same quartile scores over time. Dramatic shifts in the rankings of any given neighborhood were also exceptional.

Concerning income between 1970 and 1974, only one area that did not have the highest rating in 1970 did so in 1974. Two areas gained better ratings, but still remained below the median neighborhood, while one neighborhood moved from below to above the median. Differences in scores for housing violations between 1972 and 1976 resulted in two neighborhoods moving into the

Table 5.2. Basic Changes in Neighborhoods: Relative Rankings and First Quartile Rankings

	Income	*Housing Quality*
Relative Improvements	Soho (2-1)	Lincoln Square (2-1)
	Morningside Heights (3-2)	Union-Herald (3-1)
	Polo Grounds (4-3)	West Side (3-2)
	Lower East Harlem (4-3)	Marble Hill (3-2)
Relative Deterioration	West Side (1-2)	Chelsea (1-2)
	Upper West Side (2-3)	Two Bridges (1-2)
	Manhattanville (3-4)	Inwood (2-3)
	Lower East Side (3-4)	Clinton (2-3)
		North Washington Heights (2-3)
	Real Estate Sales	*% Population Change*
First Quartile Rankings	1. West Side	1. Gramercy
	2. East Side	2. Lincoln Square
	3. Yorkville	3. Marble Hill
	4. West Village	4. Murray Hill
	5. Upper East Harlem	5. Turtle Bay
	6. East Village	6. West Side
	7. South Washington Heights	7. West Village
	8. Millbank-Frawley	8. Yorkville

NOTE: The first number in parentheses denotes the 1970 quartile ranking and the second number the mid-1970 ranking. A score of 4 refers to the lowest quartile ranking, and a score of 1 to the highest quartile ranking. The median score was placed in the third quartile.

highest ranking, one from a submedian score and the other from the second quartile. Two neighborhoods rose from below the median to the quartile just above the median. No neighborhoods in the lowest quartile made improvements that placed them in the third quartile. It is important to note that, for the eight neighborhoods making relative improvements, not one had positive changes in both income and housing.

Information concerning real estate sales in 1970 was not available; consequently, neighborhoods were merely ranked in terms of their sales activity between 1974 and 1976. Those in the first quartile, with sales ranging from 87 to 242, were considered to provide the strongest evidence that revitalization was occuring (see table 5.2). Because rankings in actual population size in 1970 and 1975 were not meaningful, since some neighborhoods were geographically larger than others, the neighborhoods that achieved percentage increases or minor percentage decreases were of most interest. The neighborhoods in the first quartile of population change, listed in table 5.2, ranged from a decrease of less than –0.5 percent to an increase of 4.5 percent. Three neighborhoods had both high ratings in population change and real estate sales.

All of the quartile rankings of neighborhoods were used in the revitalization scale. In regard to income and housing, neighborhoods that improved in rankings were scored +1, no change was scored 0, and those that declined in rankings were scored –1. Population change and sales were scored +1 if rankings were in the first quartiles and 0 if they were out. The total scores for each neighborhood could thus range from +4 to –2. The sums for these four variables are recorded in table 5.3. The data indicate that Manhattan has only a few neighborhoods in which a moderate amount of positive change has occured. A majority of areas experienced decline, no change, or only marginal improvements. Five neighborhoods had a total score of +2 and are considered revitalized because relative improvements were evident in at least two domains.

There are major differences among the revitalized neighborhoods. Lincoln Square and Yorkville received the highest ranking in income in 1970 and the mid-1970s. They underwent other changes during the decade to consolidate their relative strength. Lincoln Square moved into the first quartile in housing quality, which Yorkville already occupied. Yorkville had substantial real estate activity and each area maintained among the most favorable migration patterns. The growth in public assistance cases were below borough-wide averages. Occupancy rates declined, but this may be because each neighborhood underwent residential construction. Surprisingly, tax

Table 5.3. Overall Neighborhood Scores Derived From Revitalization Scale

	Income Change	Housing Quality Change	Population Change	Sales	Total
Marble Hill	0	+1	+1	0	+2
West Side	-1	+1	+1	+1	+2
Lincoln Square	0	+1	+1	0	+2
West Village	0	0	+1	+1	+2
Yorkville	0	0	+1	+1	+2
Harlem River	+1	0	0	0	+1
Morningside Heights	+1	0	0	0	+1
Millbank-Frawley	0	0	0	+1	+1
Union-Herald	0	+1	0	0	+1
Turtle Bay	0	0	+1	0	+1
Murray Hill	0	0	+1	0	+1
Gramercy	0	0	+1	0	+1
East Village	0	0	0	+1	+1
Soho	+1	0	0	0	+1
East Side	0	0	0	+1	+1
Lower East Harlem	+1	0	0	0	+1
Upper East Harlem	0	0	0	+1	+1
S. Washington Heights	0	0	0	+1	+1
Polo Grounds	0	0	0	0	0
Hamilton Height	0	0	0	0	0
St. Nicholas	0	0	0	0	0
Harlem Drive	0	0	0	0	0
West Harlem	0	0	0	0	0
Midtown	0	0	0	0	0
Chinatown-Little Italy	0	0	0	0	0
Lower East Side	-1	0	0	0	-1
Inwood	0	-1	0	0	-1
Manhattanville	-1	0	0	0	-1
Upper West Side	-1	0	0	0	-1
Clinton	0	-1	0	0	-1
Chelsea	0	-1	0	0	-1
Two Bridges	0	-1	0	0	-1
N. Washington Heights	0	-1	0	0	-1

arrears increased considerably in Lincoln Square and Yorkville, indicating the existence of unprofitable lower-income housing even in these areas.

The West Side and West Village, by contrast, were neighborhoods just above the mid-1970 median per capita income. The West Side experienced relative improvement in housing conditions, moving in rank from below to above the median, while the West Village remained steadily above the median. Both neighborhoods increased in population size and had a high number of real estate sales. Tax arrears and public assistance cases did not increase in these areas as fast as did borough-wide rates. Occupancy rates declined somewhat, but new housing was again built in these areas.

Marble Hill represents very different conditions, since it is found far below the median in per capita income during both 1970 and mid-1970. However, population increase and relative housing improvements are evident. Other signs of improvement were a decrease in public assistance cases, no growth in tax arrears, and a less than average decline in the occupancy rate. There was little real estate activity between 1974 and 1976.

DISCUSSION

The research suggests, as predicted, that neighborhood revitalization has occurred in the inner city to an extent that is quite limited. The basic and secondary indicators point to continued decline in Manhattan during the 1970s. Within this context, we found evidence that some neighborhoods have improved at the expense of others.

The study found that a rise in income, or any other single factor, cannot be used to determine neighborhood revitalization. In our sample, areas in which residents experienced economic gains did not uniformly exhibit turnaround qualities. A method that takes into account multiple indicators of neighborhood revitalization and relative advances in the standing of an area is thus necessary. The revitalization scale that was developed ranked five neighborhoods above all others in relative improvement during the 1970s, although these areas fell short of the highest possible score. Sixty percent of all neighborhoods were rated as stable or moderately improved, and about one-forth had declined. Considering the characteristics of each revitalized area separately, the scale appears to have validity.

The revitalizing neighborhoods selected provide support for the view that different types of neighborhood revitalization are now occuring. Yorkville and Lincoln Square are examples of upper-strata revitalization, since their improvements now place them firmly among the prime locations in Manhattan. Lower-strata revitalization seems to have occurred in Marble Hill, which continues to have one of the lowest per capita incomes in the city, yet gained new residents and improved markedly in housing quality. The West Side and West Village neighborhoods can be best understood as examples of upgrading. Housing quality on the West Side moved from below to above the median. The attractiveness for both of these areas for above average—but not the wealthiest—inner-city residents seems to have increased as measured by population gains and real estate sales. Finally, a fourth category of neighborhood improvement not studied was also evident in the three neighborhoods that were eliminated. Battery Park, Lower Manhattan, and Roosevelt Island could be described as "vitalizing," since these once vacant or nonresidential lands all experienced large population increases between 1970 and 1975, a pattern that continued throughout the decade (U.S. Bureau of the Census 1980). The substantive implication of the study is that, in all probability, neighborhood revitalization has occurred without an overall economic upturn or "back to the city" movement. The few but varied cases of revitalization reported also suggest that the phenomenon is both less common and more varied than originally reported in the literature. The method proposed has apparent utility for planners and researchers interested in measuring the extent and character of neighborhood revitalization. The implementation of this approach depends on the availability of crucial data from local agencies in order to supplement decennial census tract data and estimate local change during some portion of the decade. Future investigators may also choose to experiment with including the secondary factors in the revitalization scale or weighting some variables more than others. To a large extent, 1980 census tract data will allow for a replication of the general approach outlined here, both for New York and other major central cities. Finally, studies ought also to include the role of community perceptions, along with objective neighborhood indicators. Changes in local residents' attitudes undoubtedly help determine revitalization and its specific character.

REFERENCES

Allman, D. 1978. The urban crisis leaves town. *Harpers* (December): 41-56.
———. 1979. A city revival? *Newsweek* (15 January): 28-35.
Auger, D. 1979. The politics of revitalization in gentrifying neighborhoods: The case of Boston's South End. *Journal of the American Planning Association* 45 (4): 515-22.
Baldassare, M. 1981. *The growth dilemma*. Berkeley: University of California Press.
Barthel, D. 1979. The social economy of rehabilitation: The case of the South End. Paper presented at the Eastern Sociological Society Meetings, New York.
Black, J. 1978. *The changing economic role of central cities*. Washington, D.C.: Urban Land Institute.
Black, J., Borut, A., and Dubinsky, R. 1977. Private market housing renovation in older urban areas. *Urban Land Institute Research Report*, no. 26, Washington, D.C.
Bordewich, F. 1979. The future of New York: A tale of two cities. *New York* (23 July), pp. 32-40.
Brown, P. 1979. Preservation movement comes of age. *New York Times* 14 October, pp. 1, 8.
Burgess, E. W. 1925 (1967). The growth of the city: An introduction to a

research project. In *The city*, ed. R. E. Park, E. W. Burgess, and R. D. McKenzie, pp. 47-62. Chicago: University of Chicago Press.

Clay, P. L. 1979. *Neighborhood renewal*. Lexington, Mass.: D. C. Heath.

Downs, A. 1979. Key relationships between urban development and neighborhood change. *Journal of the American Planning Association* 45 (4): 462-72.

Fleetwood, B. 1979. The new elite and the urban renaissance. *New York Times Magazine* 14 January, pp. 17-35.

Ford, K. 1978. *Housing policy and the urban middle class*. New Brunswick: Center for Urban Policy Research.

Fuguitt, G., and Zuiches, J. 1975. Residential preferences and population distribution. *Demography* 12 (3): 491-504. Gale, D. 1979. Middle class resettlement in older urban neighborhoods. *Journal of the American Planning Association* 45 (3): 293-304.

Goetze, R. 1979. *Neighborhood monitoring and analysis*. Information Bulletin (June), Community and Economic Development Task Force, Urban Consortium, Minneapolis.

Goetze, R., Colton, K., and O'Donnell, V. 1977. Stabilizing neighborhoods: A fresh approach to housing dynamics and perceptions. Unpublished report, (November). Public Systems Evaluation, Incorporated.

Goldfield, D. R. 1980. Private neighborhood redevelopment and displacement: The case of Washington, D.C. *Urban Affairs Quarterly* 15 (4): 453-68.

Hartman, C. 1979. Comment on neighborhood revitalization and displacement: A review of the evidence. *Journal of the American Planning Association* 45 (4): 488-91.

Hawley, A. H. 1972. Population density and the city. *Demography* 9: 521-9.

Homer, L., and Rydell, C. 1973. Indicators of landlord abandonment of housing in New York City. Unpublished report (May), The New York City Rand Institute.

Hudson, J. 1980. Revitalization of inner city neighborhoods: An ecological approach. *Urban Affairs Quarterly* 15 (4): 397-408.

Hughes, J., and Bleakly, K. 1975. *Urban homesteading*. New Brunswick: Center for Urban Policy Research.

James, F. 1977. Back to the city: An appraisal of housing reinvestment and population change in urban America. Washington, D.C.: The Urban Institute.

Kasarda, J. 1972. The impact of suburban population growth on central city service functions. *American Journal of Sociology* 77: 1111-24.

⸻. 1978. Urbanization, community, and the metropolitan problem. In *Handbook of Contemporary Urban Life*, ed. D. Street, pp. 27-57. San Francisco: Jossey Bass.

Laska, S., and Spain, D. 1979. Urban policy and planning in the wake of gentrification: Anticipating renovators' demands. *Journal of the American Planning Association* 45 (4): 523-31.

Lipton, S. 1977. Evidence of central city revival. *Journal of the American Institute of Planners* 45: 136-47.

London, B. 1978. The revitalization of inner-city neighborhoods: A preliminary bibliography. October Monticello, Ill.: Vance Bibliographies.

Long, L. 1980. Back to the countryside and back to the city in the same decade. In *Back to the city: Issues in neighborhood renovation*, ed. S. Laska and D. Spain. New York: Pergamon Press.

Long, L., and Dahmann, D. 1979. Is "gentrification" narrowing the city-suburb income gap? Unpublished paper.

Meadows, G., and Call, S. 1978. Combining housing market trends and resident attitudes in planning urban revitalization. *Journal of the American Institute of Planners* 44 (3): 297-305.

Morgan, D. J., and Murray, J. R. 1974. A potential population distribution and its dynamics: The expressed preference for residential location. Unpublished Report, National Opinion Research Center.

Morrison, R. 1976. Demographic trends that will shape future housing demand. *Rand Series* P-5596.

Muller, T. 1975. *Growing and declining urban areas: A fiscal comparison.* Washington, D.C.: Urban Institute.

National Urban League 1971. *The national survey of housing abandonment.* 2nd ed., Washington, D.C.

New York City Department of City Planning 1978. *Neighborhood profiles.* Mimeographed, August.

Real Estate Research Corporation 1973. Neighborhood "balance" policy guidelines for three alternative strategies. Unpublished paper, August.

Spain, D. 1980. Black-to-white successions in central city housing: Limited evidence for urban revitalization. *Urban Affairs Quarterly* 15 (4): 381-96.

Sternleib, G., and Hughes, J., eds. 1975. *Post-industrial America: Metropolitan decline and interregional job shifts.* New Brunswick: Center for Urban Policy Research.

Sullivan, D. 1978. Great expectations. *New York*, April 17: 52-55.

Sumka, H. 1978. Displacement in revitalizing neighborhoods: A review and research strategy. In *Occasional Papers in Housing and Communty Affairs*, pp. 134-67. Washington, D.C.: U.S. Department of Housing and Urban Development.

――――. 1979. Neighborhood revitalization and displacement: A review of the evidence. *Journal of the American Planning Association* 45 (4): 480-87. Urban Land Institute. 1976. New opportunities for residential development in central cities. *Urban Land Institute Research Report* no. 25, Washington, D.C.

U.S. Bureau of the Census. 1980. Special census of lower Manhattan, New York City, New York: September 26, 1978. *Current Population Reports* P-28, No. 1567.

Zimmer, B. 1975. The urban centrifugal drift. Pp. 23-92 In *Metropolitan American in Contemporary Perspective*, ed. A. Hawley and V. Rock, New York: Wiley.

CHAPTER SIX

Renovators Two Years Later: New Orleans

DAPHNE SPAIN AND SHIRLEY BRADWAY LASKA

We know that central cities are undergoing a net decline in population and that renovators are not primarily returnees from the suburbs (U.S. Bureau of the Census 1978; Gale 1980; Nelson 1981), but the term "back to the city" may be an accurate description of a renewed interest in city living. A small but influential group of home buyers has redefined inner-city neighborhoods as having desirable qualities, and the question now is whether those people plan to stay. Is renovation a fad, a social movement (London 1980) that will fade when "urban pioneers" are faced with the arrival of children or with crime in the streets (Fegan 1979; Gans 1979)? Or is a small segment of the population engaging in behavior that challenges traditional urban ecological theory by choosing the central city and remaining there? It is the purpose of this research to consider such questions by examining the neighborhood satisfaction and intentions to move of a panel of renovators in one city that has undergone extensive gentrification.

Daphne Spain is a demographic consultant in Charlottsville, VA. Shirley Bradway Laska is Associate Professor of Sociology, University of New Orleans.
Presented at the annual meeting of the American Sociolical Association, Toronto, Canada, August 1981. Woody Valls, Melissa Bowman, and Lynn Callery conducted the interviews. Pat Creppel assisted in data analysis, funds for which were provided by the University of New Orleans. The first author was on leave from the Census Bureau, teaching at the University of Virginia, while the research was conducted.

MEASURES OF NEIGHBORHOOD SATISFACTION
AND ANTICIPATED MOBILITY

Both *compositional* characteristics of the household and *contextual* characteristics of the neighborhood are important determinants of residential satisfaction. Among the household characteristics that have been linked to neighborhood satisfaction are the stage in the family life cycle (Rossi 1955), length of residence (Kasarda and Janowitz 1974), and social class and education (Lee and Guest 1979).

The contextual qualities of the neighborhood that are linked to residential satisfaction can be divided into *objective* and *subjective* characteristics. Urban ecologists are concerned with such objective measures as population density, racial composition, and heterogeneity of social class (Wirth 1938; Durand and Eckart 1939), while community proponents emphasize membership in neighborhood associations, the existence of close friends and acquaintances, and the crime rate as determinants of community attachment (Clark and Cadwallader 1973; Kasarda and Janowitz 1974; Galster and Hesser 1979).

Physical qualities of the neighborhood, such as its spatial location relative to other places, have also been found to contribute to neighborhood satisfaction. Dimensions of this spatial quality include centrality (Lansing and Barth 1964) and distance from work (Clark and Cadwallader 1973).

Finally, the subjective perceptions of members of the household toward their neighborhood are also related to satisfaction. These include perceptions of the condition of the neighborhood (Lansing, Marans, and Zehner 1970), the perceived degree of personal safety and level of crime (Guterbock 1976; Droettboom et al. 1971), and perceived changes in social class and racial composition (Goodman 1978).

Two of the most significant predictors of residential mobility are housing tenure and prior mobility, for which we have no variance. All respondents are homeowners, and all have lived in the same house for at least three years. The current study, therefore, examines the effects of other demographic and neighborhood variables on anticipated mobility. The literature on intentions to move indicates that housing and neighborhood satisfaction are two important subjective predictors of whether a household anticipates moving within several years (Speare 1981; Heaton et al. 1979; Newman and Duncan 1979). Other subjective measures we have added are perceptions of neighborhood safety, perceptions of community spirit, and perceptions of racial and social class changes.

Compositional household characteristics that predict intentions to move include age of the household head and family size (Roistacher 1975). Level of educational attainment and income have also been positively linked to anticipated mobility (Foote et al. 1960; Duncan and Newman 1975). Among objective contextual neighborhood variables that have been shown to affect future mobility are friendship ties and membership in neighborhood clubs (Duncan and Newman 1975), the existence of crime in the neighborhood (Newman and Duncan 1979), and distance from work (Duncan and Newman 1975).

HYPOTHESES

Survey research conducted in the 1970s indicates that renovators are young, often single individuals or small families with young children (Fichter 1977; Gale 1976, 1977). They are generally highly educated and employed in professional occupations. Renovators often work in the central city and consider proximity to cultural and recreational urban amenities to be important (Houstoun 1976). While some of these characteristics make renovators atypical of metropolitan households—single marital status, high degree of education, and choice of the central city—other characteristics, such as the presence of young children, central city employment, and purchase of a house, reflect similarities with other urban residents. Thus, with some qualifications, determinants of their satisfaction with the neighborhood and predictors of their expectations for moving should be comparable to those for metropolitan home-owners in general.

Another issue is whether renovators' highly visible wealth in the midst of low-income or transition neighborhoods makes them special targets of crime (Cybriwsky 1978). The possibility of crime is tacitly acknowledged by renovators every time the installation of bars on the windows accompanies a newly restored facade. We examine whether crime is a problem big enough to affect renovators' satisfaction with their neighborhoods or their intentions to stay in the neighborhood

Much of the current study is descriptive and intended to add to the knowledge of renovators that is possible only through case studies. However, four hypotheses in reference to the national metropolitan population are also examined.

1. Neighborhood satisfaction is higher for renovators than for other metropolitan homeowners.
2. Renovators will express less of an intention to move than other metropolitan homeowners, possibly as a

result of strong community attachments and higher than average neighborhood satisfaction.

3. Renovators are more likely to have been victims of crime than other metropolitan residents, due partially to their visibility in previously low-income areas.

4. Determinants of neighborhood satisfaction and intentions to move are similar for renovators and other metropolitan residents.

SURVEYS AND SAMPLE

The Survey

The research reported here comprised two telephone surveys administered approximately two years apart (winter 1978 and spring 1980) to the same sample of recent home buyers in old neighborhoods in New Orleans, Louisiana.

The initial questionnaire contained items specifically focused on the respondent's compositional household characteristics, reasons for selecting an inner-city residential location, and satisfaction with the existing local and city-wide services (Laska and Spain 1979). With some questions pertaining to house and neighborhood satisfaction repeated, the second questionnaire also included subjective questions about crime, perceived changes in the racial and class composition of the neighborhood, its community spirit and safety, and objective questions about the respondent's involvement in the neighborhood's social network.

In addition to the survey data, contextual measures of the tract or neighborhood were assigned to each case. The measures used in this analysis include the proximity of the tract to the central business district (CBD) (see Laska, Seaman, and McSeveney [1982], racial composition of the tract (U.S. Bureau of the Census 1981), block density of the neighborhood (U.S. Bureau of the Census, 1981; City of New Orleans 1980),[1] and degree of renovation.[2]

The Sample

The original sample was based on characteristics of neighborhoods rather than individuals. This approach was necessary because only a few case studies about the characteristics of renovators were available when the research was initiated (Gale 1976; Bradley 1977; Fichter 1977; Thayer and Waidhas 1977). Neighborhoods designated on the Banks map of 1863 (see Lewis [1976]) were considered eligible for renovation by virtue of the age of their housing stock. From a "windshield" survey and consultation with a local housing expert, ten of those neighborhoods were determined to be undergoing extensive renovation.

Ninety-seven interviews were completed from a sampling frame of 504 individuals identified by the *City Directory* as new homeowners in the renovating neighborhoods (Polk 1977). Twenty-five percent of those in the original sample were ineligible because of Directory errors, and another 38 percent were not reached as a result of missing or incorrect telephone numbers, or no answer after repeated calls. These considerations reduced the sample size to 166 individuals, 58 percent of whom completed interviews. Ninety-two percent of the respondents were white. The final sample was undoubtedly biased in favor of people enthusiastic about renovation and thus willing to discuss it.

As a result of the eligibility criteria for inclusion in the sample— all new homeowners in the designated neighborhoods—the sample included new owners with social-class characteristics similar to those of traditional residents, as well as new owners who were higher in social class (the stereotypical renovator). Approximately 15 percent of the sample had one or more of the following characteristics: a high school education *or less;* an income of *less* than $20,000; an occupational status of *less* than managerial; and self-identification as *lower*-class. These respondents were kept in the sample because they are homeowners, which distinguishes them from other original residents of these old neighborhoods, most of whom are renters.[3] In addition, their decision to buy a home in an old city neighborhood rather than in a suburban subdivision may reflect their participation in the reinvestment trend, similar to the incumbent upgrading described by Clay (1979a). While upper-middle class, college-educated households may dominate the movement, there is also often a spinoff effect to lower-status homebuyers, especially at the early stages of the process before speculation and demand cause prices to escalate.

In the spring of 1980, 67 of the original 97 respondents were reinterviewed. Eighteen of the respondents could not be located, seven had moved to other central-city neighborhoods, four had moved to the suburbs, and one had left the area. Of the eighteen not located, it is estimated by the difficulty encountered—for example unanswered rings versus disconnected numbers—that five had probably moved. This would result in a mobility rate of 17.5 percent for two years. A more conservative estimate including half of all unreached respondents (N=9) and the known movers (N=12) results in a mobility rate of 21.6 percent for the two years. National data for a two-year period indicate a moving rate for central-city white adults of 27.0 percent (U.S. Bureau of the Census 1978). Given that the national data include both renters and owners, and that owners typically have far lower mobility than renters, New Orleans renovators appear to be in line with national rates.

A comparison of the respondents who were reinterviewed with those no longer in the sample in 1980 suggests some differences between stayers and movers in age, education, and income (see table 6.1). Those who stayed tended to be younger than those who left. The percentage of respondents with a high school degree or less is about the same for stayers and movers; but those with a college degree or some college predominate in stayers, while those with a professional education were more likely to leave. In the same trend, respondents with incomes of less than $20,000 comprise a larger percentage of stayers than movers. On the fourth characteristic, stage of life cycle, the stayers' and movers' profiles were similar.

Table 6.1. Comparison of Stayers versus Movers/Lost (Data Expressed in Percentages)

Characteristics	Movers/Lost[a] (n=30)	Stayers[b] (n=67)
Age		
24-34	30.7	56.7
35-39	36.9	13.3
40+	32.3	30.0
Education		
High school (some or graduate)	17.2	16.9
College (some or graduate)	24.1	41.5
Professional (some or degree)	58.6	41.5
Annual Family Income		
<$20.00	29.6	35.6
$20,000 to 39,000	44.4	40.7
≥$40,000	25.9	23.7
Stage of Life Cycle		
Singles	20.0	19.0
Young couples	10.0	11.1
Families	60.0	63.5
Older couples	10.0	6.4

[a]Respondents who had moved or were not located in 1980.
[b]Respondents who were interviewed both in 1978 and 1980.

While it is only possible to speculate on the reasons for these differences, the existence of a pattern in which the younger, less affluent but college-educated remain may suggest that renovators are investing in inner-city homes as an economical way of becoming homeowners. Those renovators who are in a higher income category may have more options in the real estate market. Interviews completed with three of the seven movers to other inner-city neighborhoods give support to this speculation. All three had graduate degrees, earned over $20,000 and had a preschool child. Two sought larger houses and the third "couldn't resist the offer" made by a real estate agent. In addition to greater purchasing options, those with a professional education are likely to be more inner-city geographically mobile for career opportunities (U.S. Bureau of the Census 1979). Thus, while they may have chosen an inner-city home for its architectural attractiveness and proximity to urban employment and amenities, their tenure may be more limited. Finally, there appears to be neither a flight to the suburbs of known movers (only four of the twelve movers) nor an exodus of families with children.[4]

A second set of stayer/mover comparisons was made on the panel data by analyzing responses to questions asked in both surveys (table 6.2). The questions included two on satisfaction—with the neighborhood and the house—and two tapping contextual variables—perceptions of safety and involvement in the local social network.

Table 6.2. Comparative Data for New Orleans Renovators: 1978, 1980 (Data Expressed in Percentages)

	1978 Movers[a] & Lost (N=30)	Stayers[b] (N=67)	1980 Stayers (N=67)
Neighborhood Satisfaction "Very satisfied"	60.0	65.2	79.1
Housing Satisfaction "Very satisfied with investment"	58.6	76.1	82.1
Perceived Neighborhood Safety "Safe place to walk at night"	75.9	58.5	52.2
Neighborhood Association Affiliation Members[c]	47.8	36.5	62.2

[a]Respondents who had moved or were not located for the second interview.
[b]Respondents who were interviewed both in 1978 and 1980.
[c]Percentage of members when neighborhood association exists (movers n = 23, stayers n = 52).

It appears that stayers were more satisfied in 1978, both with the neighborhood and the investment value of the house, than were movers. Furthermore, satisfaction increased over time. It is especially interesting to note the increased satisfaction with investment value in light of rising interest rates, which have dampened the real estate market.

Perceptions of safety and involvement in the neighborhood are more puzzling. The movers/lost were considerably more positive about their neighborhood's safety and more were members of neighborhood associations. In addition, the perception of safety of the stayers declined between 1978 and 1980. Conversely, their neighborhood association membership increased by 70 percent between the two surveys. Perhaps the low perceived safety and increasing membership in neighborhood associations are linked, association membership being perceived as instrumental in improving neighborhood conditions. Other data (below) support this speculation.

RESULTS

Our first three hypotheses were that: neighborhood satisfaction for renovators would be higher than average; their intentions to move would be lower than average; and their crime victimization rates would be higher than average. Table 6.3 presents data comparing the New Orleans sample with national samples on each of these topics.

Table 6.3. New Orleans Renovators Compared with National Samples (data expressed in percentages)

	New Orleans (N=67)	National
Neighborhood Satisfaction		
"Very satisfied"	79.1	36.1[a]
Anticipated Mobility		
Within 5 years	23.1	23.0[b]
Victimization		
Household rate	44.4/2 years	30/year[c]
Crimes		
Contribution to total victimization by		
Violent crimes	20	15
Personal larceny	13	36
Burglary	37	17
Theft	20	26
Car theft	0	5
Vandalism	10	0

[a]"Indicators of Housing...," Annual Housing Survey, data for white homeowners in central cities, 1977 (N=9,633,000) (U.S. Bureau of the Census 1979).
[b]Panel Study of Income Dynamics data for metropolitan homeowners, 1971 (N=1,947) (Roistacher 1975).
[c]"The Prevalence of Crime" (N=80,622,000). (U.S. Department of Justice 1981).

As anticipated, neighborhood satisfaction is extremely high among renovators. The proportion of New Orleans renovators who were "very satisfied" with their neighborhoods is over twice the national average for white central-city homeowners. Renovators often choose a specific neighborhood, either low-income or in transition, and help to make it a "gentrified" area. This active involvement in the creation of a neighborhood's character may be one of the intangible aspects that increases renovators' levels of neighborhood satisfaction.

At first glance, renovators appear no more likely to plan to stay in their neighborhoods than are other households. They exhibit no higher level of community attachment than a national sample of metropolitan homeowners, 23 percent of whom say they expect to move within 5 years. But the national figure includes homeowners of all ages and socioeconomic status, whereas renovators tend to be young and well educated. These two groups—the young and the highly educated—have higher than average mobility. For example, 43.5 percent of central-city, college-educated adults aged 30 to 34 moved between 1975 and 1977, compared with 29.7 percent of all central-city residents aged 18 and over (U.S. Bureau of the Census 1978). If comparable national data on *anticipated* mobility were available by such demographic groups, a similar relationship between age, educational level, and anticipated mobility might emerge. If so, an anticipated mobility rate of 23 percent of renovators would be very low compared with the actual mobility rate of 43.5 percent for a group of comparable age and education.

We hypothesized that renovators would be less likely to move because of community attachments. Community ties do emerge as important determinants of anticipated mobility, as demonstrated later in table 6.5. Regardless of community involvement or high neighborhood satisfaction, however, a young professional may recognize that a job-related move is likely within the next five years. So the results of this hypothesis are mixed. There is some evidence that, for their demographic group, renovators may have lower than average anticipated mobility. But realistically, young professionals may not expect to stay in one place for more than five years for career considerations. The very characteristics of the renovators that encourage them to create their neighborhoods are also those that contribute to an individual's eventual mobility.

The third hypothesis concerned rates of victimization. It was expected that renovators would be victims of crime dispropor-tionately because of their high visibility in largely lower-income neighborhoods. Higher crime victimization was also expected as a result of the animosity and frustration felt by the lower-income residents toward the renovators as residential displacement occurs and community services change to serve renovators' needs (Chernoff 1980). The respondents were asked if they or any member of their families had been a victim of crime within their homes or neighborhoods during the past 2 years. Of the 60 respondents from whom answers were obtained, 44.4 percent (N=27) indicated victimization, approximately the same rate a found for a national household sample (U.S. Department of Justice 1981), although the national study did not restrict the household's victimization to the environs of the home and neighborhood.[5]

While the overall rates appear comparable, the breakdown by type of crime indicates differences. The New Orleans renovators are victims of serious crimes more often than other households. Violent crimes against persons were 25 percent higher than the national findings and burglary of households, 54 percent higher; vandalism was also higher. Thus, it appears that renovators are more seriously affected by crime than the national average. We will consider below the extent to which victimization rates are a cause of alarm and disenchantment with the inner-city locations the renovators have chosen.

The fourth hypothesis on determinants of neighborhood satisfaction and predictors of anticipated mobility is dealt with separately in the following sections.

Neighborhood Satisfaction

Each of the variables reviewed as a predictor of neighborhood satisfaction in previous research was included in the second interview with New Orleans renovators. The question on neighborhood satisfaction was worded, "How satisfied are you with this neighborhood as a place to live?" It provided four closed-ended response options, ranging from "very satisfied" to "not at all satisfied."

Table 6.4. Determinants of Neighborhood Satisfaction: 1980 (Data Expressed in Percentages)

	Very Satisfied With Neighborhood
Total (N=67)[a]	79.1
Compositional Household Characteristics	
Stage of life cycle	
Singles (N=12)	75.0
Childless couples (N=7)	71.0
Couples with children (N=41)	84.8
Elderly couples (N=4)	100.0
Length of residence in neighborhood	
Less than five years (N=30)	66.7
Five years or more (N=37)	89.2

Social class identification
  Lower (N=7) 85.7
  Middle (N=47) 83.0
  Upper (N=7) 71.4
Educational attainment
  High School (some or graduate) (N=10) 90.0
  College (some or graduate) (N=28) 71.4
  Professional (some or degree) (N=27) 81.5

Contextual Neighborhood Characteristics
Objective:
Member of neighborhood association
  Yes (N=28) 85.7
  No (N=17) 82.4
Number of close friends in neighborhood
  None (N=32) 75.0
  One or two (N=13) 84.6
  Several (N=22) 81.8
Victim of neighborhood crime
  Yes (N=27) 70.4
  No (N=33) 85.3
Work in central city
  Yes (N=55) 76.4
  No (N=12) 91.7
Proximity of tract to CBD
  Closest (N=24) 79.2
  Middle (N=21) 76.2
  Most distant (N=22) 81.8
Racial composition of neighborhood (1980)
  4-24% black (N=26) 84.0
  25-42% black (N=12) 75.0
  43-84% black (N=29) 75.9
Block density of neighborhood (1980)
  Low (N=14) 71.4
  Middle (N=24) 82.6
  High (N=29) 79.3

Subjective:
Perceived safety of neighborhood*
  Yes (N=34) 94.1
  No (N=33) 63.6
Perceived racial changes
  Yes (N=12) 66.7
  No (N=53) 83.0
Perceived social class changes
  Yes (N=15) 80.0
  No (N=52) 78.8
Perceived community spirit*
  Strong (N=22) 90.9
  Some (N=35) 80.0
  None (N=10) 50.0

*Significant at $\leq$ .05.
[a]N represents the total number of respondents in a category from which the percentage of "very satisfied" is calculated. The total for all categories of a variable does not always tally to 67 because of missing data.

Beginning with compositional variables, the largest differences exist between households with children and those without. Couples with children are approximately 10 percentage points more likely to be very pleased with their neighborhoods than those without children. The presence of children in the household probably indicates a greater reliance on the neighborhood for such services as parks and social networks than for households without children. Also, if singles, or couples, without children, do need something not provided, they are usually more mobile than families with children and can find it more easily outside the immediate area. In addition, a selection process is expected to occur in which families with children would more likely select neighborhoods in more advanced stages of renovation (Pattison 1977) and thus be more satisfied with them. In considering this question for New Orleans renovators, we found the families with children located disproportionately in the neighborhoods with more renovation occurring (see note 2).

As expected, those who have lived in the neighborhood the longest are the most satisfied with it (89.2 percent vs. 66.7 percent). Living in the same neighborhood does not imply having lived in the same house: everyone in the sample has lived in the same house for at least 3 years, but 55.2 percent had lived in their current neighborhood for more than five years. This suggests that neighborhood satisfaction was so high for movers that they chose another house within the same neighborhood—possibly shifting from renter to owner status. Although large in percentage point differences, the differences on length of residence are not statistically significant.

The data on social class are not consistent with what was expected from the literature. There is only slight variation in neighborhood satisfaction by class as measured by the Duncan SEI scale, with upper-class respondents slightly but not significantly more satisfied than other groups. A possible explanation is the homogeneity of the sample. There are very few respondents in the "lower" category (N=7) and very few in the "upper" category (N=7).

Educational attainment presents a somewhat more puzzling picture. Satisfaction is highest among the small minority (N=10) who are high school graduates. In general, the higher the educational attainment, the greater the neighborhood satisfaction. This is the case for the remainder of the sample, with professionals expressing a higher level of satisfaction than college-educated respondents.

Turning to the contextual neighborhood variables, membership in a neighborhood association appears to make little difference in level of satisfaction. However, there is a difference depending on whether there are close friends in the neighborhood: respondents with one or more close friends were more satisfied than those with no friends in the neighborhood. Apparently, secondary ties such as association memberships are not as predictive of satisfaction as are the closer bonds of friendship. One might speculate, of course, that friendships are formed *within* neighborhood associations, in which case the two variables may not be independent of one another.

Interestingly, having been the victim of a crime does *not* significantly affect neighborhood satisfaction, although there is a difference of 15 percentage points between victims and others. This rate of 70.4 percent "very satisfied" is no lower than for those respondents who happen to be childless couples or had lived in the neighborhood less than five years. In other words, having been mugged or having property stolen is not the strong predictor of dissatisfaction one might expect from such an unpleasant experience, or from the strong fear of crime usually expressed in opinion polls by urban respondents in general.

As for the spatial location of the neighborhood, neither closeness to work nor centrality to the central business district (in this case, including the French Quarter) were significant predictors of satisfaction. The fact that such a high percentage (91.7) of those whose work is outside the central city are still highly satisfied with their neighborhoods indicates an even stronger commitment on their part to city living. Despite a longer (reverse) commute to a suburban job than that of their neighbors employed in the city, these people whose home and workplace are farthest separated are extremely satisfied with their residential choices. The actual number of these people is very small, however (N=12, only 18 percent of the sample), and hence their work locations are not typical of the larger sample.

There appears to be a slight preference for neighborhoods farthest from the central business district, although the percentage differences are not large. The actual physical area of the New Orleans central city is fairly small, resulting in little variance in the distance of neighborhoods from "urban amenities," unlike in most metropolitan areas with much larger central cities. All of the neighborhoods in the sample are within a fifteen-minute drive or within easy walking distance of the French Quarter. Those that are farthest out are closer to other places like Audubon Park (with a zoo) or City Park (location of the art museum).

Two of the three linear characteristics of urbanism—hetero-geneity and density—were examined. Those renovators in neighbor-hoods with lower proportions of black residents were more satisfied, as predicted by earlier research (Clay 1979b). The high satisfaction within the two highest categories of density was not anticipated.

Finally, it is among the subjective measures that statistically significant predictors emerge. Those who perceive their neighborhoods as a safe place to walk at night are significantly more satisfied than those who perceive some danger. This reaction occurs within an overall context of declining proportions of respondents perceiving their neighborhoods as safe (58.5 percent in 1978 vs. 52.2 percent in 1980). It is also interesting that *perceptions* of safety are more important than actual experience with crime; as long as the neighborhood is defined as safe, people are satisfied regardless of whether they themselves have been victimized (40 percent of those reporting their neighborhoods as safe had been victimized).

Perceptions of neighborhood change were limited to only a few respondents (N=12). However, among those perceiving racial change, a smaller percentage was satisfied with their neighborhood than among those perceiving no change in the preceding two years. Perceived social-class changes, also applying to only a few respondents, did not make as much difference in level of neighborhood satisfaction. When the pattern of responses was analyzed for the eleven and fifteen respondents, respectively, who perceived either race or class change, it was found that about half perceived the racial change as being toward increased white and half toward increased black. The consensus on direction of class change was greater: eleven of the fifteen perceived an increase of more upper-status persons. While these perceptions may on the surface appear to be contradictory, the 1980 census data on racial composition of tracts (U.S. Bureau of the Census 1981) may lend support to the co-occurrence of the two trends in the old renovating neighborhoods in New Orleans (see final section of the chap.).

Any level of "community spirit" appears to influence neighborhood satisfaction positively and significantly by at least 30 percentage point increase over a perceived lack of community spirit. A total lack was rare, however (N=10), indicating that it is an unusual neighborhood in which there is not some degree of boosterism. Given that renovators have been characterized as "pioneers" seeking to develop a middle-class neighborhood in a previously lower-class one, community spirit may be perceived as a measure of their neighbors' commitment to this goal, and thus a sign of its eventual accomplishment. In addition, renovators have been depicted as being unusual in their quest for a more traditional community (Cybriwsky 1978). Consequently, those who perceive that community spirit exists would be expected to be more satisfied.

Of all the variables found to be important in previous research on neighborhood satisfaction, only the perception of safety of the neighborhood and perceived community spirit were statistically significant predictors of satisfaction among renovators. A possible explanation for the lack of statistical significance among the other variables is the small sample size and expected cell frequencies and the small amount of variance in the dependent variable. These methodological issues do not explain the whole story, however, because the same conditions hold true for the dependent variable on anticipated mobility (see the following section) and there are several predictors that proved to be significantly linked to future mobility. The best explanation may be that renovators have a lot invested, both financially and psychologically, in the success of their neighborhoods. The strength of this commitment may override most common predictors of satisfaction for other types of metropolitan homeowners.

Anticipated Mobility

Two of the best predictors of future mobility are past mobility and housing tenure. However, since our sample consists of homeowners who have lived in the same house for at least three years, these variables are controlled in the analysis. Table 6.5 summarizes the effects of various compositional and contextual variables on anticipated mobility.[6] (Some of the variables are different from those in table 6.4 because of a different emphasis in the literature for the respective dependent variables).

Table 6.5. Determinants of Anticipated Residential Mobility: 1980 (Data Expressed in Percentages)

	Intent to stay in House > 5 years
Total (N=67)[a]	76.9
Compositional Household Characteristics	
Age of respondent*	
25 to 34 years old (N=19)	57.9
35 to 39 years old (N=24)	79.2
40 or over (N=21)	90.5
Children at home*	
Yes (N=39)	74.4
No (N=25)	80.0
Educational attainment	
High school (some or graduate) (N=10)	100.0
College (some or graduate (N=27)	66.7
Professional (some or degree) (N=26)	84.6
Annual family income	
Less than $20,000 (N=20)	75.0
$20,000 to $39,000 (N=23)	78.3
$40,000 or more (N=14)	85.7

Contextual Neighborhood Characteristics
Objective
  Member of neighborhood association*
    Yes (N=27)   88.9
    No (N=17)   76.5
  Close friends in neighborhood*
    None (N=32)   68.7
    One or two (N=12)   100.0
    Several (N=21)   76.2
  Victim of neighborhood crime
    Yes (N=27)   74.1
    No (N=31)   77.4
  Work in central city
    Yes (N=53)   77.4
    No (N=12)   75.0
  Racial composition of neighborhood (1980)
    4-24% black (N=24)   75.0
    25-42% black (N=11)   81.8
    43-84% black (N=29)   75.9
  Density of neighborhood (1980)
    Low (N=14)   71.4
    Middle (N=22)   72.7
    High (N=28)   82.1
Subjective:
  Satisfaction with neighborhood
    Very satisfied (N=52)   82.7
    Less satisfied (N=13)   53.8
  Satisfaction with house (structure)*
    Very satisfied (N=42)   78.6
    Less satisfied (N=23)   73.9
  Perceived safety of neighborhood
    Yes (N=34)   85.3
    No (N=31)   67.7
  Perceived community spirit
    Strong (N=22)   81.8
    Some (N=34)   79.4
    None (N=9)   55.6
  Perceived racial changes
    Yes (N=11)   63.6
    No (N=52)   78.8
  Perceived social class changes
    Yes (N=15)   80.0
    No (N=50)   76.0

*Significant at ≤ .05.
[a]N represents the total number of respondents in a category from which the percentage intending to remain more than 5 years is calculated. The total for all categories of a variable does not always tally to 67 because of missing data.

As predicted by the literature, age of the respondent is an important determinant of anticipated mobility: the older the individual, the more likely he/she is to plan on staying in the same house for more than five years. The actual number of people above age 40 is only 21, lending support to our earlier suggestion that it is the young age of the sample that makes their anticipated mobility low in comparison to others their age. Although actual and anticipated mobility are not identical, since actual mobility declines with age it is reasonable to expect anticipated mobility to do likewise. Our data support that assumption by showing the relationship to be statistically significant.

People with no children at home plan to stay in the neighborhood longer than those with children. The percentage differences are small but statistically significant. Those without children are more likely to be singles or young couples than older couples whose children have left home (see table 6.1). Their expressed intention to stay could mean either that children are not expected, or, if planned, that the arrival of children would not affect the decision to stay. Parents, however, may anticipate moves related to their children's schooling more realistically than those without children.

Neither education nor income proved to be statistically significant predictors of anticipated mobility. More highly educated respondents expect less residential stability than high school graduates: 100 percent of high school graduates said they plan to stay more than five years. Among respondents with higher levels of education, however, professionals appear less likely to leave than those with only a college education. This result contradicts our earlier suggestion that realistic career considerations might lead professionals to expect high future mobility. The educational data presented here indicate instead that it is the college educated who are potentially most mobile. Perhaps a dichotomy exists between local and cosmopolitan professionals: those individuals with corporate managerial positions who are not native New Orleanians would be more likely to move, while natives with professional occupations that lend themselves to stable employment—lawyers, physicians—may expect longer tenure.

Income figures indicate a positive relationship between income and anticipated mobility: the higher the family income, the longer the family expects to stay in the current house. As does professional status, a high level of income assures a degree of control over one's future that may not be possible for lower income groups. If higher-income households want to stay in the neighborhood, they will probably be able to do so despite such changes as the increased housing costs that accompany renovation.

The objective neighborhood conditions that affect anticipated mobility most strongly are membership in a neighborhood association and the presence of friends in the neighborhood. Integration into the community through formal organizational ties and informal friendships decreases the likelihood of leaving in the near future. It may also be that those who intend to stay make a commitment to the neighborhood's improvement through member-ship in the neighborhood association.

There are only slight percentage differences in expectations of moving among people who were or were not victimized by crime in the previous two years. Those who have been victimized are slightly less likely to say they expect to stay more than five years than those who were not victimized (74.1 percent vs. 77.4 percent). Just as with neighborhood satisfaction, an actual victimization experience does not significantly affect the respondent's assessment of the neighborhood (or at least not in a way that is tapped by intended mobility). Proximity of work and residence showed little effect on anticipated mobility. Likewise, the urbanism measure of heteroge-neity—percentage black—is not related. However, high density is predictive (not significantly) of anticipated tenure, just as it was for satisfaction—both contrary to the expected rejection of dense residential arrangements.

Among the subjective measures, only satisfaction with the house proved to be statistically significantly related to anticipated mobility. Those who were most satisfied with the structural qualities of their houses were most likely to anticipate staying more than five years. Neighborhood satisfaction exhibited the same pattern—those likely to say they would stay were the most satisfied. Perceived safety of the neighborhood also affected intentions to move: respondents who thought their neighborhoods were safe to walk in at night were less likely to anticipate a move than those who did not feel safe. Community spirit figures strongly (although not significantly) into future mobility plans: the percentage expecting to stay indefinitely dropped from 81.8 percent among those perceiving strong community spirit to 55.6 percent among those perceiving no community spirit.

Changes in racial and social class operate in opposite directions in their effect on anticipated mobility, just as with neighborhood satisfaction. Perceived racial change appears to inhibit stability by reducing people's expectations of staying more than five years. Perceived social-class changes, on the other hand, appear to encourage stability.

DISCUSSION

Our findings from this panel study of renovators lend support to only some of our hypotheses. Renovators do appear to be very satisfied homeowners, and their satisfaction is considerably greater than national homeower surveys reflect. Renovators who may have taken financial and crime risks by selecting an inner-city neighborhood could be expected to reduce dissonance by being overly enthusiastic. However, it is interesting to observe their greater degree of satisfaction than other homeowners, many of whom are located in neighborhoods characterized by those traits deemed desirable—low density, low crime, class homogeneity, good schools, and modern infrastructure of services. In general, the old inner-city neighborhoods exhibit a lack of such characteristics.

In proposing the second hypothesis, that renovators will be inclined to longer tenure in their current homes and neighborhoods as a result of such satisfaction, it is likely that we overlooked the career motivations for moving that might prevent them from remaining despite their satisfaction. The third phase of our panel study, to be conducted this year, will examine this question in greater depth. If the level of satisfaction and commitment is high while tenure is no more than average, the effect of relatively frequent home turnover on the stability of the neighborhood may not be detrimental. Also, with declining mobility appearing as a national trend (U.S. Bureau of Census 1977), the anticipated mobility expressed by the respondents may be less likely to occur than in the past.

The third hypothesis regarding greater crime victimization for renovators was not supported in the frequency of victimization, but appeared to be in type of crime. Accessibility of renovators' homes to lower-income residents of the same or nearby neighborhoods, who may be frustrated by the negative effect of renovation on their lives, still seems to us the best explanation.

Finally, our very broad hypothesis about renovators' characteristics and attitudes, predicting satisfaction and tenure in a fashion similar to that of homeowners, was not supported overall. With regard to neighborhood satisfaction, no compositional or objective neighborhood contextual characteristics are related significantly to satisfaction. Only the respondents' perceptions of neighborhood safety and sense of community spirit were found to be important.

With regard to anticipated mobility, the renovators did conform on more measures with earlier findings about homeowners. Older renovators, those who were members of their neighborhood associations and had close friends in the neighborhood, expected to remain, as well as those who were satisfied with the structural characteristics of their home. One significant finding was that respondents with children at home expected to move sooner than respondents without children at home.

Several findings stand out as worthy of note, and their actual and possible interrelatedness give us clues as to a response to our original question: fad or urban residential commitment?

The responses of the New Orleans renovators lead us to believe that renovators have made a long-term commitment to inner-city living. By collapsing the expected length of residence variable into the dichotomy of less than or greater than five years, we even obscured the additional enthusiasm expressed in the responses to the original *open-ended* question. Some 25 percent of the respondents indicated that they intended to stay "forever" in their current residences.

Why such enthusiasm after all of these years of popular and academic pronouncements about "white flight," fear of crime, and rejection by suburban-bound home buyers of such urban problems as inadequate services and deteriorating infrastructures? It appears the answer is twofold. First, the amenities of the inner-city locations have been found "irresistible" by this particular group of home buyers, even though the tradeoffs for such benefits are far greater than the suburban home purchaser has had to consider (Laska, Seasman, and McSeveney 1982).

The convenience of the locations for work and recreation are very important. When asked in an open-ended question what they liked most about their neighborhoods, convenience was reported by more than half the respondents. The second most frequent answer was "the people," a response we believe reflects a desire for, and a finding of, a sense of community and neighborhood in these renovation locations. The significant association between a perceived sense of community and satisfaction with the neighborhood also supports this contention.

Such positive opinions about the neighborhoods' amenities do not obscure completely the renovators' concerns about traditional problems. However, the interesting quality about their response is the lack of an alarmist orientation, coupled with a firm pro-active stance. Some 40 percent of the renovators or their families had been victims of crime in their homes or neighborhoods. Yet, having been a victim does not significantly predict either satisfaction with the neighborhood or intent to stay, although there is a 15 percentage point difference between victims and nonvictims in satisfaction. Perception of neighborhood safety does, however, predict satisfaction and is strong, although not significantly related to intent to stay.

While the focus of our research was not on the strength of various negative neighborhood characteristics in predicting neighborhood satisfaction, the renovators' reactions to crime appear to be in line with the findings of a recent study on that topic. Barrett Lee, in an analysis of the linkages between perceptions of local safety and neighborhood satisfaction for metropolitan residents, in the Annual Housing Survey, concluded that "safety variables rank below such conventional concerns as rundown housing and trash in the ability to predict overall levels of neighborhood satisfaction among metropolitan residents" (1981, p.622). New Orleans renovators expressed concern about poor streets almost as frequently as about crime (20 percent versus 26 percent) and the need for better schools almost as frequently as the need for more police (9 percent versus 12 percent).

Finally, two additional open-ended questions support the statistical findings of a concerned but not paranoid reaction to safety. When asked what might prompt them to move, only two respondents mentioned crime. But when renovators with children were asked about the problems of rearing children in an inner-city neighborhood, crime and fear for their safety were the most frequently mentioned concerns. However, of the eighteen respondents who indicated there were child-rearing problems associated with inner-city living, only five (28 percent) said they had thought of moving to the suburbs as a solution.

The proactive response to neighborhood problems to which we referred is reflected in the degree of participation in the neighborhood associations and the considerable increase over the two-year period (table 6.2).[7] A recent study of Indianapolis neighborhoods found a similar higher participation rate in gentrifying neighborhoods as opposed to other inner-city neighborhoods. The authors (Stephens, Sayre, and Grooms 1981, p. 21) attributed the participation rate to a "critical mass" of residents willing to be involved in a neighborhood association, "residents with organizational skills and experience, particularly those with college education and professional or managerial occupations." We would add that the motivation to utilize such skills at the public group level is the perception that individual efforts at home renovation will not result in a satisfying residential situation without the maintenance or the establishment of certain physical and social characteristics in the neighborhood.

Of what benefit the organizational/community efforts will be for the neighborhood as a whole is less evident than might be expected. Many renovating neighborhoods are still very mixed, both racially and with respect to class. Given current high home mortgage interest rates, such a heterogeneity may be "permanent." In a recent analysis of 1980 census data for neighborhoods in ten cities, Spain (1981) found two cities in which the percentage of blacks was increasing in the same renovating neighborhoods that had declining populations. Since renovation has not been popular among middle-class blacks, such findings may indicate increasing class as well as racial heterogeneity.

In such mixed neighborhoods, will the renovators' proactivity result in neighborhood and city-wide racial and class conflict, or will it result in an enhanced commitment to community cohesion and improvement for the "general good"? The answer to this question may help us to determine the extent of long-term residential commitment of renovators.

NOTES

1. A tract/neighborhood equivalency list developed by the city was used to determine neighborhood block density from tract data.

2. Renovation was measured by the rate of real estate transactions that occurred in the respective tracts, standardized by the number of structures in that tract. See Laska, Seaman, and McSeveney [1982] for methodology.

3. Sixty-six percent of New Orleans households are renters; for the census tract containing our respondents, the range was 45-84% renters.

4. As was discussed in an earlier analysis of the 1978 survey (Laska and Spain 1979), more families with children are involved in renovation in New Orleans than in other cities. This may be the result of the sizable private/parochial school system that is available as an alternative to the public system.

5. Best estimates are that the crime victimization for 2 years is approximately 1½ times the 1-year rate, and thus 44.4 percent for 2 years in comparable to 30 percent for 1 year.

6. Answers to an open-ended question were grouped into 4 categories which were used for the statistical analysis. The 3 categories greater than 5 years were combined for the table.

7. This increase was *not* the result of the founding of new associations between 1978-80, for the neighborhoods studied had established associations by 1978.

REFERENCES

Bradley, D. S. 1977. Neighborhood transition: middle-class home buying in an inner-city, deteriorating community. Paper presented at the annual meeting of the American Sociological Association, September 5-9. Chicago, Ill.

Chernoff, M. 1980. Social displacement in a renovating neighborhood's commercial district: Atlanta. Pp. 204-219 in S. Laska and D. Spain (eds.) *Back to the City: Issues in Neighborhood Renovation*. Elmsford, New York: Pergamon Press.

City of New Orleans. 1980. "Tract/neighborhood equivalency list." Unpublished city document.

Clark, W. A. V. and M. Cadwallader
    1973 Locational stress and residential mobility. *Environment and Behavior* (March):5 29-41.

Clay, P. L.
1979a *Neighborhood Renewal: Middle-Class Resettlement and Incumbent Upgrading in American Neighborhoods.* Lexington, Mass.: Lexington Books.
1979b The process of black surbanization. *Urban Affairs Quarterly* 14 (June): 405-424.

Cybriwsky, R. A.
1978 Social aspects of neighborhood change. *Annals of the Association of American Geographers* 68 (March): 17-33.

Droettboom, T. et al.
1971 Urban violence and residential mobility. *Journal of the American Institute of Planners* 37 (September): 319-325.

Duncan, G. and Newman, S. 1975. People as planners: The fulfillment of residential mobility expectations. In *Five thousand American families: Patterns of economic progress,* ed. G. Duncan and J. Morgan. vol. 3, pp. 279-318. University of Michigan: Institute for Social Research.

Durand, R., and Eckart, D. 1973. Social rank, residential effects and community satisfaction. *Social Forces* 52 (September): 74-85.

Fegan, D. 1979. Mean streets. *The Washington Post,* 3 November 1979, p. A 11.

Fichter, R. 1977. *Young professionals and city neighborhoods.* Boston: Parkman Center for Urban Affairs.

Foote, N. et al. 1960. *Housing choices and housing constraints.* New York: McGraw Hill.

Gale, D. E. 1976. The back-to-the-city movement...or is it? A survey of recent homeowners in the Mount Pleasant neighborhood of Washington, D.C. Washington, D.C.: Department of Urban and Regional Planning, George Washington University.

———. 1977. The back-to-the-city movement revisited: a survey of recent homebuyers in the Capital Hill neighborhood of Washington, D.C. Washington, D.C.: Department of Urban and Regional Planning, George Washington University.

Galster, G. C., and Hesser, G. W. 1979. Compositional and contextual determinants of residential satisfaction. Paper presented at the Annual Meeting of the American Sociological Association, Boston, Mass.

Gans, H. 1979. Gentrification: a mixed blessing? *The New York Times Magazine* 11 February 1979.

Goodman, J. L. 1978. *Urban residential mobility: Places, people, and policy.* Washington, D.C.: The Urban Institute.

Guterbock, T. 1976. Push hypothesis: Minority presence, crime and urban deconcentration. In *The Changing Face of the Suburbs,* ed. B. Swartz, pp. 137-61. Chicago: University of Chicago.

Heaton, T., Frederickson, C., Fuguitt, G., and Zuiches, J. 1979. Residential preferences, community satisfaction, and the intention to move. *Demography* 16 (November): 565-73.

Houstoun, L. O., Jr. 1976. Neighborhood change and city policy. *Urban Land,* 35 (July-August): 3-9.

Kasarda, J., and Janowitz, M. 1974. Community attachment in mass society. *American Sociological Review* 39 (June): 328-39.

Lansing, J. B., and Barth, N. 1964. *Residential location and urban mobility: A multivariate analysis.* Ann Arbor, Mich.: Institute for Social Research.

Lansing, J., Marans, R., and Zehner, R. 1970. *Planned Residential Environments.* Ann Arbor: Institute for Social Research, University of Michigan.

Laska, S. B., and Spain, D. 1979. Urban policy and planning in the wake of gentrification. *Journal of the American Planning Association.* 450 (October): 523-31.

Lee, B. A. 1981. The urban unease revisited: perceptions of local safety and neighborhood satisfaction among metropolitan residents. *Social Science Quarterly* 62 (December): 611-29.

Lee, B. A. and A. M. Guest
    1979 "Subjective evaluations of metropolitan neighborhood quality." Paper presented at the 74th annual meeting of the American Sociological Association, Boston, August. 27-31.

Lewis, P. 1976. *New Orleans: The making of an urban landscape.* Cambridge, Mass.: Ballinger.

London, B. 1980. Gentrification as urban reinvasion: some preliminary definitional and theoretical considerations. In *Back to the City: Issues in Neighborhood Renovation,* ed. S. B. Laska and D. Spain. Elmsford, N. Y.: Pergamon Press.

Nelson, K. 1981. Explaining changes in central-city selection and migration. Paper presented at annual meeting of Population Association of America, Washington, D.C.

Newman, S., and Duncan, G. 1979. Residential problems, dissatisfaction, and mobility. *Journal of the American Planning Association.* 45 (April): 154-66.

Pattison, T. 1977. The process of neighborhood upgrading and gentrification. M.A. diss. Cambridge: Massachusetts Institute of Technology.

Polk, R. L. 1977. *New Orleans city directory.* Dallas: Polk.

Roistacher, E. 1975. Residential mobility: planners, movers, and multiple movers. In *Five thousand American families: Patterns of economic progress,* ed. G. Duncan and J. Morgan, vol. 3, pp. 259-278. Ann Arbor: University of Michigan, Institute for Social Research.

Rossi, P. H. 1955. *Why families move.* Glencoe: Free Press.

Spain, D. 1981. A gentrification scorecard. *American Demographics* 3 (November): 14-20.

Speare, A. 1981. Residential satisfaction as an intervening variable in residential mobility. *Demography* 11 (May): 173-88.

Stephens, S. A., Sayre, C. W., and Grooms, L. 1981. The social correlates of housing rehabilitation: Indianapolis, 1980. Paper presented at the annual meeting of the American Sociological Association, August 24-28, Toronto, Canada.

Thayer, R., and Waidhas, P. 1977. What do in-town investors want? *Urban Land* (June): 19-21.

U.S. Bureau of the Census. 1977. Geographical mobility: March 1975 to March 1976. *Current Population Reports,* ser. P-20, no. 305. Washington,

D.C.: U.S. Government Printing Office.

————. 1978. Geographical mobility: March 1975 to March 1977. *Current Population Reports,* ser. P-20, no. 320. Washington, D.C.: U.S. Government Printing Office.

————. 1979. Indicators of housing and neighborhood quality for the U.S. and regions, Annual Housing Survey, Part B, *Current Housing Reports,* ser. H-150-77. Washington, D.C.: U.S. Government Printing Office.

————. 1981. *1980 Census of Population and Housing.* Advance Reports, PHc 80-V-20, Louisiana. Washington, D.C.: U.S. Government Printing Office.

U.S. Department of Justice. 1981. The prevalence of crime. *Bureau of Justice Statistics Bulletin.*

Wirth, L. 1938. Urbanism as a way of life. *American Journal of Sociology,* 44 (July): 1-24.

CHAPTER SEVEN

Revitalization in a Working-Class Neighborhood

J. JOHN PALEN AND CHAVA NACHMIAS

The existence of this volume testifies to a growing interest in, and research on, patterns of urban regeneration and revitalization. Not since the era of the Chicago School have researchers had such an explicit and concentrated focus on change in city neighborhoods. The pattern of recent decades, one in which urban studies often were a shorthand for studying central-city social problems, has given way to an expanding concern with patterns of urban residential change. We are beginning to accumulate data on such questions as: the amount of revitalization (Baldassare, chapt. 5), the effects of such revitalization on neighborhoods (DeGiovanni, chapt. 4), the attitudes of renovators (Spain and Laska, chapt. 6) and the amount and effects of displacement (Lee and Hodge, and Henig, chapts. 8 and 9). From these studies an overview of urban revitalization is beginning to emerge.

To date, research on the characteristics of the population in revitalizing areas had focused on the newcomers moving into the area (Bradley 1977; Gale 1980). While there has been only limited research on who is likely to be displaced (U.S. Department of

J. John Palen is Professor of Sociology, Virginia Commonwealth University.
Chava Nachmias is Associate Professor of Sociology and Urban Affairs, University of Wisconsin-Milwaukee.
Research for this paper was carried out under Grant ROM35520-01, National Institutes of Mental Health, Center for Work and Mental Health.

Housing and Urban Development 1981) there is even less on existing residents who, by choice or otherwise, remain in a revitalizing area (Clay 1979; Cybriwsky 1978). This paper will discuss differences between old-timers and newcomers, renters and owners, in a revitalizing working-class neighborhood. We were particularly interested in how their responses to, and involvement in, community revitalization differed.

The assumption, generally supported by both media and research, appears to be that revitalization of a neighborhood means a change in both its physical and socioeconomic characteristics. The commonly used term "gentrification" reinforces this assumption. The gentrifiers are perceived as being young professionals or white-collar, white, upwardly mobile middle-class, single or, if married, with no or at most young children. Data indicate that this near stereotype has some basis in fact (Gale 1980, Bradley 1977; Grier and Grier 1978; Clay 1979; Goldfield 1980). To this should be added the assumption that the "urban pioneers," or gentrifiers, are both newcomers to the area and homeowners rather than renters. As a rule, their current incomes for housing are not as lofty as their housing aspirations.

Newcomers involved in renovation activities are assumed to be active in associational activities involved both with neighborhood preservation and protection of residential property values (Schoenberg and Rosenbaum 1980). In fact, community restoration and preservation groups are often discussed as if they were composed entirely of new middle-class renovators. Such groups push hard for upgrading city services, such as street lighting, police protection, housing code enforcement, street repair, and garbage pickup. Such young adult newcomers are generally less concerned with shortcomings that do not touch them directly, such as poor schools or inadequate recreational space (Clay 1979). Longer-term residents, on the other hand, are more likely to hold membership in neighborhood churches, ethnic associations, and long-term social and/or recreational associations (Nachmias and Palen 1982). Even in successful neighborhoods, conflicts are not uncommon between newcomers and longer established residents (Schoenberg and Rosenbaum 1980). In such conflicts neighborhood restoration associations are usually viewed as representing the economic and social interests of the newcomers. Churches and ethnic associations, by contrast, represent older residents.

Concerning less affluent neighborhoods where new middle-class gentrification has not occurred, but which have nonetheless experienced upgrading and rehabilitation of their housing stock, the term "incumbent upgrading" is usually used (Clay 1979). Incumbent upgraders, in contrast to newcomers, are characterized as older, likely to be white ethnic or minority, and non-upwardly mobile working-class (Clay 1979). By definition, such incumbents have a considerable temporal as well as economic investment in the neighborhood.

The term "incumbent upgrader" appears reasonable and useful, but it can be misleading. The difficulty is the modifier "incumbent." It implies that the alternative to gentrification is long-term working-class residents remaining and upgrading their residences. This is attractive imagery, but it is usually an inaccurate reflection of demographic and social reality. Far from being stable islands of immobility, working-class neighborhoods continually undergo residental movement both in and out. One-fifth of all households move each year, and nearly 40 percent of all renters do so (U.S. Department of Housing and Urban Development 1981, p. 32). Working-class neighborhoods are not immune to this pattern. At any given time a substantial proportion of any working-class neighborhood's residents are likely to be newcomers. This is particularly true of renters. What maintains an area's character is thus not the absence of residential movement, but rather that the characteristics of the entering newcomers are not sharply different from those who are leaving. In working-class areas, upgraders may thus be long-term incumbents, or they may be newcomers of relatively similar status. One of the areas this research examines is the extent to which incumbents and newcomers are similar or different in demographic characteristics, attitudes, and community participation.

RESEARCH SITE

The site of this research is an older working-class neighborhood in the industrial city of Milwaukee, Wisconsin. The continuing working-class nature of the neighborhood sets this research a bit apart from those articles dealing with gentrifying neighborhoods. Most discussions of urban revitalization tend to concentrate on once elite housing areas of some architectural, and perhaps historic, merit that are being restored to their former glory (Bradley 1977; Gale 1980). However such areas, fascinating as they are, are but a small fraction of any city's housing stock. What occurs in elite areas may have only limited relevance to the rest of the city. Most neighborhoods in most cities are far more plebian, and it is the fate of these numerous working-class "gray areas" that will determine the future of the city as a place of residence.

The research area does not appear to be perceptibly different from other working-class areas in other cities throughout the industrial heartland. The area was selected in part because of this absence of unique locational, architectural, or social characteristics. The area went under a variety of names a decade ago, but it is now commonly identified as the Riverwest neighborhood. The process of becoming a named place symbolizes the growing self-identification of the neighborhood. Riverwest is an aging community of largely frame, single-family and duplex units constructed before 1924. The houses, originally built for an ethnic working-class population, crowd their narrow 25-or 30-foot lots. The homes are solidly built and without architectural distinction.

The neighborhood contains some 12,000 persons in 5 census tracts. Prior to the population decline beginning after World War II, Riverwest held twice as many residents at extremely high densities. Originally settled by Poles, with Germans at the northern end, the area has since attracted Italians and, during the last decade blacks and Hispanics. The latter, mostly Puerto Rican, are viewed by some older residents as a buffer against invasion by abutting black inner-city areas. During the 1970s Riverwest also had an influx of young counter-culture and social-activist whites attracted by the area's diversity and low rents. Overall, one-third (33 percent) of those interviewed identified themselves as Polish; a quarter (23 percent) as German; eight percent, Italian; 5 percent as black; and 3 percent, Hispanic. The latter two populations are increasing while the others are declining.

Riverwest's ethnic and racial diversity, while socially laudable, would not traditionally recommend the area for neighborhood upgrading. Those inner-city neighborhoods identified as having best survived the turmoil and decline of the last decades are usually identified with a particular ethnic group (Schoenberg and Rosenbaum 1980). Realtors have long held that ethnically and socially homogeneous areas are most likely to remain stable and increase, or at least hold, their property values. This view, which was explicitly stated prior to the passage of open occupancy legislation, still affects residents' willingness to remain in a neighborhood (Farley 1977).

As an older central-city neighborhood of mixed ethnicity adjacent to the city's growing black ghetto, Riverwest would appear to be a candidate, not for revitalization, but rather for inevitable decline and deterioration. Such was the expectation within the city planning establishment. It also fits the conventional academic wisdom as to how central-city residential neighborhoods move through an evolutionary pattern of increasingly less prestigious tenancy (Burgess 1925; Hoyt 1939; Hoover and Vernon 1959; Schnore 1965; Downs 1979).

METHODOLOGY

Data for this study were gathered as part of a larger project designed to examine the nature, processes, and extent of urban regeneration and revitalization in older, working-class neighborhoods. Telephone interviews were conducted by professional interviewers from the Wisconsin Survey Research Laboratory, using a pretested structural interview schedule that included mostly fixed-alternative questions. Data were collected from respondents in a sample of households having numbers listed in the reverse telephone directory.

A proportionate, stratified random sample of 855 numbers was drawn, with an overall sampling rate of 1 in 9.65. A total of 185 phone numbers might have yielded an interview but did not. Refusal accounted for 133 of these. The response rate for this sample was 73 percent, the total number of completed interviews was 495. A supplemental sample of housing units with unlisted telephones, or with no phone, was included and personal interviews were taken where necessary. Respondents were selected using a controlled selection procedure designed to balance the respondent by age and sex. The response rate for this sample was 52 percent.

FINDINGS

General Characteristics

Upgraders, whether newcomers or old-timers, are usually assumed to be owners, not renters. These two populations are believed to have differing interests and priorities. In terms of attitudes and behaviors, renters are perceived as more marginal, transient, and detatched from the community. This should be reflected in their having fewer relatives and friendship ties within the neighborhood. It would also suggest a lower rate of membership in local associations, block clubs, churches, and other groups. Renters' participation in these organizations should also more often be at a nominal, or less active, level. Renters, having fewer ties binding them to the area, would also be expected to be less likely to participate in such activities as petitioning, writing, contacting politicians, picketing, or other activities designed to meet perceived threats to the neighborhood.

Owners by contrast, would be expected to have more relatives and friends as neighbors, to belong to, and participate in, more local groups and associations, and to respond more actively to perceived threats to the neighborhood.

Since the conversion of rented properties to owner occupancy is reportedly a characteristic of revitalizing areas (U.S. Department of Housing and Urban Development 1981, pp. 28-30), it is important to know if, and how, these populations differ. It is also useful to know whether working-class neighborhoods in the process of upgrading follow the pattern of renter to owner-occupancy found in gentrifying areas. If so, the amount of renter displacement could dramatically accelerate as working-class areas revitalize.

In table 7.1 we have compared demographic characteristics of renters and owners for newcomers and old-timers in Riverwest. The findings demonstrate some significant differences between the two groups. Homeowners are on the average 12 years older than renters and earn $5,000 more each year. Newcomers, whether homeowners or renters, tend to be between 10 and 15 years younger than old-timers. Also, newcomers in each of the groups earn more than old-timers, with the newcomer-homeowners earning the most, approximately $24,000 annually (1980 dollars). The newcomer-homeowner is also the best educated, with an average of 16.8 years of schooling completed. Not surprisingly, the old-timer-homeowner had the least amount of formal schooling with approximately 12 years completed. Similarly, while newcomer-homeowners are concentrated in professional occupations (48 percent), the old-timer-homeowners are mostly in lower-status occupations. Thus, the demographic analysis supports earlier gentrification studies in which the newcomer-homeowner emerges as well-educated, more heavily professional, and with a (relatively) high income. It should be noted, however, that our use of the census category "professional" may create an erroneous impression of the actual social composition of the newcomers. They are not doctors and lawyers. Generally they are white-collar technical and kindred workers.

Attitudinal Differences

The success of any neighborhood depends to a large extent on the attitudes of its residents. As is indicated in table 7.2, there are substantial differences in the attitudes of renters and owners. Almost 51 percent of the owners take a great deal of pride in Riverwest, compared with only 28 percent of the renters. Moreover, whether owner or renter, the old-timers in Riverwest have more pride in the neighborhood than the newcomers. For example, 44 percent of the owner-newcomers take great pride in Riverwest compared with 18 percent of the renter-newcomers. Among old-timers, the proportions are higher, 53 percent and 31 percent, respectively.

Table 7.1. Demographic Profile of Riverwest Homeowners and Renters

Demographic Characteristics	Homeowners			Renters		
	All	Newcomers	Old-timers	All	Newcomers	Old-timers
Age						
Mean (x)	46.7	33.2	48.8	34.8	27.3	37.6
Education						
Highest grade Completed (x)	13	16.8	12.5	13.8	14.9	13.4
Occupation						
Professional technical and kindred	17%	48%	11%	25%	27%	28%
Clerical and Managerial	28%	20%	30%	20%	26%	21%
Sales and Operators	31%	28%	33%	22%	15%	30%
Other	24%	4%	26%	33%	32%	21%
Income						
Annual (Median)	$18,987	$23,975	$17,962	$13,017	$15,050	$12,000
N	228	25	203	304	89	215

Owners rank the quality of life in Riverwest considerably higher than do renters (table 7.3). Almost half of the owners, compared with three in ten of the renters, have rated the quality of life in the neighborhood as excellent. Similarly, owners are consistently more satisfied with local services and are renters. More owners than renters have rated as excellent the quality of parochial school, fire protection, garbage collection, and the local churches.

Table 7.2. Pride in Riverwest: Homeowners and Renters

Extent of Pride	Homeowners			Renters		
	All	Newcomers	Old-timers	All	Newcomers	Old-timers
Great deal	50.7	44.0	53.1	28.1	18.4	31.4
Little or less	49.3	56.0	46.9	71.9	81.6	68.6
N	227	25	202	307	87	220

Consistent with these differences is the greater optimism of owners regarding the area. Twenty-four percent of the owners feel that the neighborhood has improved a lot over the last few years. This feeling is shared by only 14 percent of the renters.

Table 7.3. Ratings of Neighborhood Quality and Services By Owners and Renters (Percentage Rating Excellent)

Dimension	Owners	Renters
Parochial school	37.7	14.1
Fire protection	24.6	13.0
Garbage collection	40.5	31.0
Local churches	73.2	55.0
Quality of life	48.9	29.9
N	225	304

Community Participation

Neighborhood voluntary associations are closely tied to the process of urban revitalization. Whether fighting freeways and displacement or trying to reduce the burdens of local taxation, they are now regarded as a factor in urban progess and can play a major role in controlling neighborhood transformation (Van Til 1980). Neighborhood associations are being examined against a backdrop of demand for community control (Altschuler 1970) and are increasingly recognized as the urban interest group (Yates 1977).

A recent study showed that membership in local Riverwest associations plays a major role in residents' perceptions of the neighborhood and in the extent to which they are directly involved in the revitalization (Nachmias and Palen, 1982). In table 7.4 differences are shown in membership rates and participation in a local neighborhood association—ESHAC, the Eastside Housing Action Coalition. ESHAC has a history as an activist organization that has evolved into a broad-based neighborhood association of homeowners and renters engaged in resolving such local issues as closing "rowdy taverns and organizing block clubs." It has played a crucial role in organizing and supporting economic development activities.

The data in table 7.4 indicate as expected that, overall, home-owners are more active than renters in the neighborhood associa-tion. Almost 21 percent of all homeowners, compared with about 6 percent of all renters, are members of ESHAC. Similarly, 40 percent of homeowners and only about 22 percent of all renters take advantage of services offered by ESHAC. Comparisons between newcomers and old-timers in each of the groups reveal differences among newcomers and old-timers in the homeowner group. Actual membership of old-timers is considerably higher among home-owners. However, newcomers are heavy users of the neighborhood association's services.

Table 7.4. Membership and Participation in Neighborhood Association: Renters, Owners (In Percentages)

Association and	Homeowners			Renters		
Activity	All	Newcomers	Old-timers	All	Newcomers	Old-timers
Membership in ESHAC (East side Housing Action Coalition)	20.9	8.0	20.1	5.9	4.5	6.7
Use ESHAC services	40.0	44.0	37.9	22.4	20.9	23.6
N	229	25	204	303	90	213

Finally, table 7.5 displays findings on the attitudes and behavioral disposition regarding community participation of owners and renters. The four items measure support for social activism in the neighborhood. There are distinct differences between homeowners and renters. Homeowners are clearly more individualistic and *less* inclined to support collective action in the neighborhood. This was the opposite of the expected pattern. About 31 percent of the homeowners, compared to a little over 17 percent of the renters, feel social needs are not a community responsibility. A major difference was that one-fifth of the older homeowners, but *none* of the newcomers feel the community would be better off if residents spent less time on community projects. Similarly, homeowners are less willing to get involved in such activities as signing petitions or picketing. Only 20 percent of homeowners are very willing to sign petitions, compared with 32 percent of renters. Surprisingly, both groups are more willing to picket than to sign petitions. Yet, here too, there is more willingness among renters (46 percent) than among homeowners (32 percent).

A closer examination of table 7.5 reveals substantial differences in responses of newcomers and old-timers to the items presented. For old-timers, home ownership is related to their attitudes toward community participation. Old-timers who are homeowners are far less inclined to support collective action in the community. Almost 35 percent of the homeowner-old-timers agree that social needs are a personal rather than a community responsibility, compared with only 19 percent of the old-timer renters. Differences of the same magnitude are observed for the other items. Among newcomers, however, there are only slight differences between owners and renters, excepting renters' greater willingness to picket. Few newcomers believe social needs are an individual responsibility, and practically no newcomers advocate less commitment to community

Table 7.5. Community Participation: Renters, Owners (In Percentages)

	Owners			Renters		
Question	All	Newcomers	Old-timers	All	Newcomers	Old-Timer
The social needs of the people who live here are their own responsibility and not the community.*	31.3	12.0	34.7	17.6	12.4	19.3
Riverwest would be better if fewer people would spend time on important community projects.*	18.7	0	21.6	9.5	2.2	12.3
Very willing to sign petitions	19.9	33.3	15.5	31.7	31.3	31.6
Very willing to picket a city office	32.0	42.9	28.4	45.6	53.7	42.3
N	225	24	201	301	90	211

*The percentage of respondents who agreed with this statement.

projects. Similarly, there is more willingness among all newcomers to support such activities as signing petitions and picketing.

Interestingly, the marked social conservatism of the old-timer-homeowners in Riverwest stands in contrast to their relatively high representation in the most central voluntary organization of the neighborhood, ESHAC (see table 7.4). Both membership in neighborhood associations and attitudes toward social activism can be seen as expressions of forms of community participation. However, our data suggest that community participation is not a unitary phenomenon; rather, it exhibits distinct, analytical and empirical dimensions. Neighborhood residents cannot be seen simply as more or less active, but as pursuing many types of activities with different consequences.

IMPLICATIONS

We are reluctant to push too far beyond the findings presented here, but the implications for better understanding both revitalization and social policy are considerable.

Older community residents and newcomers do in fact differ, but not always in the direction expected. For example, new homeowners and renters have less pride in the area than older homeowners and renters. This could be considered somewhat unexpected since newcomers have made a voluntary decision to enter this neighborhood rather than another. Nor are newcomers the compulsive joiners sometimes portrayed. Newcomers are less likely to join the local neighborhood organization than are long-term residents.

Another, more important, discovery was the difference between established homeowners and older renters. Professional studies, as well as popular articles, have tended to assume that old-timers are a generally homogeneous group—at least as far as attitudes and social participations. Apparently they are not. In terms of attitudes toward community participation and projects, longer-term owners have by far the highest proportion of those with conservative views. Longer-term renters as a group express themselves as considerably more activist in orientation.

On this basis one would then expect that renters would be most active in the local neighborhood association, whereas homeowners would be far less so. Since the Eastside Housing Action Coalition originated as a militant antilandlord renters' organization, this would be a reasonable assumption. However, the facts are otherwise. A full fifth of all old-timer-owners belong to ESHAC, and 38 percent use its services. This is not only a remarkably high rate of participation for any neighborhood organization, but it is a rate of membership three times that of longer-term renters.

It is possible that homeowner activity is aimed more at outcomes of individual benefits, while for renters supporting community involvement and activities, such as signing petitions and picketing, is directed more at outcomes of a collective nature. In any case, the data argue against facile stereotypes of existing homeowners and renters. Old-timer homeowners may express the greatest opposition to community-wide responsibility and projects, but, nonetheless, in rather remarkable numbers they have joined a community organization with a strong activist political orientation.

REFERENCES

Altschuler, A. 1970. *Community control: The black demand for participation in large American cities.* Indianapolis: Bobbs-Merrill.
Bradley, D. 1977. Neighborhood transition: Middle class home buying in an inner city deteriorating community. Paper presented at 72nd Annual Meeting of American Sociological Association, Sept. 8, 1977, Chicago, Ill.

Burgess, E. W. 1925. The Growth of the City. In *The city*, ed. R. E. Park, E. W. Burgess, and R. McKenzie. Chicago: University of Chicago Press.

Clay, P. L. 1979. *Neighborhood renewal: Middle class resettlement and incumbent upgrading in American neighborhoods.* Lexington, Mass.: Lexington Books.

Cybriwsky, R. 1978. Social aspects of neighborhood change, *Annals, Association of American Geographers*, 68, (1, March): 17-33.

Downs, A. 1979. *Urban Problems and Prospects.* Chicago: Markham.

Farley, R. et al. Chocolate city, vanilla suburbs. Paper presented at 72nd Annual Meeting of American Sociological Association, Sept. 8, 1977. Chicago.

Gale, D. E. Neighborhood Resettlement in Washington, D.C. In *Back to the City*, ed. Laska and Spain, New York: Pergamon Press.

Goldfield, D. R. 1980. Private neighborhood redevelopment and displacement in Washington, D.C. *Urban Affairs Quarterly* 15 (4 June): 453-68.

Grier, G., and Grier, E. 1978 Urban displacement: A reconnaissance. Report prepared for the U.S. Department of Housing and Urban Development.

Hoover, M., and Vernon, R. 1959. *Anatomy of a metropolis.* Cambridge, Mass.: Harvard University Press.

Hoyt, H. 1939. The structure and growth of residential neighborhoods in American cities. Washington, D.C.: U.S. Federal Housing Administration.

Nachmias, C., and Palen, J. J. 1982. Membership in voluntary neighborhood associations and urban revitalization. *Policy Studies* 14, (Spring): 179-93.

Schoenberg, S. P. and Rosenbaum, P. L. 1980. *Neighborhoods that work.* New Brunswick, N. J.: Rutgers University Press.

Schnore, L. 1965. *The urban scene.* New York: Free Press.

U.S. Department of Housing and Urban Development. 1981. *Residential displacement: An update report to Congress*, October. Washington, D.C.: Office of Policy Development and Research.

CHAPTER EIGHT

Social Differentials in Metropolitan Residential Displacement

BARRETT A. LEE AND DAVID C. HODGE

Residential displacement is not a new phenomenon in the American metropolis, nor is it a topic that has been totally overlooked by students of intraurban mobility. Almost three decades ago, for example, Rossi (1955) reported that approximately one-fifth of the recent movers in his Philadelphia sample were forced to leave their previous dwellings because of fire, eviction, or other events beyond their control. Subsequent investigations (Fried 1963; Hartman 1964; Kantor 1965) have focused on the potentially harmful social and psychological consequences associated with involuntary mobility. Aside from such occasional inquiries, however, displacement has traditionally been relegated to the footnotes of the mobility literature. This lack of attention is not surprising when one considers the rarity of involuntary changes of address compared to voluntary ones (Goodman 1978, 1979; Grier and Grier 1980; Newman and Owen 1981; Sumka 1979; U.S. Department of Housing and Urban Development 1979a, 1981). The

Barrett A. Lee is Assistant Professor of Sociology, Vanderbilt University. David C. Hodge is Associate Professor of Geography, University of Washington, Seattle.
An earlier version of this paper was presented at the Annual Meeting of the Population Association of America, Washington, D.C., March 1981. Suggestions by Daniel B. Cornfield, Jack P. Gibbs, Avery M. Guest, and Daphne Spain were helpful in revising the manuscript. A grant from the Graduate Research Fund of the University of Washington made possible the purchase of the Annual Housing Survey data tapes used in the analysis.

popularity of rational decision-making models of mobility may also have dampened enthusiasm for displacement research, since forced moves represent bothersome exceptions to the logic of the decision-making approach.[1]

Whatever the reason for the traditional neglect of the topic, the past five years have witnessed mounting scholarly concern over the volume and impact of displacement. The stimulus prompting this concern is easy to pinpoint. Sometime during the early to mid-1970s, a variety of social and demographic trends converged to produce the much publicized "back-to-the-city"—or more accurately, "stay-in-the-city"—movement. (For a sampling of the revitalization literature, see Black [1975]; Clay [1979]; Gale [1979]; James [1980]; Laska and Spain [1980]; Lipton [1977]; London, Bradley, and Hudson [1980]; Rosenthal [1980]; Stegman [1979]; Zeitz [1979]). Within the context of revitalization, the displacement of poor and powerless residents through eviction, condominium conversion, and massive rent or property tax increases constitutes an unfortunate side effect of middle-class reinvestment in central-city housing. At least implicitly, then, residential displacement is thought by some observers to signal a new era of urban health.

Current levels of popular and academic interest in revitalization tend to obscure the sobering possibility that displacement might just as easily be interpreted as an indicator of continued central-city decay. Indeed, prevailing official opinion seems to be that demolition, abandonment, and other forms of residential *dis*investment remain major—if not *the* major—causes of displacement mobility (U.S. Department of Housing and Urban Development 1979a, 1979b, 1981).[2] This conclusion draws support from several sources. Population redistribution patterns during the 1970s demonstrate that the flow of people away from the nation's central cities is far from over, with older, larger centers in the northeast and north-central regions sustaining the greatest losses (Berry and Dahmann 1980; Goodman 1980; Kasarda 1980; Long 1980; Nelson 1980a). More pertinently, a study of 150 declining cities conducted by Sternlieb (1979; cited in U.S. Department of Housing and Urban Development 1979a) found housing abandonment rates to exceed 15 percent of the total supply in some places. And at the subcity level, the authors of a recent HUD working paper (U.S. Department of Housing and Urban Development 1979b, p. 21) remark that "many more neighborhoods have gone through disinvestment, decline, and sometimes abandonment, than have experienced middle or upper-income reinvestment." Against this grim backdrop, the presumably high proportion of all displacement mobility generated by revitalization must by viewed with suspicion.

Despite differences of opinion over the housing market dynamics responsible for displacement, most investigators agree on one fundamental point: involuntary moves are *not* distributed evenly among all segments of the metropolitan population. Throughout the literature on the subject, one encounters the claim that members of the urban "underclass"—elderly, lower income, black, and female-headed households—bear a disproportionate share of the displacement burden. As our review in the next two sections makes clear, however, the empirical evidence and theoretical perspectives supporting this contention can be challenged on a number of counts. Thus, the goal of the present analysis is to submit the *underclass hypothesis* to as decisive a test as possible. Employing aggregate-level data from the 1974-76 rounds of the Annual Housing Survey, (AHS) we attempt to determine if disadvantaged movers experience higher rates of displacement than their better-off counterparts in metropolitan areas and central cities across the country. In addition, a final, exploratory portion of the analysis specifies some of the structural conditions under which large and small social differentials in displacement can be expected to occur.

Empirical and Theoretical Support for the Underclass Hypothesis

At first glance, available empirical studies leave little room for doubting the underclass hypothesis, so unanimous do they appear to be in their pattern of findings. One of the first inquiries of broad scope to provide information about displacement differentials was undertaken by the National Urban Coalition (1978). Obtaining data on sixty-five revitalizing neighborhoods in forty-four cities from planning officials, realtors, and other informants, the Urban Coalition survey revealed major to minor declines in the representation of lower-income households, elderly residents, and families with children during the course of neighborhood change. The Griers' (1980) nationwide "reconnaissance" suggests a similar picture.

More concrete evidence on social differentials in displacement comes from Goodman's (1978, 1979) analysis of 1973 Annual Housing Survey data, in which comparatively high percentages of elderly and black intrametropolitan movers reported eviction, abandonment, or some other displacement-related action as the main reason for moving. Not surprisingly, the differentials sharpen in Metropolitan Statistical Areas (MSAs) and cities known for their tight housing markets. Hodge (1979, 1981), for example, found that over a five-year period in Seattle, displacement was experienced twice as often as other forms of mobility by lower-income than higher-income households, by unmarried than married residents, and by those above age sixty than by those below age thirty. Even in the case of smaller geographical units, broadbased support exists for the underclass hypothesis, with numerous studies of specific neighborhoods (Gale 1980; Hodge 1980; Laska and Spain 1979; Tournier 1980) or of neighborhood-level processes (Clay 1979; Cybriwsky 1980; Goldfield 1980; LeGates and Hartman 1981; Newsom 1971; Weiler 1979; Zeitz 1979) citing the threat that displacement poses to local diversity, in general, and to disadvantaged residents, in particular.

While several different theoretical explanations of displacement mobility have been offered, these explanations—like the empirical findings above—converge on the prediction that displacement rates will be greatest among underclass segments of the metropolitan population. The most popular type of explanation stresses the economic underpinnings of the displacement problem. From the vantage point of conventional economics, the disproportionate displacement suffered by blacks, the elderly, and other underclass groups can be traced to a state of disequilibrium between housing supply and demand in a given neighborhood. When housing units are in run-down condition and demand for these units is low, as in some ghetto or slum areas, landlords may decide that the price of upgrading and maintaining the units will preclude a reasonable profit and may demolish or abandon them as a result, forcing out underclass tenants (National Urban League 1971; Sternlieb 1972; Sternlieb and Burchell 1973). Of course, displacement moves also occur because of an excess of demand over supply. Once an older, inner-city neighborhood becomes attractive to middle-class households, subsequent revitalization may quickly lead to tenure conversions and an escalation of rents and property taxes, displacing those residents who lack the ability to pay (Cicin-Sain 1980; Clay 1979; Gale 1980; London 1980; National Urban Coalition 1978; Sumka 1979; Weiler 1979; Zeitz 1979).

A second explanation, consistent with Marxist and political economy perspectives, arrives at the same conclusion about the direction of displacement differentials as the conventional approach does, but by an alternate route. Proponents of the more radical explanation remain skeptical of the idea that the housing market pressures generating displacement are unintentional or "invisible." Instead, financial institutions, developers, and others who do the bidding of the holders of power are thought to consciously seek out the neighborhood investment strategy that not only maximizes their own gain but also paves the way for the "flow of capital" (Molotch 1979: Smith 1979). Local government presumably fills the role of tacit accomplice in whatever this strategy might be (Guterbock 1980). From a radical economic perspective, then, social differentials in reinvestment-stimulated displacement can be understood in terms of the following scenario:

> ...powerful interest groups follow a policy of neglect of the inner city until such time as they become aware that policy changes could yield tremendous profits. Then, policies change accordingly, with little regard for those powerless inner-city residents who will be displaced from their homes (London 1980, p.86).

Some Criticisms

Despite the apparent consensus that our review of empirical findings and theoretical explanations has turned up, there remain enough chinks in the armor of the displacement literature to warrant further investigation of the underclass hypothesis. Perhaps the most serious challenges to the hypothesis are posed by methodological problems. With respect to sampling, the tendency of researchers to focus on a single neighborhood may yield valuable insights into the sequence of events culminating in displacement, but the resultant small Ns preclude accurate measurement of variation in displacement rates by age, race, income, or other social characteristics. Case studies of entire cities are likely to convey a misleading impression as well, since investigators often select places such as Washington, D.C. (Gale 1980; Goldfield 1980) or Seattle (Hodge 1979, 1981) where an unusually high incidence of involuntary mobility has attracted public attention. Finally, no data base of sufficient scope has yet been analyzed to permit one to determine whether central-city differentials in displacement are greater than those found in the suburbs, as the underclass hypothesis implies.

Assuming that sampling deficiencies could be corrected, other problems that complicate the interpretation of the literature would persist. It is difficult to know what to make, for example, of the "soft" evidence gathered in some of the national displacement surveys, such as those conducted by the National Urban Coalition (1978) or by Grier and Grier (1980). How knowledgeable were the informants utilized in these studies? By what rules did the researchers quantify informant perceptions and mold them into findings? Another type of "softness" centers on the definition of the displacement concept itself. Beyond general agreement that displacement refers to involuntary mobility instigated by forces external to the household, considerable variation exists in the detailed meanings attached to the term. Under a liberal definition, rent increases, harrassment by landlords, or other factors that prevent future tenants from being of the same status as those moving out may qualify as legitimate causes of displacement (Clay 1979; Grier and Grier 1980; Hodge 1979, 1981).[3] A conservative definition, on the other hand, would question whether any moves aside from those due to eviction or destruction of the dwelling unit could be classified as truly involuntary. Without further belaboring the fine line between voluntary and involuntary mobility, suffice it to say that the magnitude of displacement differentials depends rather heavily upon where this line is drawn. To date, few investigators have drawn it in precisely the same place.

Methodological and conceptual difficulties do not provide the only grounds for being suspicious of the underclass hypothesis; contrary empirical findings also cast the hypothesis in doubt. Several studies (Bradley 1978; Hodge 1979, 1981; National Urban Coalition 1978; Nelson 1980b), for example, have been unable to marshal support for the proposition that blacks are particularly vulnerable to displacement. In fact, of the revitalizing neighborhoods covered in the Urban Coalition survey, half experienced either an increase or no change in minority composition, as whites often replaced whites and blacks competed among themselves or with members of other minority groups for scarce housing. In similar fashion, another piece of research utilizing neighborhood-level units (Henig 1980) found changes in the proportions of blue-collar, retired, and female-headed households living in gentrifying census tracts to be unaffected by the arrival of professional families.

At the very least, ambiguous or exceptional findings such as these call into question a major assumption underlying much of the literature, that the displacement of poor and powerless residents is an inevitable consequence of neighborhood change. Clay (1979), among others, has pointed out that substantial revitalization can be accomplished through incumbent upgrading or middle-class reinvestment in abandoned units; neither type of action directly produces displacement, let alone displacement differentials. The ongoing process of voluntary mobility might also contribute to displacement-free neighborhood change. As old-timers move out at a normal rate, their units could be left vacant or demolished if the area is undergoing decline, or they may be filled by newcomers of higher status if reinvestment is the dominant trend (Cicin-Sain 1980). In either case, neighborhood transition takes place without underclass households having to endure disproportionate levels of involuntary mobility.[4]

An alternative rationale for minimal or nonexistent differentials in displacement has been put forth by proponents of the sociocultural perspective on revitalization (Allen 1980; Gale 1979; London 1980). The sociocultural view holds that shifts in tastes and values within the middle class—including a rejection of suburbia and desire for diversity—are the decisive factors behind the the back-to-the-city movement. On the one hand, a growing disenchantment with suburban living on the part of middle-class households could conceivably open up new housing opportunities for disadvantaged city dwellers, permitting some to fulfill long-held aspirations and voluntarily move to suburbia (Cicin-Sain 1980; James 1980; Pattison 1977). At the same time, the interest in diversity professed by many gentrifiers may be strong enough to encourage both old-timers and newcomers in a revitalizing area to act collectively—via resident associations or other voluntary groups—to arrest the forced exodus of underclass members, thus maintaining the economically and/or racially mixed character of the neighborhood.

Despite the good intentions attributed to the middle class by the sociocultural perspective, it is probably unrealistic to conclude that changes in tastes and values have a benign effect on the susceptibility of underclass groups to displacement. If anything, minimal differences in displacement rates can be expected because tight housing markets have increased the risk of involuntary mobility among segments of the metropolitan population previously thought immune to such moves. A special HUD report on displacement notes:

> Land and building material costs have skyrocketed, producing an aggregate effect on the amount of available housing for persons of all income brackets. Increased costs are not limited to the central city, but are also a factor in suburban communities and smaller cities (U.S. Department of Housing and Urban Development 1979a, pp. 2-11).

Aside from general market conditions, neither the HUD report nor the rest of the literature offers many clues as to which urban structural characteristics are most likely to be associated with large or small differences in displacement rates across social categories. A later section addresses this key issue. For the time being, it should be emphasized that on theoretical grounds the underclass hypothesis is challenged by a housing market explanation as well as by models of sociocultural and neighborhood change.

The Data

To test the underclass hypothesis, we utilize aggregate-level information drawn from the early rounds of the Annual Housing

Survey (AHS), relying primarily on the separate surveys conducted from 1974 through 1976 in sixty different metropolitan areas.[5] Not all of the sixty metropolitan data bases available for that time period are included in our study, however. Given the amount of interest currently directed toward reinvestment- and disinvestment-induced displacement in inner-city neighborhoods, we have selected forty-two SMSAs for which central-city or suburban place of residence has been coded to serve as the cases in the analysis.[6] Adherence to such a selection criterion has the unintended consequence of overrepresenting moves that occur within larger, more densely settled metropolitan areas. Fortunately, it is the residents of these larger SMSAs who are believed to be most vulnerable to displacement and who therefore collectively constitute appropriate target populations.

Only a handful of variables from the AHS interview is needed to evaluate the underclass hypothesis. Naturally, the incidence of displacement must be estimated separately for movers with differing social characteristics so that underclass segments of the metropolitan population can be compared with their more advantaged counterparts. On the basis of the literature reviewed earlier, three characteristics appear particularly germane: (1) age of the household head (broken down into four categories), (2) socioeconomic status, measured by total family income during the year prior to the interview (five categories), and (3) race of the household head (white vs. black). A fourth variable, sex of the household head, has not received much attention from displacement researchers, but we incorporate it into the analysis on the assumption that a disproportionate number of financially burdened, single-parent families—a group identified by Sternlieb and Hughes (1979) as the most troubled segment of the urban underclass—will be represented among mobile female heads of household. Because the number of recent movers in a particular age, income, race, or sex category can become quite small for certain SMSAs, we present results for all movers within each category rather than by housing tenure group. A major difficulty that arises from treating owners and renters together is discussed later in the analysis.

A single AHS item asks respondents who moved during the twelve months preceding the interview to indicate their main reason for moving.[7] The dependent variables in our study are derived from this question, consisting of the percentages—and in some instances, ratios of percentages—of intrametropolitan movers (i.e., those whose origin *and* destination addresses fall inside the boundaries of the SMSA) with selected social characteristics citing "displacement by private action" as the principal reason. A number of specific actions that reflect the operation of both disinvestment and reinvestment processes are included in the "private displacement" category: abandonment, demolition, eviction, condominium conversion, mortgage default, and the termination of a rental contract. Excluded from the category are such things as drastic rent or property tax increases, or public works projects—urban renewal, highway construction, and the like—which may lead to government-sponsored relocation.[8] As these examples indicate, the operational definition of displacement employed here leans toward the conservative end of the continuum, stressing forced moves generated by the dynamics of the private market.

While constructing all of our dependent variables from a single reason-for-move item may be convenient, the credibility of such a strategy hinges on the strength of that particular item. Thus, the major weaknesses of the AHS question should be made explicit (for other discussions of these weaknesses, see Goering [1979]; Goodman [1979]). One set of problems has to do with the retrospective nature of the question. When thinking about a move which took place in the distant past, a respondent might be unable to remember specific details, or he might modify these details— unintentionally or otherwise—so that they mesh with the fabric of subsequent experience. Of course, the maximum length of time that could have elapsed between a move and the AHS interview is only twelve months, a period short enough to minimize the risk from recall error. Temporal propinquity, in conjuction with the vivid impression left by most forms of involuntary mobility, should also curb tendencies toward rationalization and the selective reconstruction of events. Another problem centers on the fact that the AHS question limits the respondent to one answer, to the *main* reason for moving; the danger with this is that a particular reason may be overlooked in the course of considering the many factors that could have prompted a move. Again, however, the strength of the "push" associated with eviction or demolition probably makes displacement a very salient factor, and thus one of the reasons most likely to be mentioned. Moreover, the frequency with which multiple reasons for moving are reported by survey respondents appears relatively low to begin with (U.S. Bureau of the Census 1966).

Keeping the above methodological limitations in mind, we can now take a first look at the AHS data on metropolitan residential displacement. Table 8.1 reports mean displacement rates for the 42 SMSAs in our sample, broken down by social category and residence of origin. As the top figures in the first and second columns indicate, displacement moves do not constitute a large share of the total volume of intrametropolitan mobility: across all SMSAs, an average of only 4.24 percent of all recent movers and 4.58 percent of those movers whose prior residence was in the central city cited eviction, demolition, condominium conversion, or some other action beyond their control as the principal reason for moving.[9] This low incidence of displacement comes as no surprise, since most previous investigations (Gale 1979; Goodman 1978, 1979; Grier and Grier 1980; Newman and Owen 1981; Sumka 1979; U.S. Department of Housing and Urban Development 1979a, 1981) have arrived at similar estimates. What needs to be emphasized, however, is that despite the small relative number (percentage) of moves that are classified as involuntary, a large absolute number may be involved as a result of the high overall level of mobility in the U.S. As a matter of fact, HUD tabulations spanning the same time period as our analysis show the number of metropolitan households displaced annually to exceed 350,000 (U.S. Department of Housing and Urban Development 1979a), and estimates for more recent years suggest an annual volume of displacement as high as 2.5 million persons (LeGates and Hartman 1981; U.S. Department of Housing and Urban Development 1981).

Table 8.1. Mean Displacement Rates for Intrametropolitan Movers in 42 SMSAs by Age, Income, Race, Sex, and Residence of Origin

| | *Residence of Origin* | |
	SMSA	Central City
Total	4.24	4.58
Age[a]		
≤25 years	3.02	3.55
26-45	4.06	4.17
46-65	6.09	6.20
66+	7.12	8.87
Income[b]		
≤$4,000	6.03	6.57
4,000-7,999	4.84	4.64
8,000-11,999	4.75	5.08
12,000-15,999	4.08	4.03
16,000+	2.36	2.45
Race[a]		
Black	4.49	4.25
White	4.19	4.64
Sex[a]		
Female	4.84	5.10
Male	4.00	4.33

SOURCE: Annual Housing Survey SMSA tapes, 1974-76 rounds.
NOTE: Figures in the table indicate mean percentages of recent movers across 42 SMSAs, giving "displacement by private action" as main reason for move.
[a]Household head.
[b]Total family income in year preceding interview.

A Test of the Underclass Hypothesis

The primary goal of our study is to shed light on the underclass hypothesis: do elderly, lower-income, black, and female-headed households experience higher rates of involuntary mobility than other segments of the metropolitan population? In general, the answer to this question appears to be yes, although differentials are greater on some social characteristics than others. As the figures for all intrametropolitan movers in the left column of table 8.1 illustrate, differences in displacement by age and income lend the strongest support to the hypothesis. With respect to head's age, an average of only 3.02 percent of the movers in the under-26 category reported being displaced across the 42 SMSAs, but the percentage climbs steadily to over 7 percent for those above age 65. The disparity reaches similar proportions when income groups are compared. On average, slightly more than 2 percent of the intrametropolitan moves made by households with annual incomes of $16,000+ qualify as displacement, in contrast to the 6 percent rate found for households with incomes under $4,000. Results for race and sex groups are less straightforward. Again considering all intrametropolitan movers in the left column of the table, it can be seen that the mean displacement rate among black movers (4.49 percent) exceeds that among whites (4.19 percent), and the rate among female-headed households (4.84 percent) exceeds that among male-headed households (4.00 percent). However, while the directions of these differences are consistent with the underclass hypothesis, their magnitudes do not come close to matching those that occur by age or income.

One way to clarify the somewhat ambiguous results for race and sex groups might be to focus exclusively on the central city portions of the forty-two SMSA populations in our sample or, more precisely, on those intrametropolitan movers whose previous residence was inside central-city boundaries. As previously noted, many observers contend that the disinvestment- and reinvestment-related activities commonly associated with displacement are concentrated in the central city; given present patterns of residential segregation, the inclusion of moves of suburban origin in the calculation of displacement rates may only serve to obscure rather clear-cut, hypothesis-confirming differentials. The central city data presented in the right-hand column of table 8.1 allow us to evaluate this possibility. The lower half of this column makes it apparent that race and sex differences in displacement levels continue to be problematic. In fact, the gap between mean black and white displacement rates for movers of central-city origin directly contradicts the underclass hypothesis, with whites (4.64 percent) slightly more susceptible to involuntary mobility than blacks (4.25 percent).

Stronger evidence favoring the underclass hypothesis appears in the top half of the second column. As with the metropolitan-level data, mean central-city displacement rates are markedly higher for the old than the young and for the poor than the well-to-do. Indeed, perhaps the most striking feature of table 8.1 in its entirety is the close similarity between the central-city results and those reported for all intrametropolitan movers in the first column. Both in terms of variation across, and levels within, comparable social categories, there may be some tendency for the incidence of central-city displacement to outstrip metropolitan rates, but this tendency is weak and subject to several exceptions. The obvious inference to be drawn from such similar results is that displacement should *not* be viewed as a problem limited solely to the urban core, as the literature on neighborhood decline and revitalization seems to suggest. In line with this inference, another anaylsis conducted by the authors (Hodge and Lee 1980) has shown that displacement often accounts for a larger share of suburban than central-city mobility. Our present findings imply that suburban displacement may also rival that of the central city in selectivity, with elderly and lower-income households the underclass groups most likely to move involuntarily.[10]

Before any final conclusion about the accuracy of the underclass hypothesis can be reached, two distinct challenges to the data must be confronted. The first challenge concerns differences in the tenure composition of the various social categories comprising metropolitan and central-city mover populations. Specifically, is the greater vulnerability to displacement experienced by the poor and elderly attributable to the lower rates of home ownership among members of these groups? Although such an explanation may account for some of the displacement moves made by lower-income residents, it seems less applicable to the situation of the elderly, for several reasons. First, the incidence of home ownership among older metropolitan residents remains rather substantial, exceeding the rates for both of the under-45 age categories. Second, while the home ownership rate actually is quite low for household heads in the youngest age group, the incidence of displacement in the group amounts to less than half that for urban dwellers over age 65 (see table 8.1). Third, low overall levels of mobility among the elderly hint that part of the age differential may be the result of a propensity to "hang on" to a particular dwelling unit at all costs, moving only when forced to do so. This propensity may be especially strong among elderly owners, whose greater investment in home and neighborhood could keep them in a deteriorating or revitalizing area past the point of no return, or at least of voluntary exit. Finally, the lack of significant race and sex differences indirectly enhances the confidence one can place in the findings for age groups. Despite a clear disadvantage in levels of home ownership, neither black nor female-headed households exhibit displacement rates markedly higher than those for their white or male-headed household counterparts. Ideally, of course, the effects of tenure composition should be checked by examining social differentials in displacement separately within owner and renter subpopulations. As mentioned earlier, however, small numbers of movers in some SMSAs, and the associated problem of case attrition, preclude such a detailed breakdown.

Small Ns also leave our results open to a second challenge, this one having to do with the handling of missing data. Throughout table 8.1, scattered zeroes have been included in the calculation of mean displacement rates. We believe this procedure is justified on statistical grounds, since with a larger sample of movers for an SMSA the expected value of the missing rate would fall somewhere between zero and the inordinately high percentage yielded by a social category with a small number of recent movers but several instances of displacement. Nevertheless, to the degree that unusually low and high values do not counter-balance one another in the smaller underclass cells, it might be argued that some social differentials have been artificially exaggerated and others attenuated. In table 8.2, we report the kind of information needed to assess this claim. Each figure in the table represents a mean ratio, computed by dividing a specific underclass displacement rate by that of a contrasting social category and then averaging across SMSA or central-city populations with nonzero ratios. Thus, the value in the upper left-hand corner tells us that, for the 37 eligible SMSAs, the displacement rate among all intrametropolitan movers in the 66+ age category is on the average 2½ times greater than the rate for the 26-45 category.[11] A quick perusal of the ratios indicates little reason for drastic revision of our previous conclusions. Even when cases with missing data are omitted, age and income differences remain substantial, race and sex differences unimpressive, and SMSA and central-city results similar.[12]

Because they only weakly support the underclass hypothesis, the minimal race and sex differences in displacement must be judged the most perplexing of the three findings above. The explanation for the nonexistent sex differences may lie partly in the crudeness of our categories; given the changing distribution of household types

Table 8.2. Mean Age, Income, Race, and Sex Displacement Ratios for Intrametropolitan Movers, by Residence of Origin

	Residence of Origin	
	SMSA	Central City
66+ years/26-45	2.57	4.17
	(37)	(34)
≤$4,000/$16,000+	3.35	3.28
	(40)	(35)
Black/white	1.32	1.20
	(37)	(35)
Female/male	1.41	1.29
	(42)	(42)

SOURCE: Annual Housing SMSA tapes, 1974-76 rounds.
NOTE: Figures in table are mean ratios, computed by dividing displacement rate for category to left of slash by that for category to right of slash and then averaging across SMSAs with nonzero ratios; numbers of cases are shown in parentheses.

in the U.S., any attempt to capture as elusive a segment of the urban underclass as the impoverished single-parent family by relying on the sex of the household head would seem foolhardy at best. As a case in point, the female-headed household category inadvertently reflects the mobility experiences of young, single, working women, who as a group might be relatively insulated from displacement. On the other hand, elderly widows also fall within the category but suffer numerous disadvantages in the housing market and should therefore contribute to a widening of the differential. More compelling methodological reasons can be offered for the slight racial difference in displacement. Since AHS sampling and interviewing procedures resemble those employed in the decennial census, the undernumeration of black males may artificially depress the incidence of involuntary mobility among black households. A similar bias could arise from the ability of black residents to absorb displacement through temporary living arrangements with family members or friends. To the extent that this time-tested adaptive strategy softens the impact of displacement, black respondents may be less likely than whites to describe a recent move as forced or involuntary in nature.

Before the modest magnitude of the black displacement rate is dismissed as artifact, however, possible substantive interpretations of the findings should be contemplated. Taking an optimistic perspective, one might speculate that inner-city revitalization has arrested black displacement through decline and abandonment and that, furthermore, the process of revitalization itself has generated few displacement moves, as whites seeking integrated neighborhoods gradually fill the vacancies that occur as a result of normal residential turnover. But the optimistic view runs counter to several pieces of evidence: (1) black-to-white successions, while accounting for only a small proportion of all housing occupancy changes in central cities, have gradually increased at the same time that black households are becoming less concentrated in inner-city areas undergoing gentrification (Spain 1980); (2) despite their preferences, few middle-class renovators expect their new neighborhoods to remain integrated once the later stages of revitalization are reached (Laska and Spain 1979; Zeitz 1979); and (3) the presumed desire among whites for racial diversity is probably overstated in the first place, judging from the results of recent studies (Cybriwsky 1978; Farley et al. 1978).

In light of such criticisms, we believe current conditions in the metropolitan housing market provide the most defensible substantive explanation for the small racial differential and, to a lesser degree, for the magnitudes of the other differentials, most of which are less pronounced than they might be or which reflect low rates of displacement. According to the market explanation advanced previously, high metropolitan-wide demand, coupled with inadequate supply, serves to intensify competition for available housing. Ultimately, one consequence of this tight situation is a more even distribution of involuntary moves across all segments of the population, with well-to-do or powerful groups gaining ground on their underclass counterparts in susceptibility to displacement. Tentative empirical support for the market explanation comes from an inspection of zero-order correlations between the total displacement rate for all intrametropolitan movers (mean shown at the top of the left-hand column in table 8.1) and specific displacement ratios (means shown in the left-hand column of table 8.2): for the race ratio $r = -.19$, for the sex ratio $r = -.36$, and for both the age and income ratios $r = -.29$. In short, as the overall level of displacement expands, social differentials in displacement contract. But, while these relationships are suggestive, we cannot tell for certain whether they occur primarily because of a tight housing market or because of other characteristics of the metropolitan setting. The purpose of the next section is to explore this issue in a more direct manner.

Explaining Displacement Rates and Differentials

Despite a consensus among researchers that underclass residents experience high levels of displacement both absolutely and relative to other urban dwellers, there has been little attempt to identify the factors responsible for variation in displacement rates and ratios across metropolitan areas. Indeed, aside from a few hints found in the growing body of work on revitalization, the literature provides virtually no leads as to the structural antecedents of displacement mobility. Out of necessity, then, the remainder of the chapter relies heavily on speculative rationale and intuition, and it should be considered an initial treatment of—rather than final word on—the subject.

The displacement rates for edlerly, lower-income, black, and female-headed households displayed in table 8.1, and the displacement ratios for contrasting social categories summarized in table 8.2, constitute the dependent variables in the final portion of our analysis. We regard six different dimensions of urban structure as likely predictors of these rates and ratios. The first dimension is a general urbanism category, which we have named *metropolitan character*, and which includes the population size, density, growth rate, and age of a metropolitan area or central city. These attributes can be used to evaluate the contention that the displacement-generating forces of decline and revitalization are concentrated in older, larger urban centers (Black 1975; Cicin-Sain 1980; Lipton 1977; Sumka 1979). One might expect that the incidence of displacement among elderly, lower-income, and other underclass residents would be high in such areas, but that differentials would be low because of widespread competition for a diminishing supply of housing. Elements of *population composition* constitute the second structural dimension, and refer to the distribution of occupational, educational, and racial groups across locational and tenure categories, as well as to their representation in the overall population. The potential importance of compositional factors has been suggested by Clay (1979) and Lipton (1977), who note the pressures toward revitalization and underclass displacement that the presence of higher-status people and jobs in the central city can create.

The third and fourth categories of urban structural characteristics focus on the nature of the metropolitan housing market. In the third category, here labeled *housing availability*, the supply and demand sides of the market are observable in vacancy and mobility rates and changes over time in the number of units. Presumably, the looser or more fluid the housing situation—that is, the higher the vacancy and mobility rates and the larger the growth in supply—the lower the displacement levels will be across all segments of the metropolitan population, and hence the smaller the differentials (Hodge 1981; Grier and Grier 1980; Zeitz 1979). Besides its availability, the *characteristics of existing housing* may play a key role. Occupants of older dwellings, for example, are susceptible not only to abandonment and demolition but also to revitalization-induced displacement, given renovators' preferences for architecturally sound units constructed during a previous era (Black 1975; Cicin-Sain 1980; Clay 1979; National Urban Coalition 1978; Zeitz 1979). Moreover, most investigators agree that rental status enhances one's vulnerability to displacement. To the extent that members of the underclass are disproportionately located in older and/or rental housing, the representation of such units in SMSA or central-city housing stocks should be directly related to displacement rates and ratios.

It seems reasonable to propose that the quality of the larger residential setting may influence demand for housing—and ultimately displacement—independent of the effects of such dwelling unit characteristics as age or tenure. In support of this view, Clay (1979) has argued that increasingly favorable perceptions of central-city neighborhoods—deriving in part from the belief that crime and other urban problems have stabilized—may be one of the major forces behind the revitalization movement. Similarly, Lipton's (1977) tract-level analysis indicates that the revival of downtown-area neighborhoods is associated with the absence of industrial activity. Whether the types of desirable residential conditions described by Clay and Lipton contribute to large or small displacement rates and ratios cannot be readily anticipated, however, since their effects depend upon the prior distribution of amenities among locational and tenure groups. Nevertheless, by examining two final dimensions of urban areas—perceived *neighborhood quality* and the presence of *manufacturing activity*—we hope to estimate the direction and magnitude of the displacement impact attributable to the residential environment.

The exploratory nature of the analysis has prompted us to start with a large number of alternative measures of each of the six dimensions of urban structure and then systematically narrow the field to the strongest determinants of underclass rates and displacement ratios.[13] Those independent variable that survived the screening process are operationally defined in table 8.3 and 8.5. Examining tables 8.4 and 8.5 together, one can see that better—though quite modest—results have been obtained in the age and income equations than in the race and sex equations. With respect to overall explanatory power, the bottom rows of tables 8.4 and 8.5 reveal R^2s typically above .4 for age and income regressions, but below .3 for race and sex groups. Furthermore, such a pattern holds, regardless of whether the dependent variable is an underclass rate (table 8.4) or displacement ratio (table 8.5), and regardless of whether all intrametropolitan movers (left half of each table) or

Table 8.3. Description of Independent Variables Included in Regression Analysis

Metropolitan Context
POP SMSA population, 1975
AGE Year CC first reached 50,000
     population

Population Composition
WC1 % SMSA workers in white-
     collar occupations, 1970
WC2 % SMSA white-collar workers
     employed in CC, 1970
HSG % CC adults graduated from
     high school ÷ % suburban
     adults graduated from high
     school, 1970
BL1 % SMSA household heads black,
     1974-6
BL2 % CC household heads black ÷
     % suburban household heads
     black, 1974-6
BL3 % SMSA renter-occupied units
     black ÷ % SMSA owner-
     occupied units black, 1974-6

Housing Availability
MOV % SMSA households moving in
     past year, 1974-6
VAC % SMSA rental units vacant,
     1974-6
GRO % Growth in number of SMSA
     units since 1970, 1974-6

Housing Characteristics
REN % SMSA units renter-
     occupied, 1974-6
UN1 % SMSA units built before
     1940, 1974-6

UN2 % CC units built before
     1940, 1974-6
UN3 % CC units built before
     1940 ÷ % suburban units
     built before 1940, 1974-6

Neighborhood Quality
NX1 % SMSA households rating
     neighborhood excellent,
     1974-6
NX2 % CC households rating
     neighborhood excellent,
     1974-6
NX3 % CC households rating
     neighborhood excellent ÷
     % suburban households
     rating neighborhood
     excellent, 1974-6
NX4 % renter households rating
     neighborhood excellent ÷
     % owner households rating
     neighborhood excellent,
     1974-6

Manufacturing Activity
MF1 % SMSA workers in manufac-
     turing, 1970
MF2 % SMSA manufacturing work-
     ers employed in CC, 1970
MF3 Number of manufacturing
     establishments per 10,000
     CC residents, 1975

NOTE: Figures at the end of each description indicate year of observation; for variables drawn from Annual Housing Survey published volumes, observation was made in only one of the years from 1974 through 1976.

only those originating in the central city (right half) are considered. On the basis of explained variance alone, we can tentatively conclude that the six sets of structural characteristics provide a better understanding of levels and contrasts in displacement mobility by age and income across metroplitan areas than by race and sex.

But focusing solely on R²s proves theoretically unsatisfying since the question of which structural dimensions most strongly influence displacement is left open. To answer this question, we turn to the standardized regression coefficients in tables 8.4 and 8.5. For some of the structural categories, the coefficients tend to be erratic in sign, contrary to expectations, and/or minimal in magnitude, rarely qualifying their variables as top predictors of an underclass rate or displacement ratio. An inspection of the coefficients for the metropolitan character measures in table 8.4, for example, indicates that while SMSA population size (POP) has the predicted positive—but weak—effect on the displacement rate of female-headed households, it is negatively related to the incidence of displacement among elderly movers. A second measure, central city age (AGE), enters only a single equation, and then its sign implies the displacement of blacks to be more severe in younger metropolitan areas, not in the older areas supposedly marked by extensive disinvestment and reinvestment. As a rule, housing characteristics and neighborhood quality variables also exhibit small or ambiguous regression coefficients throughout both tables.

A more coherent picture emerges in the case of the manufacturing and housing availability dimensions. In table 8.4, three of the four coefficients for two separate measures of manufacturing concentration in the central city (MF2, MF3) are strong and in the expected direction: as manufacturing activity increases, displace-

Table 8.4. Standardized Regression Coefficients for Best Predictors of Underclass Displacement Rates, by Residence of Origin

| | Residence of Origin | | | | | | | |
| | SMSA | | | | Central City | | | |
	66+ yrs (N=37)	≤$4,000 (N=42)	Black (N=37)	Female (N=42)	66+ yrs (N=34)	≤$4,000 (N=42)	Black (N=35)	Female (N=42)
POP	–	–	–	–	-.42	–	–	.16
AGE	–	–	–	–	–	–	.20	–
WC2	–	–	-.30	–	-.20	–	-.29	–
HSG	–	–	–	–	–	-.22	–	–
BL2	.28	.32	-.20	.26	–	.23	-.21	.21
BL3	–	.58	.10	–	–	.53	–	–
VAC	-.31	–	–	-.16	-.27	–	–	-.16
GRO	–	–	–	–	–	-.12	–	–
REN	.29	.18	-.28	–	–	–	-.28	–
UN1	–	.25	–	–	–	–	–	–
UN2	–	–	–	.16	–	–	–	–
UN3	-.26	–	.19	.12	-.40	–	–	.18
NX2	–	–	–	–	–	–	–	-.24
NX4	–	–	–	–	-.49	.11	–	–
MF2	–	–	–	-.27	–	–	–	–
MF3	-.32	-.32	–	–	–	–	.14	–
R²	.39	.63	.27	.29	.58	.41	.26	.27
Adjusted R²	.29	.58	.15	.20	.51	.33	.13	.16

NOTES: See table 8.3 for description of variables. Age is of household head.
SOURCE: Annual Housing Survey tapes, 1974-76 rounds; U.S. Bureau of the Census 1973, 1976, 1977, 1978a, 1978b.

Table 8.5. Standardized Regression Coefficients for Best Predictors of Displacement Ratios, by Residence of Origin

| | Residence of Origin | | | | | | | |
| | SMSA | | | | Central City | | | |
	66+ yrs (N=37)	≤$4,000 (N=42)	Black (N=37)	Female (N=42)	66+ yrs (N=34)	≤$4,000 (N=42)	Black (N=35)	Female (N=42)
POP	-.13	-.21	-	-	-.36	-	-	-
AGE	-	-	-	-	-	-	.34	-
WC1	-	-	-.13	-	-	-	-	-
WC2	-	.16	-	-	-.40	-	-.17	-
BL1	-	-	-	-	-	-.19	-	-
BL2	.54	.57	-.24	.19	.46	.79	-.26	.17
BL3	-	-	-	-	-	-	-	-.20
MOV	-	-	-	-	-	-.16	-	-
REN	-	-	-.40	-	-	-	-.32	-
UN3	-.08	-	-	.16	-.34	-.07	-	-
NX1	-	-	-	-	-.28	-	-	-.21
NX2	-	-	-	-	-	-	-	-.21
NX3	.12	-.23	-	-.27	-	-	-	-
NX4	.12	-	-	.29	-	-.09	-	.32
MF1	-	.17	-	-	-	-	-	-
MF3	-	-	.37	.15	-	-	.24	-
R^2	.42	.55	.41	.26	.56	.68	.34	.24
Adjusted R^2	.33	.48	.31	.16	.48	.62	.23	.13

SOURCE: Annual Housing Survey tapes, 1974-76 rounds; U.S. Bureau of the Census 1973, 1976, 1977, 1978a, 1978b.
NOTES: See table 8.3 for descriptions of variables; note for table 8.2.

ment rates among elderly, lower-income, and female-headed households decline, due in part, we would argue, to the lessened desireability of and demand for residential settings proximate to industry. The MF1 and MF3 coefficients in table 8.5 lend further credibility to this interpretation. That manufacturing activity influences displacement ratios in a positive manner, widening the gap between underclass members and their better-off counterparts, seems consistent with the selective processes of abandonment, demolition, and other forms of displacement common to decaying industrial centers. The regression coefficients for the housing availability variables make intuitive sense as well, although the impacts of these variables are weaker and appear to be limited primarily to underclass displacement rates. As the negative signs in the seventh and eighth rows of table 8.4 demonstrate, a loose market characterized by a high vacancy rate (VAC) and a growing supply of housing (GRO) is less likely to generate displacement among disadvantaged segments of the metropolitan population than is a tight market with few vacancies and a shortage of units.

The results for the population composition dimension shed further light on the market-oriented explanation of displacement rates and differentials. Contrary to the arguments of Clay and Lipton, an abundance of higher-status jobs in the central city (WC2) does not promote competition for housing to the point of elevating underclass displacement. In fact, on the several occasions when this variable ranks among the top five predictors, it usually has the opposite effect: the employment of a high percentage of all metropolitan white-collar workers in the central city tends to reduce the rate of involuntary mobility among blacks and the aged (table 8.4, row 3) and minimizes differentials by race and sex (table 8.5, row 4). But regardless of its impact on underclass displacement patterns, the importance of WC2 pales beside that of BL2, an index of blacks' proportional representation in the central city relative to their representation in the suburbs. This crude measure of geographic concentration is included among the five best predictors in 15 of the 16 equations in tables 8.4 and 8.5, and seven times exerts the strongest or second strongest effect on a displacement rate or ratio. Moreover, the BL2 coefficient is consistently positive for nonracial social categories: as black concentration increases, mobile elderly, lower-income, and female-headed households experience higher levels of displacement, both in absolute terms and in comparison to metropolitan dwellers with contrasting social characteristics. At the same time, however, the coefficient takes a negative sign in every equation involving black movers or racial groups.

Two different interpretations can be offered for the somewhat contradictory effects of the racial concentration variable. One interpretation holds that pent-up residential demand among central-city blacks—a situation created by the operation of economic forces and institutional gatekeepers in the dual housing market—is being released into white underclass neighborhoods (Molotch 1972). The obvious problem with this "spillover" interpretation centers on the direction of BL2's impact in the racial equations. If demand is intense, why don't blacks compete with and displace one another more than they appear to? Are the anticipated gains in housing quality to be had beyond the boundaries of the black community great enough to restrict competition to such external locations? A second explanation views the geographic concentration of the black population as symptomatic of central-city decay. While disinvestment takes a heavy toll on the housing supply of other underclass groups, the sheer volume of black demand may be sufficient to retard the pace of abandonment, demolition, and subsequent displacement within black neighborhoods. In addition middle-class reinvestment activity may be selective of underclass housing opportunities outside the ghetto, given the previously mentioned aversion of many whites to integrated residential environments. Unfortunately, without more refined data on the disinvestment- and reinvestment-related causes of involuntary moves, the task of choosing between these alternative interpretations—or of deciding that both have some validity—remains extremely difficult.

Discussion

The preceding analysis of Annual Housing Survey data yields three tentative conclusions about social differentials in metropolitan residential displacement. Most central to our research is the conclusion that displacement moves are distributed unevenly across segments of the metropolitan population, often occurring disproportionately among elderly and lower income movers. Such a statement should be qualified by noting that some underclass households—specifically, those with black and female heads— experience levels of displacement only marginally higher than their advantaged white and male counterparts. Despite the small magnitude of its differential, race does manage to figure prominently in a second conclusion: out of the large number of urban structural characteristics evaluated in the exploratory portion of the analysis, the concentration of blacks inside central-city boundaries represents the single strongest determinant of displacement rates and ratios. Finally, the similarity of SMSA and central city results throughout the investigation suggests that the existence of social differentials in displacement—and for that matter, the frequency of displacement itself—should be treated as a metropolitan-wide phenomenon rather than as a problem peculiar to the inner city.

Because the underclass hypothesis constitutes the focal point of our study, an appropriate question at this time is whether we have submitted the hypothesis to as fair and thorough a test as possible. Not surprisingly, we think that we have, within the limits of the data set and analytic procedures employed. But before the definitive test of the underclass hypothesis can be conducted, these limits must be stretched in several important ways. At a conceptual level, future investigators should formulate alternative definintions of displacement and try them out in their work. In light of the conservative nature of our own definition, one useful strategy would entail liberalizing the meaning of displacement so that exorbitant rent increases, harassment by landlords, government action, and other "gray-area" events are counted as inducements to forced mobility. Investigators must also broaden the temporal scope of displacement research beyond the narrow cross-sectional approach taken here, since the accuracy of the underclass hypothesis may vary with swings in the business cycle and investment climate. Indeed, the likelihood of increasing stiff competition among urban dwellers for affordable housing in the coming years hints that involuntary moves will eventually comprise a larger share of the total volume of mobility than is currently the case.

Another limitation of the present study that should be addressed in subsequent research concerns an aspect of the reason-for-move methodology employed. Among students of residential mobility, it is common practice to proceed as we have in table 8.1, comparing the frequency of moves made for one type of reason (displacement) with that of all moves made by households within a particular social category. However, in the course of avoiding the problem of miniscule percentages, this practice manages to neglect the risk of displacement experienced by members of the category as a whole. With respect to mobile elderly households, for example, a disproportionate displacement rate is apparent, but we know that few elderly households move for any reason. Therefore, the *probability* of an elderly individual's or couple's being displaced could conceivably be less than that of a member of another group that exhibits a low displacement rate but a high overall level of mobility. Determining the social and demographic predictors of such probabilities via logit analysis or some simlar technique would provide a more refined test of the underclass hypothesis.

Finally, and perhaps most seriously, our research fails to shed any light on the personal consequences of displacement. In a recent article, Michelson (1980) has warned that while most types of residential adjustment have negligible effects, forced moves may generate substantial tensions and stress for the households involved. Moreover, if certain social groups are especially susceptible to such moves, and if members of these groups live on fixed incomes, possess strong neighborhood ties, or have other characteristics that might hinder their adaptation to new surroundings, the harmful consequences of involuntary mobility could be greatly compounded. To date, the evidence on this subject remains rather sketchy, although there is some indication that students of mobility have tended to exaggerate the disruptive impact associated with displacement (Collier et al. 1979; Development Economics Group 1975; Hodge 1981; Hu 1979; U.S. Department of Housing and Urban Development 1979a 1981). Nevertheless, the possibility that hardship may result from forced moves would seem to provide the ultimate justification for continued interest in the underclass hypothesis in particular and residential displacement in general.

NOTES

1. An excellent illustration of the decision-making line of research is found in Speare, Goldstein, and Frey (1975). For a critique of mobility decision-making models, see Lee (1978).

2. The 1979 HUD reports clearly identify neighborhood disinvestment as the principal market force generating displacement. In the 1981 update report, however, the significance of disinvestment is de-emphasized considerably.

3. It is not imperative, of course, that displacement be defined in terms of its immediate causes or antecedents; such an approach may even prove undesirable from a logical standpoint. Nevertheless, a recent review (Lee 1981) has shown that the factors precipitating displacement moves are often included in conceptual treatments of the phenomenon.

4. Molotch (1969, 1972) has provided a detailed analysis of the role played by normal turnover in neighborhood change, although he focuses on the more typical case of an area undergoing the transition from white to black occupancy.

5. The AHS data-gathering effort, which began in 1973, is a two-pronged operation. Each year under HUD and AHS auspices, the Census Bureau interviews members of a multistage sample that consists of over 50,000 elements and is designed to represent all housing units in the United States. Besides the national sample, the Bureau also generates and contacts independent samples of 5,000 or 15,000 households for sixty different metropolitan areas, with twenty of these SMSAs receiving coverage on a rotating basis every third year.

6. The 42 SMSAs are distributed across census-defined regions in the following manner: (1) Northeast: Albany-Schenectady-Troy, Allentown-Bethlehem-Easton, Boston, Buffalo, Newark, Paterson-Clifton-Passaic, Philadelphia, Pittsburgh, Providence-Pawtucket-Warwick, and Rochester; (2) North Central: Chicago, Cincinnati, Cleveland, Columbus, Detroit, Grand Rapids, Indianapolis, Minneapolis-St. Paul, Omaha, and St. Louis; (3) South: Atlanta, Baltimore, Birmingham, Dallas, Ft. Worth, Houston, Louisville, Miami, New Orleans, Oklahoma City, Raleigh, and Washington, D.C.; (4) West: Anaheim-Santa Ana-Garden Grove, Denver, Honolulu, Las Vegas, Phoenix, Sacramento, San Francisco-Oakland, and Seattle-Everett.

7. The exact question and its thirty-one response categories have been reproduced in full by Goodman (1979, p. 409).

8. We have omitted displacement by public action from our estimates partly because the current emphasis in the literature is on private-market displacement and partly because government programs at all levels appear to contribute little to the overall magnitude of the displacement problem. A recent HUD analysis, for example, suggests that government activity was directly responsible for less than 20 percent of the displacement moves occurring in any region of the country from 1974 through 1976 (U.S.

Department of Housing and Urban Development 1979a), although the indirect effect of government programs remains ambiguous (Schnare 1979). For contrary views on the magnitude of government-sponsored displacement, see Berndt (1978), Grier and Grier (1980), and Lilley and Clark (1972).

9. This finding holds for SMSAs located in every region of the country as well, with mean displacement rates ranging from 3.80 percent for all intrametropolitan movers in the 11 north central SMSAs to 4.82 percent for those in the 9 western SMSAs. Regional variation in the incidence of displacement among the subsets of movers originating in the central city is even more limited, ranging from 4.07% in the 12 southern SMSAs to 5.03 percent in the north central areas.

10. Although only total findings are shown in table 8.1, an analysis of displacement rates by region lends additional support to this conclusion, confirming the underclass hypothesis for elderly and lower-income movers but not for black and female-headed households. (Regional results are available upon request from the first author.)

11. Because of the frequent and, in many ways, unique mobility experiences of individuals in the under-26 age category, we have decided to let the displacement rate for household heads 26-45 years old serve as the denominator in the age ratio.

12. That such a pattern of findings is not due to the distorting effect that a few exceptionally large or small values may have on mean rates can be seen in the following case-by-case comparisons. For SMSA mover populations, the displacement ratio exceeds one (favors underclass movers) 30 out of 37 times with respect to age and 36 out of 40 times with respect to income, but only 24 of 37 and 29 of 42 SMSA ratios exceed one for the race and sex comparisons, respectively. For central-city populations, the following proportions obtain: (1) age—30/34 cases in which the displacement ratio exceeds one; (2) income—30/35; (3) race—19/35; and (4) sex—26/42.

13. As the first step in the process, a data set consisting of 75 potential independent variables was assembled from AHS published volumes, the 1970 Census, and the 1977 County-City Data Book. This pool of variables was pared down by retaining only those measures that exhibited zero-order correlations of .2 or more with one of the underclass displacement rates or ratios contained in tables 8.1 and 8.2. Stepwise regression procedures were then used to isolate the variables exerting the greatest effects on each of the rates and ratios. Because of the aggregate level of analysis, the small number of cases, and the prevalence of redundant or overlapping measures, multicollinearity posed a serious problem during the early regression runs. Thus, our final step was to weed out those variables that were correlated in excess of .5 with other predictors in the best 5-variable equation for a particular rate or ratio.

REFERENCES

Allen, I. 1980. The ideology of dense neighborhood redevelopment: Cultural diversity and transcendent community experience. *Urban Affairs Quarterly* **15:** 409-28.

Berndt, H. E. 1978. *Displacement and relocation practices in five midwestern cities.* St. Louis: Metro Housing Resources.

Berry, B. J. L., and Dahmann, D. C. 1980. Population redistribution in the United States in the 1970s. Pp. 8-49 In *Population Redistribution and Public Policy,* ed. B. J. L. Berry and L. P. Silverman. Washington, D.C.: National Academy of Science.

Black, J. T. 1975. Private market housing renovation in central cities. *Urban Land* **34:** 3-9.

Bradley, D. S. 1978. Back to the city? *Atlanta Economic Review* 28:15-20.

Cicin-Sain, B. 1980. The costs and benefits of neighborhood revitalization. In *Urban Revitalization,* ed. D. B. Rosenthal. Urban Affairs Annual Reviews, vol. 18, pp. 49-75, Beverly Hills: Sage.

Clay, P. L. 1979. *Neighborhood renewal: Middle-class resettlement and incumbent upgrading in American neighborhoods.* Lexington, Mass.: Lexington Books.

Collier, B. J., Gabbin, A. Lawrence, C., and White, M. 1979. From theory to praxis: An analysis of some aspects of the displacement process in the District of Columbia. Working Paper no. 11. Washington, D.C.: Department of Economics, University of the District of Columbia.

Cybriwsky, R. A. 1978. Social aspects of neighborhood change. *Annuals of the Association of American Geographers* 68:17-33.

―――. 1980. Revitalization trends in downtown-area neighborhoods. In *The American metropolitan system: Present and future,* ed. S. D. Brunn and J. O. Wheeler, pp. 21-36. New York: V. H. Winston.

Development Economics Group. 1975. *Condominiums in the District of Columbia: The impact of conversions on Washington's citizens, neighborhoods, and housing stock.* Washington, D.C.: Center for Urban Policy Research, Raymond, Parish, and Pine, Inc.

Farley, R., Schuman, H., Bianchi, S., Colasanto, D., and Hatchett, S. 1978. "Chocolate city, vanilla suburbs": Will the trend toward racially separate communities continue? *Social Science Research* 7:319-44.

Fried, M. 1963. Grieving for a lost home. In *The urban condition: People and policy in the metropolis,* ed. L. J. Duhl, pp. 151-71. New York: Basic Books.

Gale, D. E. 1979. Middle class resettlement in older urban neighborhoods: the evidence and the implications. *Journal of the American Planning Association* 45:293-304.

―――. 1980 "Neighborhood resettlement: Washington, D.C." Pp. 95-115 in Shirley Bradway Laska and Daphne Spain (eds.), *Back to the City: Issues in Neighborhood Renovation.* New York: Pergamon.

Goering, J. M. 1979. *Housing in America: The characteristics and uses of the annual housing survey.* Annual Housing Survey Studies, no. 6. Washington, D.C.: Office of Policy Development and Research, U.S. Department of Housing and Urban Development.

Goldfield, D. R. 1980. Private neighborhood redevelopment and displacement: the case of Washington, D.C. *Urban Affairs Quarterly* 15:453-68.

Goodman, J. L., Jr. 1978. *Urban residential mobility: Places, people, policy.* Washington, D.C.: Urban Institute.

———. 1979. Reasons for moves out of and into large cities. *Journal of the American Planning Association* 45:407-16.

———. 1980. People of the city. *American Demographics* 2 (September):14-7.

Grier, G. and Grier, E. 1980. Urban displacement: A reconnaissance. In *Back to the City: Issues in Neighborhood Renovation,* ed. S. B. Laska and D. Spain, pp. 252-68. New York: Pergamon.

Guterbock, T. M. 1980. The political economy of urban revitalization: competing theories. *Urban Affairs Quarterly* 15:429-38.

Hartman, C. 1964. The housing of relocated families. *Journal of the American Institute of Planners* 30:266-86.

Henig, J. R. 1980. Gentrification and displacement within cities: a comparative analysis. *Social Science Quarterly* 61:638-52.

Hodge, D. C. 1979. *The Seattle displacement study.* Seattle: Office of Policy Planning, City of Seattle.

Hodge, D. C. 1980. Inner-city revitalization as a challenge to diversity? Seattle. In *Back to the city: Issues in neighborhood renovation,* ed. S. B. Laska and D. Spain, pp. 187-203. New York: Pergamon.

———. 1981. Inner-city revitalization and displacement in a growth region. *Geographical Review* 71:188-200.

Hodge, D.C., and Lee, B.A. 1980. Structural determinants of displacement in the U.S. Paper presented at the Annual Meeting of the Regional Science Association, Milwaukee.

Hu, J. C. 1979. A survey study of FNMA's pilot city lending program in St. Louis. Paper presented at the Annual Meeting of the Midwest Economics Association, Chicago.

James, F. J. 1980. The revitalization of older urban housing and neighborhoods. In *The prospective city: economic, population, energy, and environmental developments,* ed. A. P. Solomon, pp. 130-60. Cambridge: Massachusetts Institute of Technology Press.

Kantor, M. B., ed. 1965. *Mobility and mental health.* Springfield: Charles C. Thomas.

Kasarda, J. D. 1980. The implications of contemporary redistribution trends for national urban policy. *Social Science Quarterly* 61:373-400.

Laska, S. B., and Spain, D. 1979. Urban policy and planning in the wake of gentrification: anticipating renovators' demands. *Journal of the American Planning Association* 45:523-31.

———eds. 1980. *Back to the city: Issues in neighborhood renovation.* New York: Pergamon.

Lee, B. A. 1978. Residential mobility on skid row: Disaffiliation, powerlessness, and decision making. *Demography* 15:285-300.

———. 1981. Research on residential displacement: a review and an agenda. Paper presented at the Annual Meeting of the Southern Regional Demographic Group, Little Rock.

LeGates, R., and Hartman, C. 1981. *Displacement.* Berkeley: Legal Services Anti-Displacement Project.

Lilley, W., III, and Clark, T. B. 1972. Federal programs spur abandonment of housing in major cities. *National Journal* 4:26-33.

Lipton, S. G. 1977. Evidence of central city revival. *Journal of the American Planning Association* 45:136-47.

London, B. 1980. Gentrification as urban reinvasion: Some preliminary definitional and theoretical considerations. In *Back to the city: Issues in neighborhood renovation*, ed. S. B. Laska and D. Spain, pp. 77-92. New York: Pergamon.

London, B., Bradley, D. S., and Hudson, J. R., ed. 1980. Special issue, The revitalization of inner-city neighborhoods. *Urban Affairs Quarterly* 15:373-487.

Long, L. H. 1980. What the census will tell us about gentrification. *American Demographics* 2 (September):18-21.

Michelson, W. 1980. Residential mobility and urban policy: Some sociological considerations. In *Residential Mobility and Public Policy*, ed. W. A. V. Clark and E. G. Moore, pp. 79-99. Urban Affairs Annual Reviews, vol. 19. Beverly Hills: Sage.

Molotch, H. L. 1969. Racial change in a stable community. *American Journal of Sociology* 75:226-38.

――――. 1972. *Managed integration: Dilemmas of doing good in the city*. Berkeley: University of California Press.

――――. 1979. Capital and neighborhood in the United States: Some conceptual links. *Urban Affairs Quarterly* 14:289-312.

National Urban Coalition. 1978. *Displacement: City neighborhoods in transition*. Washington, D.C.: National Urban Coalition.

National Urban League. 1971. *National survey of housing abandonment*. New York: Center for Community Change.

Nelson, K. P. 1980a. *Back to the city? Trends in white intrametropolitan migration*. Annual Housing Survey Studies, no. 8. Washington, D.C.: Office of Policy Development and Research, U.S. Department of Housing and Urban Development.

――――. 1980b. Recent suburbanization of blacks: how much, who, and where? *Journal of the American Planning Association* 46:287-300.

Newman, S. J., and Owen, M. S. 1981. Residential displacement in the U.S., 1970-1977. Paper presented at the Annual Meeting of the Population Association of America, Washington, D.C.

Newsom, M. D. 1971. Blacks and historic preservation. *Law and Contemporary Problems* 36:423-31.

Pattison, T. 1977. The Process of neighborhood upgrading and gentrification. M.A. diss. Cambridge: Massachusetts Institute of Technology.

Rosenthal, D. B., ed. 1980. *Urban revitalization*. Urban Affairs Annual Reviews, vol. 18. Beverly Hills: Sage.

Rossi, P. 1955. *Why families move: A study in the social psychology of urban residential mobility*. Glencoe: Free Press.

Schnare, A. B. 1979. *Household mobility in urban homesteading neighborhoods: Implications for displacement*. Washington, D.C.: Office of Policy Development and Research, U.S. Department of Housing and Urban Development.

Smith, N. 1979. Toward a theory of gentrification: A back to the city movement by capital, not people. *Journal of the American Planning Association* 45:538-48.

Spain, D. 1980. Black-to-white successions in central city housing: Limited evidence of urban revitalization. *Urban Affairs Quarterly* 15:381-96.
_____. 1981. A gentrification scorecard. *American Demographics* 3 (November):14-9.
Speare, A., Jr., Goldstein, S., and Frey, W. H. 1975. *Residential mobility, migration and metropolitan change.* Cambridge: Ballinger.
Stegman, M. A., ed. 1979. Special supplement on "neighborhood revitalization." *Journal of the American Planning Association* 45:458-556.
Sternlieb, G. 1972. Abandoned housing: what is to be done? *Urban Land* 31 (March):3-17.
_____. 1979. A brief statement on the nature and magnitude of the abandonment problem. New Brunswick: Center for Urban Policy Research, Rutgers University.
Sternlieb, G., and Burchell, R. W. 1973. *Residential abandonment: The tenement landlord revisited.* New Brunswick: Center for Urban Policy Research, Rutgers University.
Sternlieb, G., and Hughes, J. W. 1979. New dimensions of the urban crisis. Prepared statement before the Subcommittee on Fiscal and Intergovernmental Policy. Joint Economic Committee of the U.S. Congress, March 20th.
Sumka, H. J. 1979. Neighborhood revitalization and displacement: A review of the evidence. Journal of the American Planning Association 45:480-7.
Tournier, R. E. 1980. Historic preservation as a force in urban change: Charleston. Pp. 173-86. In *Back to the city: Issues in neighborhood renovation,* ed. S. B. Laska and D. Spain. New York: Pergamon.
U.S. Bureau of the Census. 1966. Reasons for moving, March 1962 to March 1963. Current Population Reports, ser. P-20, no. 154. Washington, D.C.: U.S. Government Printing Office.
_____. 1973. Census of population, 1970: State volumes. Characteristics of the population, vol. 1, pts. 2-51. Washington, D.C.: U.S. Government Printing Office.
_____. 1976. Annual housing survey, 1974: Housing characteristics for selected metropolitan areas. Current Housing Reports, ser. H-170-74, nos. 1-19. Washington, D.C.: U.S. Government Printnig Office.
_____. 1977. Annual housing survey, 1975: Housing characteristics for selected metropolitan areas. Current Housing Reports, ser. H-170-75, nos. 20-40. Washington, D.C.: U.S. Government Printing Office.
_____. 1978a. Annual housing survey, 1976: Housing characteristics for selected metropolitan areas. Current Housing Reports, ser. H-150-76, nos. 41-60. Washington, D.C.: U.S. Government Printing Office.
_____. 1978b. County and city data book, 1977. Washington, D.C.: U.S. Government Printing Office.
U.S. Department of Housing and Urban Development. 1979a. Displacement report. Washington, D.C.: Office of Policy Development and Research, U.S. Department of Housing and Urban Development.
_____. 1979b. Whither or whether urban distress. Urban Policy and Evaluation Working Paper. Washington, D.C.: Office of Community

Planning and Development, U.S. Department of Housing and Urban Development.

———. 1981. Residential displacement: An update. Washington, D.C.: Office of Policy Development and Research, U.S. Department of Housing and Urban Development.

Weiler, C. 1979. NAN handbok on reinvestment displacement: The public role in a new housing issue. Washington, D.C.: National Association of Neighborhoods.

Zeitz, E. 1979. *Private urban renewal: A different residential trend.* Lexington, Mass.: Lexington Books.

CHAPTER NINE

Gentrification and Displacement of the Elderly: An Empirical Analysis

JEFFREY R. HENIG

Gentrification, to some, represents the successful culmination of two and one-half decades of Federal and local policy efforts aimed at attracting upper-income families into the deteriorating urban core. But, while aspects of this phenomenon are worthy of celebration, gentrification has a darker side. Rising rents, rising property tax assessments, and the conversion of rental housing into owner-occupied and condominium units—factors associated with gen-trification—threaten to displace existing residents unable to compete in the accelerated housing market.

The elderly, especially those on fixed incomes, are believed to be particularly vulnerable to gentrification-induced displacement (City of Seattle 1979; U.S. Dept. of Housing and Urban Development 1979; Grier and Grier 1978; Hartman 1979; James 1978). The risks of gentrification-induced displacement are especially worthy of concern because the elderly appear to be doubly jeopardized. They are, it is theorized, more likely than other central-city residents to be displaced by the market pressures gentrification brings to bear; and, once displaced, they are believed to be more vulnerable than others to the physical and emotional costs that forced relocation can impose.

Jeffrey R. Henig is Assistant Professor, Department of Political Science, George Washington University.
Reprinted by permission with changes, from *The Gerontologist*, Vol. 21, No. 1, 1981: 67-75.

The lack of strong empirical backing to the claim that gentrification and displacement are widespread and significant forces reshaping the cities today, however, has encouraged a counterthesis to emerge. This counterthesis suggests that the gentrification/displacement issue has, in general, been overplayed.

How widespread is gentrification, and how severe a threat does it currently represent to the urban aged? This article analyzes data based on migration patterns in 967 census tracts across nine cities. The findings provide some new support to the contentions that gentrification does exist, that gentrification-induced displacement is a threat to the elderly, that the elderly may be more at risk than other groups, and that the threat may be increasing over time.

Displacement and the Elderly: The Double Threat

The impact of displacement. Everyone needs a certain amount of stability. An unpredictable environment robs us of the comforts and efficiencies that can derive from convention, habit, and routine. While it is, of course, true that an unchanging environment can also lower the quality of living, swift and erratic change can be a life-threatening source of physiological and psychological stress (Lowenthal 1964).

The expectation that the elderly person suffers more when displaced by gentrification (Besser 1979; Chadwick 1979; Hartman 1979; Holman 1978; Sumka and Cicin-Sain 1978) is based, at least in part, on the presumption that the elderly have a more pronounced dependence on stable and predictable environments than other groups. There are physiological and sociological bases for accepting such a presumption. Physiological changes associated with the aging process—diminished visual capacity (Birren and Shock 1950; Bouma 1947), hearing difficulties (Melrose, Webb and Lauterman 1963), diminution of balance and slowed response time (Exton-Smith 1977) may make adjustments to environmental change more difficult. Changes in the brain and nervous system—slowing of blood flow to the brain, shrinkage of the brain, progressive loss of neurons (Terry 1978)—while they need not be debilitating, may erode some of the elderly person's capacity for adaptation and may lessen the capacity to absorb stress.

The elderly may be particularly vulnerable, too, to the social costs of forced relocation. Friends and neighbors form an integral part of the network of support upon which many elderly must rely. A network of friends, some evidence suggests, can make the difference between whether or not persons over 70 consider themselves to be "old" (Blau 1973). Social isolation has been hypothesized to be related to mental depression and is believed to be a factor in the high rate of suicide among the aged (Anderson and Davidson 1975; Batchelor and Napier 1953).

These physiological and sociological impacts of forced relocation are likely to be exacerbated, moreover, by additional economic costs that displaced elderly persons can be expected to incur. An analysis of the impact of displacement on the elderly in Denver, for example, found that displacement necessitated an average of about $127 in moving costs; $138 in social service counseling, referral, and assistance; and monthly rents an average of $38 above those previously paid.

Perhaps because of these factors, the elderly, when left to their own devices, generally choose not to move. The elderly are about one-half as likely to move as is the population at large, and about one-fifth as likely to move as the highly mobile 20- to 24-year age bracket (Siegel 1975). The 1970 U.S. Census found that over 44 percent of all homeowners over 65 had lived in the same house since 1949 or before. This need for stability is further evidenced in the consistently observed tendency of the elderly to express high levels of satisfaction for their housing and neighborhood conditions, even when independent observers have judged them to be poor (Britton 1966; Carp 1976; Lawton, Neban, and Carlson 1973; Lycan, Pendleton, and Weiss 1978; Winiecke 1973).

Relocation can pose a significant threat to the health and well-being of the elderly, as has been empirically confirmed (Aldrich and Mendkoff 1963; Blenkner 1967; Brand and Smith 1974; Killian 1970; Lieberman 1969; Markus et al. 1972; Yawney and Slover 1973). These studies—which focus, for the most part, on the correlates of the move into a nursing home, moves among nursing homes, or moves from one residence to another—demonstrate that relocation can have negative effects on activity levels, mental health, life satisfaction, and mortality. The impacts of relocation are especially likely to be harmful when the factors precipitating relocation are—as is gentrification-induced displacement—outside the individual's control (Schulz and Brenner 1977).

The likelihood of displacement. In addition to being more vulnerable to the physical and psychic costs of displacement, the elderly may be more likely to be displaced by gentrification in the first place. There are both spatial and economic reasons for expecting this to be so. The spatial explanation evolves from the observation that there are high concentrations of the elderly in the older, deteriorating neighborhoods near the central business districts (CBD) of the major cities. These are the very neighborhoods that the younger and wealthier gentry—attracted by the areas' convenience, often superior architecture, historical significance, and relatively low cost—find appealing (Clay 1979; National Urban Coalition 1978). This spatial factor probably works in conjunction with economic factors. Many elderly households financially overextend themselves already, simply to hold onto the housing they have. Elderly households are twice as likely as the general population to spend over 35% of their income for housing (Struyk 1977). These households are not in the position to absorb the increased rents, increased taxes, or other expenses that gentrification can impose. Relocation, for them, may be the only feasible response.

There is some empirical evidence to substantiate the expectation that these spatial and economic factors leave the elderly especially likely to be victimized by gentrification-induced displacement. A study of those displaced by condominium conversion in Washington, D.C., found that 45% of the displacees were elderly (Development Economics Group 1976). A survey of Seattle households found that 34% of the elderly households who moved did so because they were displaced (City of Seattle 1979). And, in one of the few multicity, multineighborhood studies of gentrification, the National Urban Coalition surveyed city planners, realtors, housing specialists, and neighborhoods representatives in 44 cities. "Almost 80% of the neighborhoods reporting elderly residents," according to that study, "indicated a decline in their number after rehabilitation" (1978). The findings, however, have not been unanimous. A study in Portland concluded that the elderly in that city were *not* being displaced at especially high rates (City of Portland 1978).

While suggestive, these studies do not offer a firm empirical base from which to estimate the extent of gentrication-induced displacement among the elderly. First, the single case-study mode of several of the analyses limits the generalizability of the conclusions that can legitimately be drawn. This problem is exacerbated by the fact that the highly studied cities—Washington, Seattle, Portland, and a few others—are widely regarded as being unusual in the degree of gentrification under way. Second, because the National Urban Coalition study is based so heavily on the subjective impressions of the respondents, the results of that comparative analysis must be regarded with caution. We cannot be sure of the precision with which the various local respondents obtained their estimates of the extent of displacement, nor can we be confident that the criteria and definitions applied were explicit and consistent throughout. None of the existing analyses, finally, provide longitudinal indicators of changes in the rate or patterns of gentrification and displacement over time.

Data and Methods

The research reported here is based primarily on census tract level data collected by R.L. Polk & Company, and made available to cities that contract for it through the published series *Profiles of Change.* Polk is a private firm that has been publishing city directories since 1870. Each year the company surveys approximately 27 million housing units and 2 million businesses. The company claims that its door-to-door canvass "generally results in obtaining information from 80 to 95% of the residents" of the cities in which they operate. The company also claims that "spot comparisons with the Bureau of Census surveys made at the same point in time show the counts to be very close...."

Each Polk *Profiles of Change* report is based on two separate canvasses, usually 1 year apart. Reports covering the mid-1970s are available through the Dept. of Housing and Urban Development, which awarded Polk a $1.6 million contract to compile reports on 318 cities. Later reports are available only from those cities that have continued to contract with Polk to develop them for use by their planning and development agencies. In July 1979, there were 10 cities with populations greater than 200,000 that had received late 1970s Polk reports. This study is based on the mid- and late-1970s surveys in 9 of those 10 cities. The 9 cities—Cincinnati, Dayton, Louisville, Memphis, Milwaukee, Minneapolis, Oklahoma City, Rochester, and St. Paul—have no claim to being "representative." They are similar, in racial makeup and income levels, to other U.S. cities of their size, but their rates of population loss from 1960 to 1975 are more severe. Signs of gentrification and its impact on the elderly, therefore, will probably be less visible in these case cities than in others, such as Washington, D.C., Seattle, Boston, Atlanta, or Manhattan, where the gentrification phenomenon is likely to be more advanced.

Figure 9.1 summarizes some of the key Polk indicators that are employed in this study. Data for each tract are based on four distinct canvasses—two, about 1 year apart, in the mid 1970s, and two, about 1 year apart, in the late 1970s. Since tracts with very small populations might undergo proportionally extreme changes that could distort some of the analysis, tracts with fewer than 200 households were not considered. A small number of additional tracts were dropped either because of boundary changes that made comparability over time infeasible or inconsistencies in the published data that indicated coding or typographic errors. The 967 tracts that are included in the analyses contain approximately 99% of the households in nine cities under review. Two key varriables

Table 9.1. Correlation Between Professional Inmigration and Selected Neighborhood Attributes—Mid-1970s and Late 1970s

	Mid-1970s	Late 1970s
I. Housing & Commercial Environment		
% housing units vacant	-.11	-.05
two-canvass vacancies	-.08	-.05
% renter-occupied	-.14	-.06
% commercial	-.04	-.01
% commercial units vacant	-.07	.03
II. Demography		
% professional/technical	+.20	+.07
% blue collar/service	-.10	-.07
% retired	+.02	+.12
% female-headed	-.10	.00
% black, 1970	-.10	.00
III. Location		
distance from central business district	+.06	+.01

SOURCE: Henig, 1980.

were added to those that the Polk reports provide. Information on the percentage of blacks within each census tract was obtained from the 1970 U.S. Census. Each tract, in addition, was coded from 0 to 5 according to its distance from the central business district.

Net inmovement of households headed by persons in professional or technical occupations provides the operational indicator of gentrification that will be employed. While the Polk reports do not present information regarding the age of outmovers, data on the mobility of households headed by a retired person provide a rough but satisfactory surrogate. For the purpose of this analysis, then, gentrification-induced displacement will be assumed to be under way in tracts that reveal a net outmigration of retired households occuring simultaneously with a net increase, due to migration, in professional/technical households. These measures provide a rather broad definition of the central concepts, so it is worth taking a moment to consider more directly what they include and do not include.

The definition of gentrification as the net inmigration of professional/technical households does not distinguish tracts in which professionals move directly into housing units theretofore occupied by lower class or older residents from tracts in which the so-called gentry are moving into previously empty or newly constructed units. This means that a neighborhood that is capable of accommodating increased numbers of professionals without dislodging the prior residents would still be classified as "gentrifying." The definition of gentrification-induced displacement as the net outmigration of retired households from gentrifying tracts does not distinguish tracts in which the outmigration is directly forced by the recycling of units for the incoming gentry from tracts in which retired households may be moving out voluntarily or moving out, for reasons unrelated to the gentrification, from units elsewhere in the census tract. In using this difinition, therefore, we risk mistaking two distinct patterns of neighborhood change—"filling in" and "segmented development"—for gentrification-induced displacement, which they may superficially resemble. Filling in occurs when professionals gradually filter into a neighborhood as units previously occupied by the elderly become available through voluntary relocation or death. This process results in the socioeconomic upgrading of the area, but without the trauma and rapidity associated with gentrification-induced displacement. Segmented development occurs when unique attributes make reinvestment appealing in one small part of a census tract while nearby areas continue to suffer disinvestment and deterioration. In some cities, for example, luxury apartment or condominium development is under way on waterfront or urban-renewal areas, while, nearby, conditions of abandonment, crime, and longstanding neighborhood decline are forcing those elderly who can afford to to flee. As with gentrification/displacement and filling in, tract level demographic trends will reveal, in such instances, net inmigration of professionals and net outmigration of elderly or retired, but those migratory streams will be causally unrelated and spatially distinct.

The breadth of the measures is imposed by the nature of the Polk reports, which provide no data on patterns of succession (who replaces whom) at the individual housing unit level, and which acquires no survey data regarding households' reasons for moving out. Gentrification and displacement must be inferred from aggregate demographic changes at the census tract level. This represents a constraint on the type and forcefulness of the conclusions we will be able to draw.

Although the breadth of the measures imposes some constraints, these should not be crippling. Filling in, by its very nature, is a gradual and evolutionary process of neighborhood change; it can have only a marginal impact on this analysis, which limits its focus to rapid demographic shifts that occur over 1- or 2-year intervals. Neighborhoods that appear, at first, to be undergoing processes of filling in or segmented development, moreover, may actually be experiencing an indirect form of gentrification/displacement sparked by the anticipation of future revitalization. Landlords and speculators who forsee the possibility of future revitalization in a neighborhood will sometimes allow their properties to deteriorate while awaiting the proper time to rehabilitate or sell. During this period of "anticipatory disinvestment," existing residents, finding themselves faced with lack of services, insufficient heat, and general disrepair, may begin an exodus. In some cases their units are allowed to lie vacant; in other cases they are rented to more transitory residents on short-term leases, or no leases at all. The result can be that, by the time revitalization begins in earnest, forced displacement of the long-term residents is no longer necessary to accommodate the wealthier inmovers. While this process resembles filling in—in both cases the so-called gentry occupy units that have been standing vacant or have been voluntarily vacated—the underlying dynamic is rooted in the same economic and social forces that drive gentrification-induced displacement of the more direct sort. Withdrawal of landlord services simply replaces eviction, sharp rent increases, and condominium conversion as the mechanism of displacement. A more narrowly conceived measure of gentrification-induced displacement might misinterpret this phenomenon. Such a narrow measure could also lead the researcher to overlook links that often exist between new, luxury construction and apparently unrelated deterioration and outmigration of the elderly nearby. Since new construction alters property values and potential land uses in surrounding areas, a spatially limited redevelopment project may spark anticipatory disinvestment in other parts of the census tract. What appears to be segmented development, in such cases, may actually represent gentrification-induced displacement caught at an early stage.

Several analysts have recommended, or experimentally employed, the Polk data for investigation of gentrification and displacement at the census tract level (Grier and Grier 1978; Houstoun 1976; Johnson, Steggert, and Metzcus 1977). It remains—in spite of the limitations discussed above (see, also, Henig [1980])—the only existing data base that provides comprehensive, cross-city census tract level data for this important time period. With these data, the following questions can be probed. Is gentrification greater in census tracts with high percentages of retired residents? Is the inmigration of professional and technical households related to the outmigration of households headed by retired persons? Are the elderly, in fact, more likely than other urban groups to be displaced by gentrification? Is the threat of gentrification-induced displacement increasing over time?

Findings

Where do the gentry go? Table 9.1 presents simple correlations between the inmigration of professional/technical households (gentrification) and selected neighborhood attributes. The correlation coefficients measure the strength and direction of the relationships between gentrification and each of the other census tract characteristics. A positive correlation (as between gentrification and the percentage of existing households that are headed by professional/technical persons) indicates that the two variables tend to rise and fall together. A negative correlation suggests that gentrification increases and decreases in inverse relationship with the other variable. While most of the correlations presented in table 9.1 are weak, the patterns they present are informative.

During the mid-1970s, the data suggest net immigration of professional and technical households was most likely to occur in tracts exhibiting what we might call more "suburban" traits. The trends indicated in column 1, I must emphasize, are not strong, but they do suggest that the so-called gentry were, at that time, shying away from tracts with high vacancy rates and commercial activity. The negative correlations indicate that they shied away, too, from tracts with higher percentages of blue-collar and service workers, female-headed families, and blacks. These professional households, instead, opted for tracts already occupied by households with occupations as prestigious as their own.

Between the middle and late 1970s an interesting shift is evident. That shift is manifested in the decreasing strength of all but one of the correlations. Both the broad decrease and the single exception have an interest to us here. The decreasing strength of the various housing, commercial, demographic, and location variables suggests that those factors may have been becoming less relevant to professional/technical households in their housing searches. While the data do not reveal the broad and forceful reversal of mobility trends that the more vivid accounts of gentrification conjure, they are consistent with an increasing readiness of the wealthier movers to locate in tracts that, previously, they would more likely have shunned.

The positive and increasing correlation between professional inmigration and the percentage of retired, in addition, is consistent with the thesis that gentrification is more likely to occur in tracts with sizable elderly populations. This is so in spite of the fact that the distance variable shows no indication that professionals are more likely to move into close-in tracts than other areas. Tracts

Table 9.2. Percentage of Households Headed by Retired Person, by Distance from CBD, Mid-1970s and Late 1970s

	CBD Tracts (N=12)	0-1 Miles (N=148)	1-2 Miles (N=233)	2-3 Miles (N=199)	34 Miles (N=128)	4+ Miles (N=247)	All Tracts
				Distance			
Mid-1970s	33.7	31.3	26.6	26.8	25.3	20.4	25.7
Late 1970s	25.2	25.0	23.0	24.4	24.1	20.1	23.0
Difference (percentage points)	8.5	6.3	3.6	2.4	1.2	0.3	2.7

with higher proportions of retired residents are—at least in these nine cities—increasingly likely to experience gentrification. If this net inmigration of professionals, however, is absorbed by previously vacant units, by units emptied by the occupant's death, or by normal turnover, gentrification need not signal a displacement threat. The next section seeks to determine whether the inmigration of professionals statistically corresponds with the outmigration of retired households from the very same tracts.

Gentrification and displacement. Table 9.2 presents information on the spatial location of retired households as indicated by the middle and late 1970s Polk canvasses. As expected, the data show that census tracts closer to the CBD have greater percentages of households headed by a retired person. More significantly, though, there appears to have been a relative shifting of retired households away from CBD cores during the second half of the decade. The percentage of housholds headed by a retired person declined, from the middle to the late 1970s, in tracts at *all* distances from the CBD, reflecting a general net outmigration of retired households from these cities. The decline, however, is progressively sharper as one moves toward the city center.

Is the observed outward shift of retired households attributable to gentrification-induced displacement? Not necessarily. The pattern evidenced in table 9.2 could reflect, instead, a voluntary flight from abandonment and urban deterioration on the part of those retired residents with the resources and willingness to escape the central-city core. We need to assess the extent to which the inmigration of professionals that we noted in the previous section directly corresponds to the outmigration witnessed here.

Table 9.3 presents simple correlations between the yearly net change in professional/technical households, due to migration, and the change in retired households. The correlations are presented, according to the distance from the CBD, for all tracts that are gaining in professionals (gentrifying tracts). A strong positive correlation would be inconsistent with the thesis that the inmovement of professionals usually sparks an outmovement of retired households. The positive correlation, instead, would indicate that the professional and retired households were tending to move into these tracts in tandem. A negative correlation, on the other

Table 9.3. Correlations Between Annual Change in Professional/Technical Households, Due to Migration, and Annual Change in Retired Households, Due to Migration. According to Distance from CBD, Late 1970s. (Tracts With Net Increases of Professional Households)

	Pearson's r
CBD Tracts (N=5)	-.90 ⎱ -.25
0-1 Miles (N=69)	-.12 ⎰
1-2 Miles (N=105)	-.01
2-3 Miles (N=89)	-.11
3-4 Miles (N=60)	+.10
4+ Miles (N=112)	+.06
All Tracts (N=440)	-.12

hand, would be consistent with, and supportive of, the thesis that gentrification exerts pressures that result in the dislocation of retired households from their homes and neighborhoods.

The data reveal that gentrification does generally correlate with the net outmigration of retired households. This is true for all 440 tracts undergoing net inmigration of professional/technical households ($r = -.12$), but it is especially true for tracts near the CBD. In the five CBD tracts undergoing gentrification the relationship to displacement is a strong one. The small number of such tracts, of course, makes the generalizability and reliability of that coefficient ($r = -.90$) problematic. When we combine the CBD tracts with those within 1 mile of the CBD, in order to increase the size of the sample, we find the correlation equals -.25—still indicating a gentrification/displacement pattern, and still indicating that pattern to be strongest in the areas closest to the CBD.

Are the retired households any more susceptible to gentrification-induced displacement than other groups? Blue-collar and service workers, and female-headed families are also believed to be vulnerable to the pressures of gentrification (National Urban Coalition 1978; Sumka and Cicin-Sain, 1978). Table 9.4 presents the correlations between professional inmigration and the migration of retired, blue-collar/service, and female-headed households for all gentrifying tracts. Only in the case of retired households is the pattern consistent with that which we expect gentrification-induced displacement to reveal.

Table 9.4. Correlations Among Migration Trends of Various Types of Households in Tracts Undergoing Net Increases of Professional Households, Late 1970s

Annual % Change	Prof./ Tech. HHs	Retired HHs	Female- Headed HHs	Blue-collar/ Service HHs
Prof./Tech. HHS	1.00	-.12	.12	.11
Retired HHs		1.00	-.06	.14
Female-headed HHs			1.00	.03
Blue-collar/ Service HHs				1.00

N=440

Summary and Conclusions

This study has added some empirical support to the increasingly heard assertion that the elderly are currently and increasingly facing the threat of gentrification-induced displacement in our central cities. The physiological and psychological needs of the elderly make the threat of forced relocation through gentrification-induced displacement all the more worrisome in their case. Given the untested nature of the Polk data in studies of this nature, and in light of possible limitations of the measures discussed earlier, firm and dramatic conclusions are not in order. The analysis does suggest, however, that, during the second half of the 1970s, net inmigration of professional households became slightly, but perceptibly, more likely to occur in areas with traits—housing and commercial vacancies, female-headed households, CBD and near-CBD locations—that previously they sought to avoid. This gentrification was more likely to occur in census tracts with higher percentages of retired households. And, especially when it occurred in tracts in and near the cities' central cores, this gentrification was associated with a simultaneous outmigration of retired households consistent with the hypothesis that gentrification-induced displacement was taking place. It is especially important that future studies develop more precise measures—perhaps based on surveys and on-site investigation—in order to better distinguish gentrification-induced displacement from patterns of filling in and segmented development. The latter two, as noted earlier, might be mistaken for gentrification-induced displacement, given the broad, tract-level measures employed in this study.

Others have argued, eloquently, that the elderly are important resources for our neighborhoods and cities (Holman 1978). Still others have prescribed specific strategies to diffuse the impact of gentrification or to better protect or compensate those who are being displaced (Clay 1979; Gale 1978b). The public policy implications of this study come in the way of highlighting and providing more precise descriptions of the problem, rather than in pinpointing specific remedies. The trends suggested in this analysis, though, are neither so forceful nor so well advanced as to pre-empt effective intervention if the committment to take action is made.

NOTES

1. The nine cities, with their canvass dates are:

	Mid 1970s	Late 1970s
Cincinnati, OH	1974-75	1977-78
Dayton, OH	1974-75	1977-78
Louisville, KY	1974-75	1977-78
Memphis, TN	1974-75	1976-77
Milwaukee, WI	1974-75	1977-78
Minneapolis, MN	1973-74	1977-78
Oklahoma City, OK	1974-75	1977-78
Rochester, NY	1973-75	1977-78
St. Paul, MI	1973-74	1976-78

REFERENCES

Aldrich, C. K., and Mendkoff, E. 1963. Relocation of the aged and disabled: A mortality study. *Journal of the American Geriatrics Society*, 2:185-95.

Anderson, W., and Davidson, R. 1975. Concomitant physical states. In *Modern perspectives in the psychology of old age*, ed. J. G. Howell. New York: Brunner/Mazel.

Batchelor, I. R. C., and Napier, M. B. 1953. Attempted suicide in old age. *British Medical Journal*, 2:1186-90.

Besser, J. D. 1979. Gentrifying the ghetto. *The Progressive* 43:30-32.

Birren, J. E., and Shock, N. 1950. Age changes in rate and level of visual dark adaptation. *Journal of Aplied Physiology*, 2:407-411.

Blau, Z. S. 1973. *Old age in a changing society*. New York: New Viewpoints.

Bouma, P. J. 1947. Perception on the road when visibility is low. *Philips Tech. Review* 9:149-59.

Blenkner, M. 1967. Environmental change and the aging individual. *Gerontologist* 7:101-105.

Brand, F., and Smith, R. 1974. Life adjustment and the relocation of the elderly. *Journal of Gerontology* 29:336-40.

Britton, J. H. 1966. Living in a rural Pennsylvania community in old age. In *Patterns of living and housing in middle-aged and older people*, ed. F. M. Carp. USGPO, Washington, D.C.

Carp, F. M. 1976. Housing and living environments of older people. In *Aging and the social sciences*, eds. R. A. Binstock and E. Shanas. New York: Van Nostrand Reinhold.

Chadwick, T. B. 1979. Displacement: Consequences of urban revitalization for the elderly. Unpublished paper presented at the Gerontological Society meetings, No.

City of Portland. 1978. *Displacement of residents of Portland due to urban reinvestment.* Office of Planning and Development.

City of Seattle. 1979. *Seattle displacement study.* Office of Policy Planning.

Clay, P. 1979.*Neighborhood renewal.* Lexington, Mass.: Lexington Books.

Development Economics Group. 1976. *Condominiums in the District of Columbia.* Prepared for the D.C. Office of Housing and Community Development, Washington, D.C.

Exton-Smith, A. N. 1977. Clinical manifestations. In *Care of the elderly*, ed. A. N. Exton-Smith and J. G. Evans. London: Academic Press.

Gale, D. E. 1976. *The back-to-the-city movement... Or is it? A survey of recent homebuyers in the Mount Pleasant neighborhood of Washington, D.C.* Dept. of Urban and Regional Planning. George Washington Univ.

Gale, D. E. 1978a. *The back-to-the-city movement revisited: A survey of recent homebuyers in the Capitol Hill neighborhood of Washington, D.C.* Dept. of Urban and Regional Planning. George Washington Univ.

————. 1978b. Dislocation of residents. *Journal of Housing* 35:232-34.

Goodman, J. L. 1978. *Urban residential mobility: Places, people, and policy,* Washington, D.C.: Urban Institute.

Grier, G., and Grier, E. 1978. *Urban displacement: A recconnaissance.* Report prepared for the U.S. Dept. of Housing and Urban Development, Washington, D.C.

Hartman, C. 1979. Displacement: A not so new problem. *Social Policy* 9:22-27.

Henig, J. R. 1980. Gentrification and displacement within cities. *Social Science Quarterly* (December): 638-52.

Holman, M. C. 1978. Older Americans in the nation's neighborhoods: Revitalization and displacement. Testimony before the U.S. Senate Committee on Aging, Dec. 1.

Houstoun, L. O., Jr. 1976. Neighborhood change and city policy. *Urban Land* 15:3-9.

James, F. 1978. The revitalization of older urban neighborhoods: Trends, forces and the future of cities. Unpublished paper by the Special Assistant to the Assistant Secretary for Community Planning and Development, U.S. Dept. of Housing and Urban Development.

Johnson, G. T., Steggert, F., and Metzcus, R. H. *South Bend on the move.* South Bend Urban Observatory, South Bend, Ind.

Killian, E. 1970. Effects of geriatric transfers on mortality rates. *Social Work* 15:19-26.

Lawton, M. P., Kleban, M. H., and Carlson, D. A. 1971. The inner-city resident: To move or not to move. *Gerontologist* 13:443-48.

Lieberman, M. 1969. Relationship of mortality rates to entrance to a home for the aged. *Geriatrics* 16:515-19.

Lipton, G. 1977. Evidence of central city revival. *Journal of the American Institute of Planners* 43:136-47.

Lowenthal, M. 1964. *Lives in distress*. New York: Basic Books.

Lycan, R., Pendleton, P., and Weiss, J. 1978. *Residential mobility study for Portland*. City of Portland, Office of Planning and Development.

Markus, E., Blenkner, M., Bloom, M., and Downs, T. 1972. Some factors and their association with post-relocation mortality among institutionalized persons. *Journal of Gerontology* 27:376-82.

Melrose, J., Welsh, O., and Lauterman, D. 1963. Auditory responses in selected elderly men. *Journal of Gerontology* 8:267-70.

National Urban Coalition. 1978. *Displacement: City neighborhood in transition* Washington, D.C.

Nelson, K. P. 1978. Movement of blacks and whites between central cities and suburbs in metropolitan areas, 1955-1975. Annual housing survey working papers, Report no. 2. Office of Economic Affairs.

New York Times Magazine. 1979. The new elite and an urban renaissance, by Blake Fleetwood, 14 January.

Schulz, R., and Brenner, G. 1977. Relocation of the aged: A review and theoretical analysis. *Journal of Gernotology*, 32:323-33.

Siegel, J. S. 1975. Some demographic aspects of aging in the United States. In *Epidemiology of aging*, ed. A. M. Ostfeld and D. C. Gibson. Washington, D.C.: U.S. Dept. of Housing and Urban Development.

Struyk, R. 1977. The housing expense burden of households headed by the elderly. *Gerontology* 17:447-52.

Sumka, H. J., and Cicin-Sain, B. 1978. Displacement in revitalizing neighborhoods: A review and research strategy. Office of Policy Development and Research, U.S. Dept. of Housing and Urban Development. Washington, D.C.

Terry, R. 1978. Physical changes of the aging brain. In *The biology of aging*, ed. J. A. Behnke, C. E. Finch, and G. B. Moment. New York: Plenum Press.

U.S. Dept. of Housing and Urban Development. 1979. *Displacement report*. Office of Policy Development and Research.

Winiecke, L. 1973. The appeal of age-segregated housing to the elderly poor. *Aging and Human Development* 4:293-306.

Yawney, B. A., and Slover, D. L. 1973. Relocation of the elderly. *Social Work* 18:86-95.

Zeitz, E. 1979. *Private urban renewal*. Lexington, Mass.: Lexington Books.

III

Comparative Cross-National Patterns

INTRODUCTION

It is commonly observed that the work of social scientists in the United States tends to be ethnocentric. We study phenomena that occur within the borders of our own nation while giving far less attention to analyses of similar phenomena in other nations. The result can be findings that are culture-specific and not generalizable.

In this section, we seek to overcome this ethnocentricity by including three papers that describe the processes of revitalization and gentrification in other nations. Canadian patterns, in Vancouver, are discussed by Ley in chapter 10. Patterns in Great Britain and in Europe are analyzed by Williams in chapter 11 and, in chapter 12, Kendig gives us some insight into patterns of gentrification in Australia.

Although these authors do specify the relevance of certain factors unique to each society, the overall impression derived from a reading of these cross-national studies is one of remarkable similarity in the demographic, ecological, sociocultural, and political economic processes attending revitalization and gentrification, regardless of whether the process is occuring in the United States or in any of the other industrialized nations considered. All the nations reviewed appear to be undergoing analogous patterns. The exact form, however, is strongly influenced by varying government policies related to housing.

CHAPTER TEN

Inner-City Revitalization in Canada: A Vancouver Case Study

DAVID LEY

While the inner-city question provided a major emphasis of American and British research and public policy during the 1970s, it has received relatively little attention in Canada, either from government or from the research community.

In this paper three related questions will be addressed concerning revitalization processes in the Canadian inner city. First, using national data from the 1976 census, general population patterns in the inner city will be assessed. Second, narrowing the focus to the Vancouver housing market, the contexts of inner-area revitalization will be considered. Third, the effects of revitalization will be examined, with particular reference to the demolition or conversion of modestly priced housing and the attendant displacement of existing residents in the Kitsilano neighborhood in Vancouver's inner city. Responses to change, both from neighborhood groups and from different levels of government, will be discussed in the context of the development of public policy.

David Ley is Associate Professor of Geography, University of British Columbia. Reprinted by permission, with changes, from *The Canadian Geographer*, Vol. 25, No. 2, 1981: 124-48.

The research for this paper was supported by a grant form the Social Sciences and Humanities Research Council. I am grateful to Ann McAfee, John Mercer, and Roman Cybriwsky for their comments on an earlier draft.

POPULATION CHANGE IN THE CANADIAN INNER CITY

Knowledge of the Canadian inner city is limited, in part no doubt because it has proven much less problematic to national administrations than have inner-city areas in the United States or Britain. To counter the exaggerated notion of a generic North American city, some of the dissimilarities between Canadian and American metropolitan areas have recently been clarified.[1] Such distinctiveness holds particularly for the inner city for, as McCann has indicated in Edmonton, the stage of widespread blight and partial abandonment included in American models of neighborhood change is far less typical of Canadian inner areas.[2] In contrast, the Canadian inner city has, in general, been characterized by continuous phases of redevelopment with each phase leading to a more intensive land use type. A national inner-city study based on the 1971 census identified neighborhoods in decline as only one variant in a fourfold typology: even then the revitalized neighborhood was recognized as a second major inner-city type.[3] It is possible, therefore, to interpret the redevelopment activity of the 1970s as simply a continuation of earlier trends rather than, as has more usually been the case in the United States, a dramatic arresting and reversal of neighborhood blight. This diagnosis may explain the more limited interest in inner-city change in Canada, though it is only partly correct; the population being rehoused by current redevelopment and conversion is not the same as the households that benefited from the redevelopment of the 1950s and 1960s.

Because of the paucity of comparative data, a full monitoring of inner-city change is not possible for the period since the 1971 census was taken. Despite its limitations, however, the partial census in 1976 does present useful data, including certain demographic, tenure, and educational traits. Inner-city data from the 1976 census have been compiled by Canadian Mortgage and Housing Corporation for the 23 Census Metropolitan Areas (CMAs) existing in both 1971 and 1976.[4] This source is not without its difficulties; the inner city in each CMA was defined primarily, but not exclusively, by the period of housing construction. This criterion has led to unevenness in the size of the inner city; over the range of CMAs, the inner city accounts for 29 percent of all households in Montreal to 9 percent in Victoria (table 10.1). However, this unevenness is not too troublesome since half the CMAs fall within five percentage points of the mean and, more importantly, because it is the relative changes between 1971 and 1976 that are of major interest; absolute values are not the only ones to be discussed.

Table 10.1. Characteristics of Canadian Inner Cities, 1971-76

	Percentage inner-city population change, 1971-76	Percentage inner-city household change, 1971-76	Percentage of CMA households in inner-city, 1976	Percentage inner-city population with some university education, 1976	Absolute gain in percentage of inner-city population with some university education, 1971-76
St John's	-23	- 9	10	11	4.2
Halifax	-12	+ 6	29	21	7.3
Saint John	-20	- 5	31	9	2.7
Quebec City	-14	- 5	30	14	6.4
Montreal	-12	+ 2	46	15	6.3
Hull	-18	- 2	28	12	5.7
Ottawa	-13	+ 3	26	25	10.6
Oshawa	- 6	+ 4	25	6	2.3
Toronto	-11	+ 1	23	17	5.6
Hamilton	-12	+ 4	18	11	4.3
St Catherines	-11	+ 2	23	10	3.7
Kitchener	-12	0	17	12	5.5
London	-16	- 2	13	12	4.6
Windsor	-13	0	29	11	4.0
Sudbury	-16	- 1	31	10	3.0
Thunder Bay	- 8	+ 2	34	12	4.3
Winnipeg	-14	- 6	16	12	5.2
Regina	-14	- 2	23	14	3.9
Saskatoon	- 7	+ 3	29	23	6.8
Calgary	-10	+ 4	31	20	6.5
Edmonton	- 6	+ 9	24	21	7.5
Vancouver	- 6	+ 4	29	21	7.2
Victoria	- 3	+10	9	16	7.0
All CMA	-11	+ 2	29	16	6.2

SOURCE: Developed from data in P. Brown and D. Burke, The Canadian Inner City 1971-1976: A Statistical Handbook (Ottawa: Canada Mortgage and Housing Corporation, 1979).

The national data show that considerable shifts took place in the composition of the Canadian inner city between 1971 and 1976 (table 10.1). Significant population loss occurred for so short a period, ranging from 23 percent in St. John's to 3 percent in Victoria, with a national mean change of -11 percent. Moreover, taking educational attainment as a surrogate for socioeconomic status, there was also a *relative* decline in the share of high-status individuals resident in the inner city, for the proportion of college-educated persons in the population grew, on average, more rapidly in CMAs as a whole than in their inner-city districts.[5] Both the population loss and the relative decrease in high-status occupancy would suggest some erosion of the Canadian inner city through the early 1970s. But this conclusion must be challenged in light of further data. Though population loss occurred, the number of *households* increased by more than 2 percent. Again this average conceals a marked variation (from –9 percent in St. John's to +10 percent in Victoria), but the general implication of these trends is that household size in the inner city is shrinking; that is, families with children are being replaced by a larger number of smaller household units. Second, the apparent loss of more-highly educated residents was relative only to the more rapid increase in the suburbs. The inner city in 1976 continued to contain an above-average per capita share of residents with some higher education; in this respect there continues to be a marked contrast between the status of the average inner-city district in Canada and that in the United States. Moreover, although inner-city socioeconomic status declined in *relative* terms, there was an *absolute* increase in better-educated residents in the inner-city areas of all 23 CMAs, from 9.9 percent with some university education in 1971 to 16.1 percent in 1976. In some cities this increase was substantial: nearly 25,000 in Toronto and nearly 20,000 in Vancouver, while in the generously defined inner city of Montreal the gain was almost 60,000 persons. As a result, by 1976 there were six CMAs where more than one-fifth of the inner-city population had received some university education; in each instance this was a substantially higher proportion than the value for the whole CMA.

Looking at the characteristics within each column of table 10.1 in more detail, we see that broad differences exist in the inner-city profiles of the separate CMAs, making it impossible to posit a nationwide trend. Nevertheless, certain groupings are evident. Cities that fall in the top quartile in the fourth and fifth columns include Ottawa, Halifax, Edmonton, Vancouver, Saskatoon, and Calgary; CMAs falling into the bottom quartile include Oshawa, Saint John, St Catharines, Sudbury, Windsor and St John's. The distinction is one between the service-oriented, white-collar, regional centers, particularly those in the western provinces, and the blue-collar, manufacturing cities of Ontario and the Atlantic provinces. These distinctions already existed in 1971, but they had become sharper by 1976. The aggregate evidence suggests that inner-city revitalization is likely to be far more a feature of the first set of cities than the second, an expectation consistent with Lipton's analysis of American SMSAs, which revealed high positive correlations between high-status, inner-city neighborhoods and the presence of downtown white-collar employment, but negative correlations against blue-collar, manufacturing centers.[6] The contrast may be developed further, since the white-collar cities also show tendencies (though these are flawed by several exceptions) to more rapid population growth, higher house prices, and a lower level of rental vacancies. Thus, it is possible to relate the geography of inner-city change to broader shifts in the national economy and society.[7]

From this outline of national trends, I turn now to a more detailed examination of the inner-city housing market in Vancouver, identified by the aggregate data as one of the group of cities characterized by inner-area revitalization.

THE CONTEXTS OF INNER-CITY REVITALIZATION IN VANCOUVER

Mirroring changes in the national economy, the British Columbia employment mix has shifted toward tertiary and quaternary occupations during the 1970s. From 55 percent of provincial occupations in 1971, they rose rapidly to 64 percent by mid-1978, with quaternary activities showing the most marked relative gains.[8] The industrial classification also showed that from 1971 to 1976 the sectors of public administration, finance, the several forms of services, construction, and trade were in excess of the British Columbia job-creation level of 20 percent; the categories of transportation, manufacturing, mining, and forestry fell behind the provincial average.[9]

The city of Vancouver is overrepresented in the fast growing tertiary and quaternary occupations with 70 percent of its work force in white-collar jobs in 1971. The city added 7,000 new jobs each year from 1971 to 1980, with perhaps 75 percent of these generated by new office construction.[10] This trend affected particularly the downtown area, which contains almost three-quarters of the city's office capacity and has undergone a development boom with a doubling of its office space in the past decade. Thus, it is possible to follow the transmission of large-scale adjustments in the economy to the pattern of job creation in Vancouver, with trends favoring white-collar job growth in the central business district. These contextual factors lie behind demographic changes in the metropolitan area and the housing demand pressures that accompanied them.

Housing Demand

Rapid growth has been associated with Vancouver's status as a white-collar, service-oriented city, as the metropolitan population increased by 13 percent, 21 percent, and 8 percent in the successive five-year periods between 1961 and 1976. Within the city itself, inmigration was highly biased. Sixty percent of net inmigrants fell into the 20-24 age cohort between 1966 and 1971, while half the net outmigration consisted of children under 5 years of age.[11] These trends have been maintained into the 1970s, with the continued loss of young children, and a net gain of 9,000-10,000 adults in the 25-34 age group up to 1976.[12] Two implications follow from the somewhat older age of adults in this rapidly gaining population cohort in the 1970s. First, as this group is of child-rearing age, and yet the younger age cohorts in the city continue to decline, it is probable that the new adult households are primarily childless. Vancouver's households are certainly becoming smaller, for while the city's population was at approximately the same level in 1976 as in 1966, there had been a gain of 5 percent in the number of households. Such shifts in household size and composition have a clear impact on the nature of housing demand.

Second, since 1971 there seems to have been a significant increase in the purchasing power of the city's residents. A decrease in child-raising costs, the greater probability of two wage-earners in the household, and the growth of high-income quaternary jobs together contribute to greater discretionary income. Almost a quarter of Vancouver households earned more than $20,000 in 1976; in constant dollars this represented a gain of over 12,000 households in this privileged category over 1972.[13] In addition, white-collar city residents have higher levels of job security. In 1977, when unemployment in British Columbia reached 9.5 percent, only 4.6 percent of quaternary jobs were affected, and 8.6 percent of workers in the tertiary sector. The combination of high household incomes and greater job security identifies a group of consumers with notable market power.

These households have been drawn in significant numbers toward the inner-city housing market. Their small family size made large suburban lots unneccessary, and the tendency toward two wage-earners in a household allowed less free time to be spent on home maintenance.[14] In addition, downtown commuting from Vancouver's suburbs is difficult, with congested bridge crossings from the north and south, and neither a freeway nor a rapid transit system within the city itself.[15] The inner city, meanwhile, has substantial attractions of its own, with access to the city's major parks, beaches, and marinas, as well as the lively cultural and retail activity of the downtown area. The neighborhoods themselves include a measure of lifestyle, ethnic, and architectural diversity, valued attributes of middle-class movers to central city. As we shall see, these desiderata of the culture of consumption should not be underestimated in interpreting the revitalization of the inner city.[16]

Housing Supply

The changing economic, demographic, and cultural orientation of the Vancouver population placed a premium on inner-city accommodation, and the rental vacancy rate in Vancouver has consistently fallen beneath that of the suburban municipalities, leading through most of the 1970s to a severe apartment shortage. From 1973 to 1976 the vacancy rate scarcely reached 0.5 percent, and pressure was even more acute in parts of the inner city, where official rates in several desirable neighborhoods stood at zero for much of 1974, 1975, and 1976.[17]

In such a market, a rapid response by the property industry to supply a new round of high-rise rental units might have been expected. But institutional and popular constraints precluded this option. Public opposition to high-rise construction was a common feature of Canadian inner-city neighborhoods after 1970, and in Vancouver, the first widespread inner-city down zoning occurred in 1974, to be quickly followed by similar by-laws in other inner areas. Rental tenure, the norm in the 1960s, was also modified as a result of government constraints and market opportunities. Federal tax revisions in 1972 removed a tax shelter that had made rental structures an attractive investment for small and moderate investors, and, responding to the rapid increase of rents, the provincial government introduced a rent freeze in 1974. Despite some exemptions that were intended to encourage new rental construction, the freeze depressed initiatives for building rental apartments.[18] The rental market enjoyed a short-lived boost between 1976 and 1978 under the initiatives of the federally funded Assisted Rental Programme, but the termination of ARP renewed the sense of crisis, and during 1979-80 the rental vacancy rate fell to 0.1-0.2 percent, representing fewer than 150 available apartment units over the entire city of Vancouver.

Acceptable returns could be guaranteed more easily and quickly through the construction of condominiums. The new middle-class housing consumer in the inner city was a logical client for ownership rather than tenancy. The condominum offered equity to the purchaser, provided a more complete range of amenities, required less upkeep, and allowed a more controlled living environment than rental apartments, for fellow owners would be more committed than tenants to social order and building maintenance. The development emphasis on condominiums within the city was revealed in the enumeration of nearly 8,000 self-owned apartments in the 1976 census. More conservative records of strata-title condominiums identify the registration of over 7,300 units up to mid-1978.[19] A profile of condominium households in Greater

Vancouver and Victoria in 1977 showed that 70 percent of households contained no children, that household heads in half of them were aged under 40 years, that a quarter of households earned over $24,000, and that the dominant employment categories fell in professional and managerial occupations.[20] These tendencies would have been accentuated in the high-priced units in the inner city, where, significantly, both purchasers and developers perceived location to be the single most important consideration in residential choice.[21]

Housing Demolition and Population Displacement

Since the passing of a city by-law in 1973, the conversion of rental units to condominiums has not been allowed except under extraordinary circumstances. Nonetheless, various forms of upgrading of rental properties have continued, removing over 1,000 units annually from the low-rental market in Vancouver. More conspicuous in the loss of low-cost housing has been the pattern of demolition. From 1973 to 1976, 4,400 residential units were demolished in Vancouver; at least 65 percent were rental units.[22] During the later part of 1975 and 1976, 85 percent of rental demolitions were located in six inner-city neighborhoods, particularly those on the west side where condominium development was concentrated. Assuming a constant level of attrition in 1973 and 1974, the inner-city districts lost over 2,400 rental units through demolition over the four-year period.

At least 90 percent of demolished units were estimated by the city planning department to be in reasonable structural repair. But, despite their generally sound quality, they were not competitive with self-owned condominums; in an inflating land market, the dogma of the highest and best use prescribed their removal. Whereas the apartment redevelopment of the 1960s had not seriously altered the status of the inner city in providing a stock of low- and moderate-income housing, condominium redevelopment involved the displacement of the existing population. In 1971, inner-city incomes and inner-city rents remained below the city mean, so that housing and population were not seriously mismatched, but by the mid-1970s it was estimated that the cost of a condominium required an income 25 to 50 percent *above* the city mean.[23] The construction of 6,000 condominiums in the inner city up to July 1978 has therefore involved a serious erosion of low-cost housing opportunities in the zone that has traditionally provided shelter for poorer households. In inner Vancouver, as elsewhere, the displacement of affordable housing is the invariable consequence of the revitalization process.[24]

In the inner-city neighborhood, Kitsilano, demolition was concentrated in the apartment-zoned district; almost 1,000 dwelling units were removed from 1968 to 1976, while at least another 270 units were converted from rental to condominium tenure. Up to 1978, replacement housing included over 1,500 expensive strata-title units. Since little is known of the relocation experience of tenants removed by inner-city revitalization, an attempt was made to interview a group of displaced tenants in Kitsilano.[25] Many households were difficult to trace through conventional means, and it is likely that a number disappeared as discrete units, either through doubling-up, as a result of leaving the region altogether, or, in the case of some of the elderly, through entering some form of institutional care. In the end, 36 households were found; they had been evicted from converted units 6 to 12 months earlier, in advance of the construction of 3 condominium projects during 1974-75.

Table 10.2. The Transition of Commercial Functions, Fourth Avenue, Kitsilano, 1966-76

	Total	New[a]	Surviving from 1966	Surviving from 1971
1966	242	150	54	38
1971	232	110	122	
1966	223			

SOURCE: City directories, 1966, 1971, and 1976.
[a]New functions were those opened within the previous five years.

The tenants included a high proportion of young, white-collar employees in low-paying jobs, with a median income of only $3,500 to $4,500. Thirty percent were married, while the remainder were single (47 percent), single parents, or living common-law. More than 40 percent had lived in their residence for more than 2 years. One-third of displaced households resettled within Kitsilano; of those who moved away, two-thirds expressed a continuing preference for Kitsilano but had been forced to move by the lack of affordable housing. Most of the few respondents who preferred their new location had also become homeowners, and their perception was no doubt colored by their new tenure status. Overall, the residential satisfaction of households declined as a result of the move; more than four out of five tenants preferred their former home. New units were generally smaller but also more expensive, even though they were in a poorer location. Over half the tenants experienced rent increases of more than 60 percent. Relocation also brought about a significant deterioration in the rent-to-income ratio of tenants. Whereas the modal category of the ratio had been less than 15 percent in Kitsilano, it rose after displacement to 50-70 percent. Given that the proportion of income allocated to rent should not exceed 30 percent, the demolition of their converted dwellings thrust a significant number of the tenants into the growing ranks of Vancouver households with a housing problem.

While the most severe impact of the revitalization process in Kitsilano has been the attrition of the stock of low- and middle-income housing, other aspects of community infrastructure have also been eroded. The replacement of family housing by adult-only condominiums has been associated with a serious decline in school enrollment. After stable enrollment levels since the 1920s, the numer of pupils at Kitsilano elementary schools dropped by 40 percent from 1967 to 1975. Other manifestations of community stability have disappeared. Two ratepayers' associations with long histories have been terminated, a workingman's hall has been converted into an experimental theatre, and a Pentecostal church and union building have been demolished to be replaced by stores and a private medical-dental building. The transformation of the residential area has also been accompanied by the embourgeoise-ment of Fourth Avenue, one of Kitilano's two major commercial streets. The number of stores, offices, and services along Fourth Avenue increased relatively little between 1966 and 1976 (table 10.2). But concealed within this overall stability is a process of rapid adjustment to the changing environment. Fewer than a quarter of stores exisiting in 1966 survived at the same location in 1976. Retail turnover was equally rapid among stores opened between 1967 and 1971, only 35 percent of them surviving to 1976. As a result, over 60 percent of Fourth Avenue's commercial functions in 1976 had been newly established in the preceding five years. Retail turnover is closely associated with the market power and consumption tastes of middle-class newcomers. Fourth Avenue had been making a comeback as a recreation and shopping area for the upwardly mobile condominium set. Trendy restaurants, clothes shops, and other specialty stores are springing up like mushrooms after a spring rain.[26] The invasion-succession process has transformed not only the Kitsilano housing market, but also neighborhood voluntary associations and the retail sector. The entire fabric of community life has undergone transition.

Neighborhood Opposition to the Transition Process

Some Kitsilano residents, notably small landowners and some homeowners, benefited from neighborhood resurgence. But, as the survey data revealed, a majority of both owners and tenants was skeptical or openly antagonistic toward redevelopment and its consequences. The high level of neighborhood satisfaction was associated with the recreational amenities of the beach and parks, ocean views, low- to moderate-density housing, the congenial nature of neighborhood people, and, for property owners, the residential stability and commitment implied by ownership. Change was a negation of their image of Kitsilano.

Community opposition to transition processes was formalized in response to a proposal to redevelop the commercial thoroughfare of West Broadway, in 1972. A developer's proposal, which entailed the demolition of some houses to provide additional parking space, was vigorously resisted by threatened homeowners who joined together to form the West Broadway Citizen's Committee. After a successful resolution to that issue, WBCC became a permanent community association, opposed to the demolition and redevelopment of Kitsilano's housing stock. Over the period from 1972 to 1975, WBCC became perhaps Vancouver's most energetic community group, resisting redevelopment pressures and urging a policy of neighborhood preservation with local control of development. It secured a downzoning that precluded additional high-rise development and was successful in neighborhood elections for the Kitsilano Community Resource Board, a provincial program for the decentralized administration of social services. WBCC also had informal links with the New Democratic Party government of British Columbia, from which it received operating funds in 1974. Although caricatured by reporters as radical and unruly, until it pursued the issue of tenant rights WBBC maintained a broad base of local support, including both tenants and owners of varied ages. Then, in 1975, through a subsidiary group, the Kitsilano Housing Society, the group purchased and rehabilitated a rental structure threatened by demolition. A second rental structure was purchased and renovated in 1977, with additional infill units featuring an innovative use of solar panels. The purchases were secured through loans from WBCC members and were supported by Canada Mortgage and Housing Corporation.[27]

This ambitious attempt to preserve affordable rental housing through purchase and construction followed a failure to check demolition. A reform city council had been elected in 1972 with a commitment to citizen participation in planning, and Kitsilano was the first neighborhood outside the downtown peninsula to be selected for a Local Area Planning Programme.[28] Little real decentralization of decision-making resulted, however. Upon the initiative of WBCC, the local planning committee several times requested city council to introduce a moratorium on housing demolition and on development permits for condominiums. These submissions were repeatedly rejected by council and WBCC withdrew from the committee in protest. Local area planning in Kitsilano therefore did little to arrest the redevelopment cycle and the attrition of affordable housing, aside from the acquisition of two sites using grants from the government of Canada.[29] Other monies from the Neighborhood Improvement Programme were channelled through the local area planning committee and permitted some expenditure on day-care services and recreational facilities. But far more significant was the independent effect of the Federal government's Residential Rehabilitation Assistance Programme. Kitsilano residents responded enthusiastically to the offer of loans and grants for home maintenance, and, by the end of 1979, more than 1,000 Kitsilano homeowners and landlords had applied for RRAP support. More than 2,000 units had been rehabilitated and the neighborhood had received over $8 million in goverment aid.[30] Each of these figures represents substantially more than half the net impact of RRAP in Vancouver, confirming the strong commitment to neighborhood maintenance and preservation expressed in the 1974 surveys.

CONCLUSION:
REVITALIZATION AND THE HOUSING PROBLEM

In many respects Kitsilano epitomizes the resurgent inner-city neighborhood. A favoured location with an aging population and older, though sound, housing stock invited redevelopment. Its initial lower-middle-class status and associated housing values made Kitsilano an attractive setting for property assembly and land speculation by absentee owners. In 1974, WBCC documented fifteen cases of land assembly, involving at least five contiguous parcels, by individuals and companies of various sizes in and around the apartment district.[31] A spatial concentration of speculative absentee owenership inflated the local land market and introduced instability to the housing stock, inviting all the consequences of a transfer from use value to exchange value in the perception of neighborhood housing. This activity by property interests in the inner city was stimulated by Vancouver's emerging status as a postindustrial city, with its privileged and growing white-collar labor force disproportionately employed in the downtown office district and exercising its market power in the inner city. That Kitsilano was one of the inner-city neighborhoods to which resurgence was selectively channelled was owing to its recreational and leisure opportunities and an attractive community ambience, including diversity and vitality. However, besides these local and regional factors, national and even international forces contributed to high levels of investment in Vancouver's core and inner-city districts. Large flows of foreign and domestic capital moved into Vancouver from Hong Kong, Europe, and central Canada from a variety of sources, including conglomerates, development and insurance companies, pension funds, and speculative interests.[32] The net effect was a psychology of over-investment leading to the typical cycle of rapidly rising values, over-building, and high vacancies in both office and condominium space by 1977. A high-rise condominium, opposed by WBCC and leading to the eviction of ninety Kitsilano tenants, encountered marketing difficulties and had failed to sell a number of suites three years after completion. It was not until the suspension of ARP that the excess condominium capacity was absorbed.

The varied contexts of the development pressures acting upon Kitsilano made neighborhood response problematic. Too often, problems and solutions were defined because they were accessible rather than because they were critical. A major objective of WBCC and (as the survey showed) the community at large was neighborhood downzoning to terminate high-rise redevelopment. This objective was secured, but it did not check the transition process because expensive high-rise units were merely succeeded by expensive low-rise and townhouse units. Indeed, any reduction of densities through rezoning *added* to neighborhood desirability and housing prices; the first Kitsilano condominiums priced at above $100,000 were town-houses, not high-rise units. The use of city by-laws proved an accessible but ineffective antidote to redevelopment. So, too, by-law amendment on demolition controls, with a moratorium on condominium construction, were advocated by WBCC and the local planning committee, but rejected by city council as a poor solution to the housing problem, as they neither diverted redevelopment pressures nor promoted the upkeep of redeemed units. "These pressures," the Planning Department noted, "are largely outside the City's Charter authority."[33] The city's role in managing the pressures generated by private redevelopment has been constrained by its modest resources, so that it has more often acted as a regulator than a director of change. New by-laws have challenged property deterioration in absentee-owned housing, but new housing initiatives have been limited to ever-diminishing sites held by the city and eligible for grants from senior governments.[34]

As a result of the city's limited resources for creating new housing, Kitsilano's local area plan has had little impact on the neighborhood's housing problems. Indeed, successful initiatives by community residents were invariably associated with agreements with higher and more powerful levels of goverment. WBCC's early history was aided by the sympathetic New Democratic Party, which then controlled the provincial housing ministry; its later successes were linked to an improving relationship with the national housing agency, CMHC.[35] From 1973 to 1978, senior governments played a more active role in the Vancouver housing market in stimulating new construction. Over these years the proportion of market units fluctuated between 32 percent and 77 percent of all housing completions[36] The median figure of almost 60 percent indicated an active public presence in the housing market, a contribution incorporating a range of nonmarket and assisted market programs. In addition, rehabilitation funds for housing and neighborhood improvement had some effect in checking redevelopment pressures in the inner-city, particularly in Kitsilano.[37] The overall impact of the state, though, was less significant than it might appear. First, moderately priced units were not necessarily constructed in the neighborhoods where they were most needed; despite its low vacancy rate and high level of demolitions, Kitsilano received the fewest new government-assisted units of any of Vancouver's inner-city districts between 1976 and 1978. Second, assisted units did not necessarily serve households with the greatest need. In 1977, over 70 percent of the city's assisted units were affordable only to households earning more than $12,000; a majority of tenants had incomes below that figure.[38] Finally, the amount of new housing in the city fell far short of demand; in 1977, completions of all forms of government-assisted housing met only 2 percent of the estimated need.[39] Economies initiated in 1979 (including the termination of Assisted Rental Programme) make it unlikely that this shortfall will be remedied.

The consequence has been a severe shortage of housing for lower-income households. The housing crisis in Vancouver is defined not by overcrowding or by quality but by affordability; a quarter of the city's households in 1978 were exceeding the desired 30 percent to 35 percent of the total income in their expenditures on housing.[40] These households include the elderly, single parents, the handicapped, and the underemployed. Their numbers are expanding with every inner-city demolition in anticipation of condominium construction; in the Kitsilano displacement survey, 24 percent of tenants evicted from their units were added to the ranks of households with problems of housing affordability as a direct result of dislocation. Almost one-half of interviewees had rent-income ratios of over *50 percent* following displacement; preceding evicition only 12 percent had comparable affordability problems. While the City Planning Department has amassed an impressive inventory of strategies to meet the housing crisis, including innovative housing and shelter allowances, these plans rest upon a significant fiscal commitment from senior government, equivalent to an additional $23 million, or $200 per annum transferred from each Vancouver household with adequate shelter. The present politics of consumption in Canada make such a transfer of resources extremely unlikely. Indeed, in an era of social and political conservatism, transfer payments are more likely to favor the middle class; for example, if the government of Canada's promise of mortgage tax credit legislation had been carried out, in 1979, it would have directed more than $2 billion in housing subsidies to middle-class homeowners by 1983. In this manner the inequity of the marketplace might be reinforced in the short term by government action. Certainly, Canadian urban policy has been less attentive to the problems of displacement in the inner city than has been the case in the United States.

Inasmuch as overinvestment and the inflationary spiral in the inner city have causes outside the housing market, they might also be addressed by policy intervention in other areas. The steep land-value gradient that exercises such control over the inner-city housing market might be eroded, either through the decentralization of quaternary activites from the downtown core or through the development of a rapid transit system to aid long-range commuting. Without such substantial public intervention, income and housing inequities in the postindustrial city are likely to continue to sharpen. The market, which has failed the disadvantaged in the industrial inner city through underinvestment, is penalizing the same group in the postindustrial city through overinvestment. For, as Weiler has observed, the problem of reinvestment displacement is a problem of the spatial over-concentration of both demand and capital.[41]

Present social, economic, and political trends are redefining the morphology inherited from the industrial city. In Vancouver, there is evidence that the income gap between the central city and its suburban municipalities is narrowing rapidly. Whereas in 1972 there was a 13 percent differential in mean income between Vancouver and its suburbs, by 1976 the city's deficit had narrowed to 4 percent.[42] Housing demand during the 1970s has been consistently higher in the city than its suburbs, as indicated both by vacancy levels and by trends in house and rental prices. These developments are associated with the changing employment structure of the postindustrial city, with a concentration of the growth sectors of quaternary and tertiary employment in the downtown core, while blue-collar employment is dispersing to the suburbs.[53] By 1971, three of Vancouver's six inner-city planning districts already claimed 78 percent to 90 percent of their work force in white-collar categories. With the revitalization process of the past decade, sections of the postindustrial inner city have begun a transformation from the home of the laboring classes toward a zone of privilege reminiscent of the innermost residential ring in Sjoberg's model of the preindustrial city. If present trends accelerate, the social geography of the nineteenth-century industrial city may even appear to urban scholars of the future as a temporary interlude to a more historically persistent pattern of higher-status segregation adjacent to the downtown core.

NOTES

1. J. Mercer. "On continentalism, distinctiveness, and comparative urban geography: Canadian and American cities." *The Canadian Geographer,* 23(1979):119-39.

2. L. D. McCann. *Neighborhoods in Transition* (Edmonton: University of Alberta, Department of Geography, Occasional Papers No. 2, 1975).

3. R. McLemore, C. Aass, and P. Keilhofer. *The Changing Canadian Inner City* (Ottawa: Ministry of State for Urban Affairs, 1975).

4. P. Brown and D. Burke. *The Canadian Inner City 1971-1976: A Statistical Handbook* (Ottawa: Canada Mortgage and Housing Corporation, 1979).

5. Education is an acceptable surrogate for socioeconomic status, particularly in an assessment of inner-city population change, for the educational attainment of residents is a particularly sensitive indicator of areas undergoing revitalization. See, for example, D. E. Gale, "Middle class resettlement in older urban neighborhoods," *Journal of the American Planning Association* 45 (1979): 293-304.

6. S. G. Lipton, "Evidence of central city revival," *Journal of the American Institute of Planners* 43 (1977): 136-47.

7. D. F. Ley, "Inner city resurgence in its societal context." Paper presented to the Association of American Geographers, New Orleans, 1978; idem. "Liberal ideology and the postindustrial city." *Annals of the Association of American Geographers,* 70 (1980): 238-58.

8. Statistics Canada, *The Labour Force* 34, no. 6 (1978). But note that nearly 10 percent of the labor force of British Columbia was unclassified in the 1971 Census. In Canada as a whole (bearing in mind the unclassified proviso) white-collar occupations rose from 54 percent to 62 percent of the labor force from 1971 to 1978.

9. Statistics Canada, *Estimates of Employees by Province and Industry, 1961-1976,* catalogue 72-516 (1978).

10. Vancouver City Planning Department, *Quarterly Review,* 7 (July 1980); 18; idem, *Employment Growth in Vancouver* (1975).

11. Vancouver City Planning Department, *Understanding Vancouver* (1977). For a discussion of similar trends in Toronto, see J. W. Simmons, "Net migration patterns," in L. S. Bourne, R. D. MacKinnon, and J. W. Simmons (eds.), *The Form of Cities in Central Canada* (Toronto: University of Toronto Press, 1973), pp. 138-48.

12. Vancouver City Planning Department, *Quarterly Review* 5 (April 1978): 16.

13. Vancouver City Planning Department, *Quarterly Review* 4 (October 1977): 19. The increase represented a growth of 50 percent over the four-year period.

14. The desire to spend less time on upkeep and maintenance was the major factor motivating former homeowners to purchase a condominium: S.W. Hamilton (ed.) *Condominiums: A Decade of Experience in B.C.* (Vancouver: British Columbia Real Estate Association, 1978), p. 87.

15. M. A. Goldberg, "Housing and land prices in Canada and the U.S.," in L. Smith and M. Walker (eds.), *Public Property? The Habitat Debate Continued* (Vancouver: Fraser Institute, 1977), pp. 207-54.

16. D. F. Ley and J. Mercer, "Locational conflict and the politics of consumption," *Economic Geography* 56 (1980): 89-109.

17. Real Estate Board of Greater Vancouver, *Real Estate Trends in Greater Vancouver* (Vancouver: 1977).

18. In 1975 one of Vancouver's leading property companies estimated that even an immediate rental increase of 50 percent would give only a 3 percent return on investment: *Block Brothers Annual Report* (Vancouver: 1975).

19. There are some differences in detail in the definition of condominium, strata-title unit, and self-owned apartment. The most general and widely used term in North America is condominium, which implies coownership, in civil law. A strata-title unit is a more precise legal definition embodied in the British Columbia Strata Titles Act, which may involve common ownership in horizontally or vertically stratified units in a single physical structure. Thus, strata-title plans may include row housing. They do not, however, include a smaller category of cooperative condominiums which have a separate legal identity. Self-owned apartments, as defined in the census, would appear to included both types of apartment condominiums, but to exclude row housing. In general, during the period covered in the analysis, there is substantial overlap between condominiums, strata-title units, and self-owned apartments.

20. Hamilton, op. cit.

21. A premium on location was also expressed by home purchasers in inner Toronto. W. Michelson, *Environmental Choice, Human Behavior, and Residential Satisfaction* (New York, Oxford University Press, 1977).

22. Vancouver City Planning Department, *Demolition Report* (Vancouver: 1977), Appendix I.

23. P. W. Stobie, "Private Inner City Redevelopment in Vancouver: A Case Study of Kitsilano," MA diss. University of British Columbia, 1979.

24. Population displacement has been identified as the most serious unanticipated consequence of inner-city revitalization in the United States: for example, R.A. Cybriwsky, "Social aspects of neighborhood change,"

Annals of the Association of American Geographers 68 (1978): 17-33: and Weiler, op. cit. However, the extent of displacement is much disputed. For an optimistic account see H. Sumka, "Neighborhood revitalization and displacement," *Journal of the American Planning Association* 45 (1979):480-7. Empirical data might challenge this optimism. A survey of 1,269 households in Seattle indicated that 25 percent of tenants, and 24 percent of the elderly who had moved between 1973 and 1978, did so involuntarily: D.C. Hodge, *Seattle Displacement Study* (Seattle: City of Seattle Office of Policy Planning, 1979).

    25. Stobie, op. cit.

    26. *Vancouver Province,* 25 May 1978.

    27. J. Khouri, "The rising cost of tearing down," *Vancouver Sun,* 29 October 1977, p. A6.

    27. For the political context of inner-city change in Vancouver, see Ley (1980), op. cit., footnote 7.

    29. Vancouver City Planning Department, *The Kitsilano Neighborhood Plan* (Vancouver: 1977).

    30. Vancouver City Planning Department, *Quarterly Review,* 7 (January 1980): 17.

    31. West Broadway Citizens Committee, "Is this your block? Next month?" (Information bulletin, January 1974).

    32. In 1973 it was estimated that $140 million of foreign funds was flowing into Vancouver real estate. Almost 70 percent originated in Hong Kong and was directed primarily at inner-city multiple family units. British and American investment favored downtown office buildings. P.S. Ross and Partners, *The Impact of Foreign Investment in Commercial and Multiple Family Residential Real Estate in the Greater Vancouver Area* (Vancouver: Real Estate Board of Greater Vancouver, 1974).

    33. Vancouver City Planning Department, *Understanding Vancouver's Housing* (Vancouver: 1979). Section III b, p. 28.

    34. For the more active role of the city of Toronto, see M. Dennis, "The work of the Toronto Housing Corporation," in C. McKee (ed.), *Innovative Strategies for the Renewal of Older Neighborhoods* (Winnipeg: University of Winnipeg, Institute of Urban Studies, 1977), pp. 117-32.

    35. For the relations between community groups and senior governments, see J.T. Lemon, "The urban community movement: moving toward public households," in D.F. Ley and M.S. Samuels (eds.), *Humanistic Geography* (Chicago: Maaroufa, 1978), pp. 319-37.

    36. Vancouver City Planning Department (1979) op. cit., Section III d, p. 10.

    37. Kitsilano residents were eager recipients of rehabilitation grants: D.A. Phillips, "Urban Housing Quality: The Importance of Attitudes in the Decision to Rehabilitate," MA diss. University of British Columbia, 1976; also Vancouver City Planning Department (1980), op. cit., footnote 40.

    38. Vancouver City Planning Department (1979), op. cit., Section IV b, p. 18.

    39. Ibid., Section IV b, p. 7.

    40. The housing situation in Vancouver has undoubtedly deteriorated

since these assessments were made. By November 1980, the rental vacancy rate had declined to 0.1-0.2 percent, while house prices had risen 35 percent over the preceding 12 months, by far the highest increase in any Canadian city.

41. Weiler, op. cit., p. 103.

42. Vancouver City Planning Department, *Understanding Vancouver* (Vancouver: 1977), pp. 3-11. It does not seem as if such income convergence had occurred with any consistency in major American cities up to 1977: L.H. Long and D.C. Dahmann, *The City-Suburb Income Gap: Is It Being Narrowed by a Back-to-the City Movement?* (Washington, DC: U.S. Department of Commerce, Bureau of the Census, 1980).

43. These trends were well established in Vancouver by the early 1970s: G.P.F. Steed, "Intrametropolitan manufacturing: spatial distribution and locational dynamics in Greater Vancouver," *The Canadian Geogapher* 17(1973): 235-58.

CHAPTER ELEVEN

Gentrification in Britain and Europe

PETER WILLIAMS

INTRODUCTION

Our understanding of the relationships between urban change and general social processes remains relatively crude. While it is fairly easy to observe the way the built form changes and develops, it is much harder to construct an adequate account of the processes involved. Cities are complex manifestations of the societies in which they are located; they are both expressions of, and influences upon, the form and structure of the society concerned. Just as society is in constant transformation, so too are the cities. Thus, in developing an account of one social process, gentrification, which dominantly but not exclusively finds expression in large metropolitan centers, it is essential to remain aware of the fact that this is just one form of contemporary urban change. Moreover, given the locally specific nature of the structure of each urban center, its economy and social patterning, it is reasonable to expect the precise form taken by any process of change to vary from center to center. Such a position probably negates any attempt to erect a

Peter Williams is Research Fellow Urban Research Unit, Research School of Social Sciences, Australian National University, Canberra.
The author gratefully acknowledges the comments and advice of Hal Kendig and Peter Spearrit in the Urban Research Unit; David McCullough, Association of Metropolitan Authorities, London; Hugh Clout, University College London; Chris Flockton, University of Surrey; and Daniel Noin, University of Paris.

universal account of gentrification, even as a recognition of complexity undermines arguments that render this process the outcome of single factors, such as the rise in fuel costs or changes in lifestyle.

In arguing for the need to place gentrification in context and to avoid extracting it from social realities and general social relations, it becomes clear that to construct an adequate account of this process would require an extensive elaboration of the relationships between the mode of production, class relations, and the processes of urbanization. In this chapter, we can only signify some of these relationships, primarily because much of the more detailed research necessary has yet to be undertaken, or in some cases, brought together. In addition, since much of exisiting research has been conducted with an emphasis on measurement with a concomitant neglect of the conceptual framework necessary to evaluate the results, it is often difficult to extend the analysis in directions that would allow a full grasp of the social processes at work.

There is a great danger that, in our concern to analyze what at times can be a conspicuous and spectacular process of social and physical change, we ignore more general questions of change in urban areas, the social processes imbedded within them, and their historical antecedents. Implicit in many discussions of gentrification is the view that it is a further sequel in the process of invasion and succession which many would argue has been typical of inner-city areas. This view immediately shifts the analysis into the very limited and constraining framework provided by the Chicago School. Such a framework has a number of serious conceptual weaknesses (see, for instance, the critiques provided by Harvey 1978; Mellor 1977) and uncertain empirical validity (Zunz 1980). Moreover, as always it would seem, the model articulated by Park, Burgess, and others as a means of understanding the social and physical impact of urbanization processes has been subsequently rendered into a static representation of what they saw as a complex social process, with the consequence that many analysts are more concerned with the degree of "fit" than with the processes at work.

Such applications have substantially impaired our understanding of residential segregation and differentiation and, in particular, have diverted attention from the relationship between these processes and the questions of inter and intra class relations and social mobility.[1] Given the substantial literature on class, it is disappointing that this divergence has arisen, especially in light of our current concern with the process of gentrification, that is, the process by which areas that have an established working-class population become increasingly occupied by persons from the middle and upper classes. In chapter 3 in this volume, a general account of gentrification as a class-based process is attempted. Thus, only certain issues will be tackled here, retaining a principal focus on the nature of the process in Britain. The chapter is organzied into four sections. First, an historical overview of class segregation in British cities is presented in order to locate these processes within the development of the social and economic structure as a whole. Having established the context, a specific examination of gentrification is presented with a focus on change in London. In the third section, consideration is given to the occurrence of this process in cities in Continental Europe. Finally, in the conclusion, the politics of urban change are addressed, with comments on the prospects for the spead of upgrading and the ineffectiveness of government intervention.

GENTRIFICATION IN BRITAIN, A BRIEF SOCIAL HISTORY

It is important to begin by situating this particular aspect of urban change within an understanding of the historical dimensions of the patterns of class-based residential segregation. Despite the limitations of the ecological model of city structure and its influence in both sociology and geography, a substantial literature has now developed regarding the distribution of classes in British cities and the ways city form and structure are both a product of, and an influence upon, general social relations (e.g., Dennis 1977; Dennis and Daniels 1981; Dyos 1968; Dyos and Wolff 1973; Foster 1974; Hollen Lees 1980; Joyce 1980; Stedman Jones 1972; White 1979; Ward 1980.). In particular, the debate has been directed toward understanding the extent of class segregation by residence arising at different stages in the development of British capitalism (commercial, industrial, monopoly) and the ways in which such processes are integral to changing class relations. Although most analysts recognize that spatial segregation presupposes a class structure and that a class structure, in all its complexities, is strongly rooted in the development of the forces and relations of production and the concomitant divisions of labor arising there, they are also concerned to avoid an overgeneralised model of differentiation and to identify the substantial differences that emerge between and within localities over time.

It is often suggested that with the mechanization of production and the introduction of factory techniques in the 19th century, the possibilities of the spatial separation between home and work became a realistic alternative to the home-centered, skill-based production of earlier eras. Such opportunities were conferred upon the owners of the means of production, who, taking advantage of developing transport facilities and an adequate management structure, were not only able to escape the squalor of districts scarred by industrial production but also to leave behind the working class, their sickness and poverty, and the class tensions that existed (though in the case of the most affluent, both town and country houses were maintained). However, as the research has shown, this simple dichotomy, the residential segregation of "the two nations" (Ward 1980) is not totally borne out in reality. In studies of a number of towns and cities, including Leeds, St. Helens, Birmingham, and Oldham, a complex spatial intermixing of classes is revealed, persisting in some areas long after separation has occurred elsewhere (Foster 1974; Gordon 1979; Joyce 1980; Lawton 1979; Perry 1969; Pooley 1977, 1979; Shaw 1977, 1979; Vance 1967). Such a mixing would not simply be of landlord and tenant but also of merchant and laborer, though admittedly, while living in the same area, social distinctions might arise through the size of the house, the quality of its furnishings, or the street on which it was located. The extent of segregation was therefore often quite limited, although, as Ward (1980) points out, there are major problems in any such evaluation, partly because of the data available and questions as to the scale at which such analysis should be conducted.

The conditions for differentiation developed throughout the nineteenth and twentieth centuries with an expanding and increasingly differentiated labor force engaged in the production of both goods and services, concentrated land ownership, a developing building industry, and an improved transport system. These developing relations were important elements in the process of suburbanization. However, in the late nineteenth and early twentieth centuries while strata of the new middle class moved onto the villa estates developing around industrial towns, others remained behind in what would now be termed the inner city, often residing in the remaining urban estates of the landed aristocracy (e.g., Belgravia and Bloomsbury, in London, and Edgbaston, in Birmingham) (Cannadine 1980). Such estates, frequently with a mix of classes, survived for a variety of reasons, but their impact upon patterns of differentiation should not be underestimated, nor their significance, in later periods when inner-city gentrification takes place.

Until the 1950s the most obvious examples of upward social and physical change, that is, gentrification, had occurred in a variety of coastal locations and in chosen villages on the periphery of metropolitan areas. As Cannadine (1980), Lewis (1980), and others have shown, during the nineteenth century a number of small towns and fishing villages were transformed into fashionable seaside resorts for the middle and upper classes (e.g., Eastbourne, Torquay) while, more recently, settlements on the metropolitan periphery have undergone equally dramatic change (e.g., Pahl [1965]; Ambrose [1974]) though this has rarely been termed gentrification (but see Eversley [1981]). As illustrated here, it is quite clear that the debate over gentrification should widen beyond social and physical change in inner urban areas in order to capture the complexity and diversity of this market process. The interelationships between changes in the form and structure of the housing market and developments in the labor market, transport, and land ownership find expression in a variety of ways in a number of places. The transformation of seaside towns, rural villages, and decaying inner areas are all part of this more general process of social and economic change.

The period of social and physical reconstruction that followed the Second World War acted to stimulate further the flow of population out of the center of metropolitan areas and into the suburbs and beyond. This outmigration from center to periphery occurred amongst all classes, though the form of movement may have differed. For many individuals, war damage and redevelopment resulted in their displacement to suburban estates provided for rent by local authorities (Merrett 1979), while for others the postwar boom enhanced opportunities for social mobility and the possibilty of becoming a homeowner, particularly during the latter half of the 1950s (Hall et al. 1973). The future of most central residential areas became quite uncertain during this time as a consequence of such factors as the expansion of commercial needs, attempts to segregate land uses, and the apparent unpopularity of the older inner areas as residential environments. One consequence of this was that remaining higher-class enclaves were most often seen as having a very limited life (Cannadine 1980). The "great estates" had been run down and much of the prewar pattern of upper-class life in London had changed substantially.

Although the early postwar era was characterized by massive public housing schemes and the continuation of rent control in the private rented sector, by the late 1950s, the Conservative government had instituted a series of policies designed to expand homeownership and remove the privately rented sector from any form of control (Nevitt 1966; Pawley 1978). Since large areas of inner London, Liverpool, and other major centers were dominated by landlordism, these moves had vital consequences.[2] Rent control had, in effect, frozen the social relationships extant in such areas, with landlords bitterly opposing restraints upon their rental income and tenants enjoying low rents but with poor conditions and little likelihood of being able to find alternative accommodation (Greve 1965). Decontrol was developed selectively, beginning with properties on which the highest rates, or property taxes, were paid. This, of course, had a significant class impact since it was the wealthy tenants who were first to feel the effects of higher rents and the pressure to buy. Since levels of home ownership were so low, even amongst such strata of the population, the possibilities of a substantial transformation of tenure patterns in the inner metropolitan market were created, especially given the general drive to expand ownership (Williams 1976a).

Throughout the fifties and the sixties, some landlords sold off substantial quantities of their property, both directly to owner-occupiers and to other entrepreneurs who began moving in on the market aware of future capital gains through sales to individuals (Francis Report 1971). Other landlords, generally those with properties in less favored locations and/or poorer condition, found themselves with little alternative but to sell out to the local authority, which in most cases intended to clear the property and redevelop the site. Such processes of purchase, clearance, and redevelopment took a very long while, not least because alternative housing had to be found by the tenants—a process exacerbated by the fact that, in some areas, they were West Indians or Asians whose position in the market was still marginal (Rex and Moore 1967).

Toward the end of the sixties it became apparent that clearance programs were expensive, slow, inefficient, and perhaps had undesirable effects on communities (see, for instance Ungerson [1971]). Slower growth in the British economy (Glyn and Sutcliffe 1972), the cost of clearance and subsequent renewal of the whole infrastructure, and curbs on state expenditure were all factors in an important shift in policy which had a profound impact on the inner areas. The direction of state intervention changed, from public expenditure and redevelopment to private intiative and rehabil-itation (Ministry of Housing and Local Government 1968). Conservation and improvement of the existing stock became watchwords, with grants being made available to individuals to assist in this process (Paris and Blackaby 1979). The intersection between such changes, the reduction in the private rented sector, the expansion in home ownership, and a rapidly restructing labor force with a shift into white-collar employment and away from factory based manual labor, all produced conditions that aided the gentrification process in many inner-city areas (Cameron 1980).

The changing fortunes of the inner city have been the subject of intense analysis in Britain through a series of government-sponsored initiatives (in particular, Community Development Projects, Inner Area Studies, and the Department of the Environment's Inner City Research Programme) and, more recently, academic initiatives by the Social Science Research Council (SSRC Inner City Working Party). This last examination has resulted in a series of reports on the relationship between inner-city problems and such matters as land values, transport, housing market processes, economic and technological change (Social Science Research Council 1980). From such work and a subsequent publication (Hall 1980), a number of the more general arguments brought forward to explain gentrification can be considered, for example the impact of changing transport costs. However, while each of these factors is clearly important in establishing the general parameters within which gentrification might arise, they do not explain the specific occurrences. In the next section we describe in some detail the extent of gentrification in London and other areas of Britain and consider the conditions that underlay this upward social and physical change.

URBAN CHANGE AND SOCIAL CHANGE

The documentation and analysis of gentrification in British cities remains quite limited. The most complete accounts exist only for London, while for other cities and towns we have only the evidence of a few small scale pieces of research and subjective impressions. Furthermore, in seeking to provide accurate measures of the extent of change, a number of very questionable assumptions must be made regarding the data available (Hamnett and Williams 1979). Even though it has now been more than 25 years that this form of upgrading has been at work in parts of London, empirical assessment remains very crude primarily because other issues have dominated the research agenda (e.g., the impact of clearances) while gentrification has until recently remained a relatively minor process.

Despite this, a series of studies of areas of London have been undertaken allowing a range of insights into the process of gentrification (Broadbent 1973; Cave 1968; Challen 1973; Hamnett 1973; Hamnett and Williams 1979, 1980; Neild 1974; Pitt 1977; Power 1972, 1973; Simpson 1972; Williams, 1976a, 1976b). Typically, working-class households have been replaced by higher-income households, often headed by persons with professional or managerial jobs. Poor, generally rented property is refurbished, ultimately emerging as totally renewed and now individually owned dwellings. This process may be mediated by entrepreneurs who buy up rented dwellings, improve, and sell on; or it can be the product of individual purchasers (Merrett 1976). Either way, it becomes clear that gentrification involves the displacement of working-class households and the diminution of the privately rented sector which has traditionally housed the mass of unskilled workers, albeit in relatively poor conditions. The research conducted has only given limited insights into the effect on the displaced, primarily because of the difficulties of tracing households who have moved. By contrast, it has provided substantial detail on the nature of the households that move in. Their higher status has already been noted. In addition, these households tend to be relatively small, often with no children, and occupy early stages in the life cycle. Often all the adults are working and many would have tertiary qualifications. All this, in conjunction with a preference for Georgian or Victorian housing, that is, those properties with the greatest architectural interest, lends much support to arguments about lifestyle. However, as argued later, that is only one element in the analysis. Both houses and flats have been gentrified and increasingly, as the supply of the older dwellings dries up, areas of newer Edwardian property are being taken over. Research indicates that most of the households engaged in the process have been resident in the inner areas before, and relatively few have moved in from outer suburbs. Questioning about motivation reveals a concern with style, convenience, and, importantly, capital gains. The purchase of cheap, rundown property that can be improved offers real possibilities of an untaxed capital gain when the dwelling is sold. This has clearly been an important component in the process, a factor that can only really be understood through an elaboration of housing and taxation policy and curbs on the expansion of real incomes.

Assessment of gentrification in this way brings out the parallels between the processes operating in London and other cities of the world. However it is obviously important not only to describe the process but also to signify its relevance to the changing social structure of London and to understand the causal mechanisms at work.

Considerable debate has ensued in the 1970s as to whether London's distinctively polarized residential class structure[3] is being transformed (e.g., Harris and Lyons 1971; Harris 1973; Lomas 1973; Willmott and Young 1973) and, if so, what role gentrification has played in the process. A whole series of complex arguments related to the falling size of households, the declining metropolitan population, and changes in employment and income groups has been advanced (Eversley and Bonnerjea 1980), all of which have relevance for this debate. With certain provisos[4] however, it is clear that gentrification is beginning to have a measurable impact at several scales of analysis.

Thus the evidence available indicates a substantial increase in the higher socioeconomic groups in inner London over the period 1961-77, a change also associated with a rise in the level of home ownership (Hamnett 1976). Using the number of economically active males as an indicator, the figures for Greater London for the period 1961-71 show an increase in the percentage of employers, managers, and professional workers, from 16 percent in 1961 to 20 percent in 1971 (Dugmore 1975). For Inner London the figures were 13 percent to 17 percent. In 1977 a National Dwelling and Housing Survey estimate for Greater London indicated that, of all economically active *persons,* 17 percent were in these socioeconomic groups (Department of the Environment 1979). Allowing for the generally lower status of female employment and for the broad definition of economically active persons, this result indicates a continuation of the trend. Similar changes are also observable at the borough level. The Inner London boroughs of Greenwich, Hammersmith, Islington, Lambeth, and Southwark (see fig. 1) all recorded increases in economically active males in these groups over the period 1966-1971, from 13 percent to 15 percent, 11 percent to 14 percent, 9 percent to 12 percent, 12 percent to 14 percent, and 9 percent to 10 percent, respectively (Hamnett and Williams 1980), while evidence from a range of surveys suggests these increases have continued over the period from 1971 to 1980.

Tenure change has also taken place, though the link between increasing levels of home ownership and higher status is by no means absolute (primarily because of purchases by relatively poor black and Asian migrants in the early 1960s in Inner London). Over the period 1961-71 ownership rose in Greater London from 36 percent to 40 percent of households, and council renting increased to 27 percent from 18 percent. Private renting fell from 45 percent to 34 percent, continuing its historic decline from the beginning of the century when approximately 90 percent of dwellings in England as a whole were rented from private landlords. The National Dwelling and Housing Survey conducted in 1977 shows 44.5 percent of households owning or buying, 30.6 percent renting from councils, and only 21.5 percent renting from private landlords (remainder from housing associations—nonprofit rental organization). This decline has proceeded apace throughout the inner areas, with boroughs such as Kensington and Chelsea recording a fall from 76 percent in 1971 to 48 percent in 1977 in the number of households in the privately rented sector.

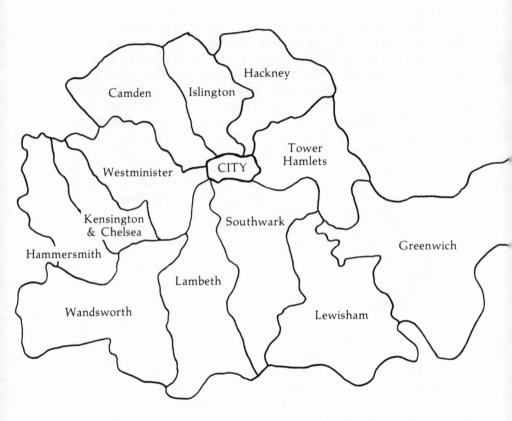

Fig. 1. Inner London Boroughs

These aggregate statistics give an indication of the changes occurring in the inner areas. More detailed research at the level of enumeration districts (the base area for the collection of census statistics) extends this substantially (Hamnett and Williams 1979; Williams 1976b) indicating both the local impact of change and the ease with which such evidence is obscured. Thus, for example, in Islington's Barnsbury area, the number of economically active males in the professional and managerial socioeconomic groups rose from 3 percent in 1961 to 16 percent in 1971 while, in Greenwich's Trafalgar area, they rose from 5 percent to 16 percent. Although gentrification has taken place in a fragmented way over a large area, some streets and squares in now well-established areas have been almost completely transformed, for example, Lonsdale Square in Barnsbury. In some respects it would seem only a matter of time before streets coalesce and whole areas are transformed. Although Islington's gentrification developed in streets within what had been middle- and upper-class residential estates in the nineteenth century, the area is unusual in that these developments took place away from any existing cores of high-status residence. Elsewhere in London, gentrification has often been on the periphery of prestigious areas such as Hampstead and Kensington. Either way, although the process may begin by a recolonization of former middle-class housing (and old estates), the process soon spreads beyond into the cottages and villas built for the working class. The market does not respect boundaries, nor is there any mechanism to retain a balance between competing needs. While local councils have in the past acted to inhibit the takeover, current restrictions on expenditure and new directions in central government policy, such as the sale of council houses, would suggest gentrification could become more rapid.

Throughout this volume, arguments have been advanced in explanation of gentrification, and, indeed, a whole range of factors can be seen to be related to it. But, as argued at the outset, a universal explanation is unlikely since this would be easily undermined by areas and cities with similar residential patterns responding to similar conditions in different ways. In London, gentrification can be attributed to a complex market restructuring deriving from the articulations between a class-based society, residential patterning, and economic and social change (Harvey 1975). The restructuring of the built environment over time, changes in production and distribution, and the emergence of what might be termed "consumption classes" have in London taken particular forms reflecting the city's role as a major financial and commercial center, the prevailing configuration of property relations, and local conflicts. Such generalizations are not attempts to obscure the intricacies of residential restructuring, but rather to locate changes firmly within a political economy of the city.

The general components of such an analysis have been elaborated at length elsewhere (see, for instance, Basset and Short [1980]; Mingione [1981]; and Saunders 1981]). Suffice it to say here that the city is not viewed as an autonomous object of analysis in which specific "urban" processes are played out, but rather as one expression of general social relations, albeit with particular local characteristics.[6] Within London one can identify a number of relations that have crucially contributed to the gentrification process. First, the economic and social sturcture of the city has been changing substantially since the Second World War. The total population has been both falling (from a peak of over 8 million in 1951 to a little more than 6½ million in 1981) and restructuring, with rises in single- and two-person households, relatively high levels of outmigration (especially from Inner London) and substantial falls in the birthrate. All these changes have meant that, though the population has fallen, the demand for housing remains at a very high level. The changing population structure clearly relates to the way London's economic base has shifted in the postwar period, with declines in manufacturing, construction, and distributive trades and increases in professional services, insurance, and banking (Foster and Richardson 1973; Dennis 1980). In addition, employment has physically shifted from the inner areas, and there has been a major increase in the number of working women (Lomas 1973). Unemployment has of course risen in recent years throughout London, but it continues to be unevenly distributed, reflecting the very different conditions pertaining across the conurbation. Significantly, Evans has recently commented

Since the higher skill groups have lower unemployment rates than the lower skill groups, the effect of gentrification—the displacement of lower skill groups by higher—will be to reduce the average unemployment rate in the area. Thus the gentrification occurring in inner-north London will lead to a reduction in unemployment there (1980, p. 227).

These changes in economic activity, employment, and related income levels are in large part a product of shifts in the competitive position of industries in home and overseas markets and subsequent patterns and processes of reorganization (Keeble 1980). While regional policies that encouraged the outmovement of industry will obviously have had an effect, it is quite clear that the decline in manufacturing is "part of the wider phenomenon of contraction and change in the manufacturing base of the UK economy" (Massey and Meegan 1980).

The impact of these changes intersect with a wide range of other factors related to gentrification, not least of which are the housing market, transportation, changing consumption patterns, and the nature of local and central government intervention, revealing throughout the contradictory nature of such processes and the tension between sustaining London's role as a center for accumulation and meeting the needs for reproduction of the labor force (Rose 1981). The heavy dependence in Inner London on the privately rented sector constitutes an important element in the explanation. As noted earlier, the progressive withdrawal of rent controls during the late fifties and sixties, at a time when more than 60% of households in the inner areas were private tenants, helped create a situation in which dramatic change became inevitable. As the Milner Holland Report of 1965 and the Francis Report of 1971 show, the demand for decent housing, combined with the pressure from landlords to remove tenants on low rents, created a conflicting situation—one that encouraged sales to owner-occupiers and the displacement of tenants (Cave 1968; McCarthy 1975; Simpson 1972).

It has often been suggested that the extension of the improvement program in 1969 stimulated interest in older property and encouraged speculators to buy up dwellings, improve by use of the grants offered, and then sell to higher income owner-occupiers—in other words, that improvement was an essential stage in the displacement of low-income renters by high-income owners. Certainly there is evidence such abuse took place (Hamnett 1973; Power 1972, 1973) and it is clear grants were one factor, but it would be inappropriate to attempt to explain the extent of change in this way (Dugmore and Williams 1974). Just as important was the relatively low price of property in these inner areas (reflecting conditions and problems of raising finance) and the much higher house prices elsewhere (Department of the Environment n.d.). Not only did the changing population and employment structure stimulate demand, but these bargain prices created excellent conditions for corporate and individual speculation as has been described in detail elsewhere (Williams 1976a). Estate agents (realtors), property companies, finance companies all moved in to take advantage of the profits available (Pitt 1977). Although there were initial problems with raising mortgage financing because of redlining (Williams 1978), these areas have now become popular with financial institutions. Given the substantial promotion of home ownership in the postwar era, through tax concessions and grants (Pawley 1978; Boddy 1980), and the expansion and increasing stratification of white-collar work in London, it is scarcely surprising that part of the demand was met by properties in such areas.

Indeed, what is significant is that studies of the gentry show that most have always lived in Inner London, moving from rented accommodations in one inner borough to ownership in another (Williams 1976b). This pattern of movement stands in contrast to arguments about "back to the city" and demonstrates to an extent the impact of displacement of higher-income groups from renting. During the 1960s these inner areas recorded above average increases in house price, indicating the way the market was adjusting to changing conditions (Department of the Environment n.d.). This trend has continued in the 1970s, although recently the entire London market has been depressed. The much reduced rented sector can no longer supply dwellings in volume and, as a consequence, prices in these areas have reached levels that preclude many would-be gentry. This, combined with the known prejudices of established lenders, continues to limit opportunities of all households other than those with two earners and middle or above income. Recent policy development related to the sale of public housing to existing tenants and urban homesteading may well ensure a flow of lower-income purchasers joins the inner London market, but both strategies are unlikely to substantially influence the general direction of change. This is not to say all existing inner-city owners are middle class. From the 1930s on some numbers of skilled workers and then semiskilled workers became owners (Burnett 1978; Gauldie 1974). These were supplemented in the 1950s and 1960s by immigrant households. But all the indications are that in many inner localities such houses pass on to households of a higher status when sold.

Such a pattern is observable in many ways and in many areas. Hamnett (1981) has recently reported on a study of the breakup of rented apartment blocks into single-unit ownerships. This process, which returns substantial profits to the block owners, has been gathering momentum throughout the 1970s. These mansion blocks have for a long time been owned by insurance companies, older property companies, or other such institutions as the Church Commissioners (the property management arm of the Church of England), providing a reliable return on investment. However, as yields have fallen (rental income in relation to capital value of the dwelling), so the owners have sought to dispose of the property to other companies or, more recently, to break up the blocks and sell them as units. This process almost inevitably results in changes in occupancy, with lower-income tenants being replaced by higher-income earners. Hamnett and Randolph (1981) argue that in central London (Camden, Kensington, and Chelsea and Westminster) "the major part of the shift to owner-occupation has been directly attributable to break-ups in the purpose-built flat sector. Thus the central London housing market has undergone a massive restructuring over the last 15 years."

The complex reshaping of the market has also been assisted by changes in the transport system. The opening of the Victoria underground line from Brixton in South London to Walthamstow in the North East and passing through central London and Islington certainly acted to open up certain areas that had previously been poorly served by public transport, and it is also apparent that change in other areas has been inhibited by the absence of such services—e.g., Hackney. However, while such developments have aided the direction of change, they are not in themselves capable of producing the changes that have arisen. The same is also true of shifts in preferences and consumption patterns. It is true that a very definite lifestyle can be identified amongst the gentry (Raban 1974) and that many have expressed a desire for old houses as well as old carpets, furniture, and paintings. But that style and the income which makes it possible can in turn be traced to developments around the mode of production, changes in the class structure, and residential differentiation; in other words, it is not an autonomous response but one that mirrors continuing social tensions and conflicts.

To move beyond this level of analysis of gentrification in London is to consider the detailed issues pertaining in specific localities.[7] Critical among these is the pattern of property ownership. In Islington, as in England as a whole, property ownership was concentrated in the hands of private landlords until the 1950s. However, over the next 30 years these estates were broken up for sale to individuals or to the council either for clearance or refurbishment. Thus, in the Canonbury district, the Northampton estate, owned by the Marquess of Northampton since the 1600s, was, in the 1950s, acquired by two property companies whose object has been to restore the estate socially and architecturally (Milner Holland Report 1965). Though a fashionable area in mid-Victorian times, Canonbury had begun a long slow decline by 1900, admittedly tempered by the fact that it was in the ownership of an aristocratic estate. Thus even in the twenties and thirties Canonbury continued to have "residents of distinction" including

Walter Sickert, Evelyn Waugh, and George Orwell (Harris 1974), who it would appear enjoyed "slumming" it with the working class. By the late 1950s Canonbury was climbing back up the social ladder, attracting more artists, architects, and lawyers. By the 1970s the estate agents were able to advertise:

> Situated in heart of Canonbury and is well known for its most elegant period houses surrounding it. All houses overlook the private square gardens with their attractive flower borders, shrubs and trees. Quick access is gained to both the City and West End....

Social and physical renewal has been achieved. The opening of a fast underground line was only part of the process, as was the provision of improvement grants. To understand the transformation of Canonbury we have to take account of its pattern of ownership, the clear speculative intentions of its recent owners (and of course in a different way, its earlier owners), middle-class lobbying regarding conservation and preservation, the changing employment structure of inner London, and shifts in the way housing finance was allocated. This last point has been discussed earlier but it is important to recognize that ownership in such areas was largely precluded until the 1960s because of the difficulties of obtaining mortgage finance. Over time, loan institutions, far from being laggards in these areas, have lent generously on the assumption that, if any property was to sustain its price, areas like Canonbury were certainties.

Despite the dramatic changes arising in specific parts of Islington, the overall level of home ownership has risen only slowly—from around 5 percent in the 1940s to 11 percent in 1961 and 15 percent in 1977. The reason for this, and for the concentration of gentrification in particular areas, is that the local council has over the years been active in the building of new council-owned dwellings for rent and, more recently, in the municipalization of dwellings from landlords who refused to improve the condition of their properties (Merrett 1979). Thus, although improvement grants made by the local authority may be seen to have aided gentrification, their program of house construction has also inhibited it, removing large areas of decayed, privately rented housing and replacing it with modern dwellings for the working class. In 1977, 50 percent of households in Islington lived in council property. No wonder, then, that the impact of change is muted at an aggregate level. Similar patterns of intervention have been repeated throughout Inner London, with council building proceeding hand in hand with other policies on improvement and the setting up of conservation areas, that is, local authorities have played a highly contradictory role in the process of gentrification. Indeed, gentrification has become a highly contentious process for many inner area councils. Their dominantly Labour party administrations have been charged with encouraging the displacement of working-class residents, a charge many find difficult to refute.

The position outside of London is more difficult to describe or evaluate because no systematic research has been published, though subjective assessments indicate "upgrading" in selected areas of other cities. Although many of the same factors would appear to be at work outside of London, albeit in different combinations, the rate of change does appear to be slower, probably because market pressure is lower. In Birmingham, gentrification has been taking place in a number of inner area locations; Edgbaston, Handsworth, Harborne, Kings Heath, Moseley, and Selly Oak. (Interestingly in Handsworth, which is better known as an area of West Indian and Asian residence, see Rex and Moore [1967]). In part, the persistence of the Calthorpe Estate, in Edgbaston, one of the remaining urban estates in the possession of the aristocracy, in this case, Lord Calthorpe, has aided the process. The estate has selectively sold off property and has generally sought to sustain its high social status. This core of property (approximately 5,000 dwellings) has encouraged change in surrounding areas, as has the presence of two early twentieth century model cottage villages, Bournville and Harborne Tenants, and the University of Birmingham—all of them in the inner Southwest sector of the city.

Within these areas considerable variation exists, pointing up the selectivity of the gentrification process. The same is also true of cities elsewhere in Britain. Thus in Bristol, Clifton has been the core area for change, and in Oxford, Jericho; similar areas exist in Reading, Leeds, Newcastle, Glasgow, Bath, Canterbury, Norwich, Manchester, Edinburgh, and elsewhere.[8] Although it might be tempting to suggest that any area of pre-1919 property that is unlikely to be cleared and is not blighted by road proposals has a possibility of undergoing this kind of "upgrading," this would be unwarranted. The condition of much of the housing stock (English House Condition Survey 1978, 1979) is such that massive repairs are necessary. Recently a working party for the Royal Town Planning Institute (1981) has suggested that 3½ billion pounds must be spent to sustain the pre-1919 stock of dwellings alone, a call which coincides with a government that has cut housing expenditure over the period 1979/80 to 1981/82 by 4 billion pounds. This, combined with rising unemployment and declining real incomes, suggests such predicitions are problematic. Furthermore, depressed circumstances and more rigid council enforcement of standards probably reduce the possibilities of capital gains on the improvement of the dwelling and resale, even by individuals who may do much of the work themselves.

Outside of the cities, gentrification has been quite widespread. The creation of the new town of Milton Keynes in the Midlands and the location there of the Open University have done much to ensure the gentrification of parts of nearby towns and villages. Such nometropolitan change has generally been analyzed in terms of the impact of newcomers in established communities (Pahl 1965). However, as noted earlier, we now need to reconsider this focus. A more detailed analysis of what has been termed "rural gentrification," in Nottinghamshire and Norfolk, has recently concluded that such a process was occurring not only in areas accessible to larger settlements but also in more remote villages favorable for retirement (Parsons 1979, 1980). Closer examination of the rural housing market reveals the extent to which households with higher wages outbid indigenous inhabitants (Dunn, Rawsonn and Rogers 1981).

Gentrification in Europe

In Western Europe the dominant concerns regarding urban change in the 1970s relate to questions of the continuing movement from rural to urban areas, the impact of "guest" workers upon sociospatial structures of cities, and, more recently the trends toward dispersal from major metropolitan areas (Vining and Kontuly 1978). Setting aside the question of changes in the residential structure of cities, it is important to recognize the enormous labor migrations that have taken place in Europe since the Second World War (King 1976). Estimates vary but a figure of 8 million has been given (Hume 1973) with particularly substantial numbers in Germany, France, and Switzerland (O'Loughlin [1980] suggests there were 3,948,000 in West Germany in 1977). Though these figures are dramatic, they are overshadowed in magnitude by internal migration within each of the countries. Since the war, there has been a rapid restructuring of the agriculture, forestry, and fishing sectors, with the consequence that substantial migration has taken place to all major urban centers (Clout 1976). The impact of these two trends and their relationship to the economy of Western European countries has presumably been sufficient to deflect attention from the smaller-scale and less pressing questions of the upgrading of inner areas (Lee and Ogden 1976; Romanos 1979).

The flow of labor from poorer regions and poorer countries has created a fairly large number of problems within cities in Europe, placing many services under strain and creating a substantial underclass who enjoy few of the benefits of an advanced economy. These inequalities, substantial enough at the outset, have been heightened by the economic depression that has existed in much of Europe since the mid-1970s (George and Lawson 1980). Thus attention has been focused upon patterns of residential segregation in Europoean cities as part of a more general concern with the residual position of foreign immigrants (e.g. Drewe et al. 1975; Koch 1977; O'Loughlin 1980). Moreover, as the work of Castells (1978), Lojkine (1976), and others indicates for France, such segregation is not only expressed in terms of a clustering of immigrants in decaying inner-city areas but also on the periphery in both public housing and very primitive shelters. Such patterning in conjunction with a general tendency for European cities to have retained higher-status inner areas makes a distinct contrast to cities elsewhere in the developed world. However, although the "traditional" pattern of vertical, rather than horizontal, segregation has persisted, most European cities experienced substantial suburbanization after the Second World War and, since many inner areas were destroyed during the war, quite substantial restructuring has taken place over the last 30 years.

It is in the context of these changes that the very small literature on gentrification must be considered. The most extensive documentation refers to Paris, with several reports on the process becoming significant in the 1960s and 1970s. Interestingly, one of the earliest publications constitutes the most substantial study. This was the report of an international study week on the *Urban Core and Inner City*, published by the University of Amsterdam (1967). Several of the papers presented deal specifically with upgrading in parts of central Paris, in areas such as Les Halles and the 5th Arrondissement. Poor, privately rented housing at controlled rents has been replaced by high-quality flats and housing owned or rented by the affluent. Significantly, as Bentham and Moseley (1980) note, this gentrification has in part been a product of renewal, with cheap, poor quality housing being torn down and new, expensive dwellings erected. They comment:

> In 1973, 50 percent of the rented housing in Inner Paris was in the rent-controlled sector, relatively cheap but often in poor condition and lacking amenities. A further 13 percent was moderate-rent public-sector housing. Thus Inner Paris had a major concentration of low-rent housing. However, this stock of relatively cheap dwellings has been

shrinking rapidly. Between 1970 and 1973 it fell from 428,000 to 311,000 units as a result of concerted policies of renewal and rehabilitation, as well as the less spectacular trends towards decontrol and amalgamation. The better quality and much more expensive dwellings which have taken the place of the cheap flats have mostly gone to feed the apparently insatiable demand amongst the affluent for an address in Paris (Bentham and Moseley 1980, p. 67). Little wonder, then, that in such recent reports as those of Damais (1978) and Chauvire and Noin (1980) substantial changes in the social structure of Paris have been noted, with Damais indicating research showing the occurrance of gentrification in Inner Paris.

Published evidence for other cities of Western Europe has not come to light, though there has been a small study of change in Amsterdam (Blauw and Pastor 1978) and one on Bordeaux (Pailhe 1978). The lack of data and reports obviously inhibits any firm statements regarding such processes, but the general move throughout Europe to conserve the historic inner areas does in all likelihood signify that such changes will arise. Many planners and architects see social upgrading as a necessary cost for the preservation of the built environment—a position well indicated by the European Campaign for Urban Renaissance, a program specifically concerned with preservation and revitalization (Department of Environment 1980).

The position in Eastern Europe is interestingly different. The inheritance of presocialist cities, the presence of substantial inequalities in influence and power and, to a lesser extent, in income, and the continuing problems of achieving high levels of service provision in all areas has resulted in significant levels of residential segregation. In a number of cities, this clustering has produced a pattern the inverse of the classic ecological model with the wealthy at the center and the poor displaced to the periphery. Hamilton and Burnett (1979) note such patterns are apparent in Lodz and Wroclaw, in Poland, paralleling Musil's findings (1968) for Prague in Czechoslovakia, in the 1960s, though they do comment that "social levelling also resulted from the loss of elite character in old areas and some advancement of workers areas" (p. 285). High-status central areas are also observable in Constanta, Romania; Warsaw, Poland; and Budapest, Hungary, though in each instance commentators note such patterns have been or are likely to be modified in the future (Hamilton and Burnett 1979; Weclawowicz 1979; Compton 1979).

Thus, while in Eastern Europe attempts have been made to

diminish the advantages of the inner areas, there is continuing evidence of social segregation and more specifically of a clustering of high-status occupations in inner residential zones. In some cases, these are perpetuations of presocialist patterns, but their reproduction under socialism indicates the extent to which nonmarket structures do not necessarily redistribute opportunities but actually reinforce the prevailing distribution of power. Though there are crucial differences between such patterns and those observable elsewhere in Europe, they do indicate the persistence of class inequalities under different modes of production. Although it would be difficult to describe this process as gentrificiation in the normal sense of the word, that is, a market-based process, the failure to redistribute these opportunities, as well as the tendency for this pattern to consolidate, at least for the present, points toward sociospatial conflicts being resolved in favor of those with the greatest power—whether measured by influence or financial resources. The parallels with gentrification then become very clear.

CONCLUSIONS

In this chapter consideration has been given to the nature and extent of gentrification processes in Britain and Europe. As will be clear now, the evidence is fragmentary and much research must still be undertaken before a conclusive account can be presented. Despite these gaps, a number of conclusions can be drawn regarding this process and its specific manifestations in the countries concerned.

First, it is apparent that gentrification is a complex process involving a wide range of factors. Thus, in Paris, upgrading has in part been associated with clearance and the construction of high-status apartments, whereas in London the links between rehabilitation and gentrification are very strong. In both countries, it is clear that middle-class gains have been at the expense of working-class residents of the inner areas. While many have been displaced to better quality housing in suburban estates, the continuing restructuring of metropolitan and national economies suggests that this is now a disadvantageous location to occupy with limited resources.

Secondly, although gentrification can be seen as an expression of middle-class lifestyles, it represents much more than this. As Harvey comments

> Residential differentiation is produced in its broad
> lineamants at least, by forces emanating from the capitalist
> production process and it is not to be construed as the

product of the autonomously and spontaneously arising preferences of people. Yet people are constantly searching to express themselves and to realise their potentialities in their day to day life-experiences in the work place, in the community, and in the home. Much of the micro variation in the urban fabric testifies to these ever present impulses. But there is a scale of action at which the individual loses control of the social conditions of existence in the face of forces mobilised through the capitalist production process.... It is at this boundary that ... social relations between people become replaced by market relations between things (1975, p. 368).

Changes in the class structure and in particular with respect to the identity of the middle class, shifts in employment patterns and economic growth, the financial market, and flows of funds into housing—all are elements embedded in this process. An over-emphasis on lifestyle would obscure these critical social relations.

Third, a much neglected aspect of gentrification has been its implications for political practices and outcomes in the areas where gentrification occurs. The progressive takeover of the councils of certain inner London boroughs by strata of the middle class has created considerable political tension and revealed a stark division of interest between original residents and newcomers with respect to forms of housing, education, and other aspects of local conditions. As the chairman of one local residents' association in Islington has commented:

People in the street didn't resent the new owners who moved into the houses Redspring managed to empty. What they did resent was the way they wanted to change the area we live in, tear up roads, put down cobbles etc. People objected to outsiders coming in, making changes and then making existing residents pay for them on the rates. They were the aggressors [cited in Pitt 1977, p. 1.]

What to the newcomers was an attractive environmental improvement was to many original inhabitants a needless expenditure and inconvience. Similarly, moves to make areas traffic free (Ferris 1973) were instigated by newcomers who benefitted from quieter streets while displacing the traffic onto others. In all such cases, control of the local council becomes critical, and thus local politics assumes new significance. Thus changes in housing policy, local property taxes, schooling, social services, and recreation—all of which in Britain are local responsibilities—can become critically tied to the changing residential housing market. Some middle-class activists have arrogantly assumed that their presence will assist an apparently inarticulate and passive working class, but they quickly discover the wide differentials in material interests that exist.

These tensions, and recent outbreaks of rioting in certain metropolitan areas in Britain, might well inhibit the gentrification process. The decline of metropolitan economies, reduced central government expenditures, and increasing concern about the financial resources available to local authorities (Bartley in progress; Glassberg 1979) could produce conditions that would deter further upgrading. The contraction of white-collar jobs, whether it be because of cuts in public service or higher education expenditure or the impact of new technologies and the restructuring of industry and commerce, may also act to diminish those strata that have provided most buyers. Equally, there is a question about whether these households will seek a change in location more commensurate with their needs later in the life cycle, that is, if they then have children. However, fundamental shifts in household structure have already occurred, suggesting that demand from child-free adults may be more than sufficient to sustain and expand this market. Furthermore, with increases in divorce and remarriage, the buying power of such new domestic units can be considerable.

In conclusion, all the evidence from Britain, France, and elsewhere in Europe suggests that this form of residential change is occuring selectively and will continue to expand for the present. The promotion of home ownership, the rapid expansion of secondary and tertiary sectors of employment, and the continued differentials in income and credit-raising ability are all factors that act to sustain gentrification and none are likely to change dramatically in the near future. In Britain, with continuing pressure to liberate sectors of the economy from intervention, there is little prospect of government seeking to intervene further in this process. Concern with the vitality of inner-city areas currently overshadows other interests in improving housing standards for the poor; while curbs on government expenditures and the move to sell local authority housing may actually help increase the rate of change. The frailty of policy interventions, inequalities in income and opportunity, and the underlying class basis of residential patterning are all exposed through an examination of gentrification, revealing arguments about social mix and balance to be totally inadequate in the light of market processes. While the inner city may be rendered a physically more attractive area through gentrification, it is essential that this should not close our eyes to either the fundamental processes at work or the costs imposed. For as Eversley commented recently in a critique of the European Campaign for Urban Renaissance (Eversley, 1981)

No doubt this [the campaign] will restore the brightness of some formerly drab townscapes, and greatly increase the value of adjoining properties. It will do nothing to ease the housing or employment prospects of the inner city populations. On the contrary, the displacement effect will grow and the end result will be longer housing waiting lists, more overcrowding and homelessness (1981, p. 149).

NOTES

1. While it is true that much Chicago School sociology was concerned with social mobility, this aspect of the analysis has played a surprisingly minor role in applications of Burgess's model.

2. In 1914, 90 percent of households in Britain lived in housing rented from private landlords with the remainder owning their own homes. In 1978, 16 percent were renting privately, 54 percent owning or buying, and 30 percent renting public housing.

3. The structure has been likened to a cross in physical terms with north/south and east/west bands of working-class residential areas stretching from the city to the furthest boundary of the inner boroughs and beyond. In the east the "arm" of working-class residence continues into the outer areas. The interstices of the cross are areas of middle-class occupancy. (See Lomas, [1973]; Willmott and Young 1973].)

4. The problems of calculation include determining the impact of occupational changes in the workforce, i.e., the extent to which socioeconomic change is simply a consequence of the changing status of the jobs held by the original population.

5. Although Greenwich is outside the defined Inner London area, much of the borough has characteristics very similar to the inner area.

6. This denial of urban autonomy is understandable given previous excesses, but there is a real danger that the role cities play as physical and social structures in the development of general social relations will be overlooked. In this paper the city is viewed as a crucible in which such relations are both expressed and restructured.

7. These local variations are very important. Differentials in the forms of ownership (freehold or leasehold), variations in the age profile of tenants, highly localized employment patterns, and the effectiveness of local market professionals are all factors that contribute to differentials in the rate of change.

8. The only study reported on cities outside London is Kersley (1975). Related work on mortgaging patterns gives some indications of such changes.

REFERENCES

Ambrose, P. 1974. *The quiet revolution.* Brighton: Sussex University Press.

Bartley, J. In progress. Research on the political consequences of gentrification, Urban and Regional Studies Unit, University of Kent at Canterbury, U.K.

Basset, K., and Short, J. 1980. Housing and residential structure. London: Routledge and Kegan Paul.

Bentham, G., and Moseley, M. 1980. Socio-economic change and disparities within the Paris agglomeration: does Paris have an inner-city problem? Regional Studies 14:(55):70.

Blauw, W., and Pastor, C. 1978. Back to the city; A research into return migration of families with children to big cities. Paper presented to the 9th World Congress of Sociology, Uppsala.

Boddy, M. 1980. The building societies. London: Macmillan.

Broadbent, W. 1973. GIA's and gentrification (a case study in Brentford). B.A. diss. School of Planning, Kingston Polytechnic, London, U.K.

Burnett, J. 1978. A social history of housing. London: Newton Abbot, David and Charles.

Cameron, G. 1980. The future of the British conurbations. London: Longman.

Cannadine, D. 1980. Lords and landlords: the aristocracy and the towns 1774-1967. Leicester: Leicester University Press.

Castells, M. 1978. City, class and power. London: Macmillan.

Cave, P. W. 1968. Landuse and residential environment in Inner London: a study of the urban morphology and functional patterns of high density areas. D.Phil diss. University of Oxford, U.K.

Challen, M. G. 1973. Causes and effects of gentrification on the existing housing stock of Inner London. M.Phil. diss. School of Environment Studies, University College London, U.K.

Chauvire, Y., and Noin, D. 1980. Socio-professional typology of Greater Paris. Bulletin de l'Association de Geographes Francais 446-467: 51-62.

Clout, H. 1976. Rural-urban migration in Western Europe. In Migration in post-war Europe, ed. J. Salt and H. Clout. London: Oxford University Press.

Compton, P. 1979. Planning and spatial change in Budapest. In The Socialist City, ed. R. French and F. Hamilton. Chichester: Wiley.

Damais, J. P. 1978. Colloque sur l'occupation sociale de l'espace urbain. Rapport de synthese. Bulletin de l'Association de Geographes Francais 449:29-31.

Dennis, R. 1977. Intercensal mobility in a Victorian city. Transactions, Institute of British Geographers, New Series 2.3:349-63.

Dennis, R. 1980. The decline of manufacturing employment in Greater London, 1966-1974. In The inner city, employment and industry, ed. A. Evans and D. Eversley. London: Heinemann.

Dennis, R., and Daniels, S. 1981. 'Community' and the social geography of Victorial cities. Urban History Yearbook 1981: 7-23. Leicester: Leicester University Press.

Department of the Environment. 1979. National dwelling and housing survey, Phase 1, London: Her Majesty's Stationery Office.

Department of the Environment. 1980. Urban renaissance, a better life in towns. London: Her Majesty's Stationery Office.

Department of the Environment. n.d. The movement of house prices in the Greater London area, 1961-1970. London: D.O.E.

Drewe, P., Van Der Knapp, G., Mik, G., and Rodgers, H. M. 1975. Segregation in Rotterdam; an explorative study on theory, data and policy. *Tijdschrift voor Econ. en Soc. Geografie* 66.4: 204-216.

Dugmore, K. ed. 1975. The migration and distribution of socio-economic groups in Greater London: Evidence from the 1961, 1966 and 1971 Censuses. Research Memorandum 443, Greater London Council, London.

Dugmore, K., and Williams, P. 1974. Improvement Grants *Area* 6.2: 159-160.

Dunn, M., Rawson, M., and Rogers, A. 1981. *Rural housing: Competition and choice.* London: Allen and Unwin.

Dyos, H. 1968. The slums of Victorian London. *Victorian Studies* 9: 5-40.

Dyos, H., and Wolff, M., ed. 1973. *The Victorian city: Images and realities.* vol. 1 and 2. London: Routledge and Kegan Paul.

English House Condition Survey. 1978. Pt. 1, Report of the physical condition survey. London: Department of the Environment, Her Majesty's Stationery Office.

English House Condition Survey. 1979. Pt. 2, Report of the social survey. London: Department of the Environment, Her Majesty's Stationery Office.

Evans, A. (with the assistance of Russell, L.) 1980. A portrait of the London labour market. In *The Inner City, Employment and Industry,* ed. A. Evans and D. Eversley. London: Heinmann.

Eversley, D. 1981. Retrospect and prospects. *The Planner* 67.6: 148, 149, and back cover.

Eversley, D., and Bonnerjea, L. 1980. Changes in the resident populations of inner areas. The Inner City in Context, paper no. 2, Social Science Research Council, London.

Ferris, J. 1973. *Participation in urban planning: The Barnsbury case.* London: Bell.

Foster, C., and Richardson, R. 1973. Employment trends in London in the 1960's and their relevance for the future. In *London: Urban patterns, problems, and politics,* ed. D. Donnison and D. Eversley. London: Heinemann.

Foster, J. 1974. *Class struggle and the Industrial Revolution.* London: Methuen.

Francis Report. 1971. Report of the Committee on the Rent Acts, Cmnd 4609. London: Her Majesty's Stationery Office.

French, R., and Hamilton, I., eds. 1979. *The socialist city.* Chichester: Wiley.

Gauldie, E. 1974. *Cruel habitations.* London: Allen and Unwin.

George, V., and Lawson, R., eds. 1980. *Poverty and inequality in Common Market countries.* London: Routledge and Kegan Paul.

Glassberg, A. 1979. The politics of middle-class return to the city; Anglo-American perspectives. Occasional Paper 79-8, Center for International Studies, University of Missouri, St. Louis.

Glyn, A., and Sutcliffe, B. 1972. *British capitalism, workers and the profits squeeze.* Harmondsworth, Middlesex: Penguin.

Gordon, G. 1979. The status areas of early to mid-Victorian Edinburgh. *Transactions, Institute of British Geographers,* New Series 4.2: 168-91.

Greve, J. 1965. *Private landlords in England.* London: Bell.

Hall, P., ed. 1980. *The inner city in context.* London: Heinemann.

Hall, P., Gracey, H., Drewett, R., and Thomas, R. 1973. *The containment of urban England,* vol. 1, *Urban and metropolitan growth processes.* London: PEP, Allen and Unwin, and Sage Publications.

Hamilton, F., and Burnett, A. 1979. Social processes and residential structure. In *The socialist city,* ed. R. French and I. Hamilton. Chichester: Wiley.

Hamnett, C. 1973. Improvement grants as an indicator of gentrification in Inner London. *Area* 5.4: 252-61.

———. 1976. Social change and social segregation in Inner London 1961-1971. *Urban Studies* 13.3:261-72.

———. 1981. Flat break-ups. *Roof* (May/June): 18,19,24.

Hamnett, C., and Randolph, B. 1981. Flat break-up and decline of the private rented sector. *Estates Gazette* 260: 31-35.

Hamnett, C., and Williams, P. 1979. Gentrification in London 1961-1971: An empirical and theoretical analysis of social change. Research Memorandum 71, Centre for Urban and Regional Studies, University of Birmingham, U.K.

———. 1980. Social change in London: A study of gentrification. *Urban Affairs Quarterly* 15.4: 469-87.

Harris, C. 1974. *Islington.* London: Hamish Hamilton.

Harris, M. 1973. Some aspects of social polarization. In *London: urban patterns, problems and policies,* ed. D. Donnison and D. Eversley. London: Heinemann.

Harris, M., and Lyons, J. 1971. Social polarization. Research Memorandum 324, Greater London Council, London.

Harvey, D. 1975. Class structure in a capitalist society and the theory of residential differentiation. In *Processes in Physical and Human Geography,* ed. R. Peel, M. Chisholm and P. Haggett. London: Heinemann.

———. 1978. On countering the Marxian myth—Chicago style. *Comparative Urban Research* 6(2 and 3): 28-45.

Hollen Lees, L. 1980. The study of social conflict in English industrial towns, *Urban History Yearbook 1980,* pp. 34-43. Leicester: Leicester University Press.

Hume, I. 1973. Migrant workers in Europe. *Finance and Development* 10: 2-6.

Joyce, P. 1980. *Work, society and politics.* Brighton: Harvester Press.

Keeble, D. 1980. Industrial decline in the inner city and the conurbation. In *The Inner City, Employment and Industry,* ed. A. Evans and D. Eversley. London: Heinemann.

Kersley, S. R. 1975. Gentrification: a case study and its implications. B.Sc. diss. Department of Town and Country Planning, Heriot-Watt University, Edinburgh.

King, R. 1976. The evolution of international labour migration movements concerning the EEC. *Tijdschrift voor Econ. en Soc. Geografie* 67.2: 66-81.

Koch, R. 1977. Migration and recession: Migration in the Federal Republic of Germany, 1974 and 1975. *Informationen zur Raumentwicklung* 12: 875-87.

Lawton, R. 1979. Mobility in nineteenth century British cities. *Geographical Journal* 145: 206-44.

Lee, R., and Ogden, P., eds. 1976. *Economy and society in the EEC.* London: Saxon House.

Lewis, R. 1980. Seaside holiday resorts in the United States and Britain: A review. *Urban History Yearbook 1980* pp. 44-52. Leicester: Leicester University Press.

Lojkine, J. 1976. Contribution to a Marxist theory of capitalist urbanisation. In *Urban Sociology, Critical Essays,* ed. C. Pickvance. London: Tavistock.

Lomas, G. 1973. Labour and life in London. In *London: Urban Patterns, problems and Policies,* ed. D. Donnison and D. Eversley. London: Heinemann.

Massey, D., and Meegan, R. 1980. Industrial restructuring versus the cities. In *The inner city, employment and industry,* ed. A. Evans and D. Eversley. London: Heinemann.

McCarthy, J. 1975. Some social implications of improvement policy in London. Internal paper, Social Research Division, Housing Development Directorate, Department of the Environment, London.

Mellor, R. 1977. *Urban sociology in an urbanized world.* London: Routledge and Kegan Paul.

Merrett, S. 1976. Gentrification. In *Political Economy of Housing Workshop, Housing and Class in Britain.* London: Conference of Socialist Economists.

————. 1979. *State housing in Britain.* London: Routledge and Kegan Paul.

Milner Holland Report. 1965. Report of the Committee on Housing in Greater London (Chairman, Sir Milner Holland), Cmnd 2405. London: Her Majesty's Stationery Office.

Mingione, E. 1981. *Social conflict and the city.* Oxford: Blackwell.

Ministry of Housing and Local Government. 1968. Old Houses into New Homes, Cmnd. 3602. London: Her Majesty's Stationery Office.

Musil, J. 1968. The development of Prague's ecological structure. In *Readings In Urban Sociology,* ed. R. Pahl. Oxford: Pergamon.

Neild, M. 1974. Urban residential change in an inner London general improvement area: Moore Park Estate, Fulham. BA diss. University of Liverpool, U.K.

Nevitt, D. 1966. *Housing, taxation and subsidies.* London: Nelson.

O'Loughlin, J. 1980. Distribution and migration of foreigners in German cities. *Geographical Review* 70.3: 253-75.

Pahl, R. 1965. Urbs in rure: The metropolitan fringe in Hertfordshire. Geographical Paper no. 2, London School of Economics and Political Science, U.K.

Pailhe, J. 1978. Recent changes in the social structure of Bordeaux. *Revue Geographique des Pyrenees et du Sud-Ouest* 49.1: 11-28.

Paris, C., and Blackby, B. 1979. *Not much improvement: Urban renewal policy in Birmingham.* London: Heinemann.

Parsons, D. J. 1979. A geographical examination of the twentieth century theory and practice of selected village development in England. Ph.D. diss. University of Nottingham, U.K.

———. 1980. Rural gentrification: The influence of rural settlement planning policies. Research Papers in Geography, University of Sussex, U.K.

Pawley, M. 1978. *Home ownership.* London: Architectural Press.

Perry, P. 1969. Working class isolation and mobility in rural Dorset, 1837-1936. *Transactions, Institute of British Geographers* 46: 121-41.

Pitt, J. 1977. *Gentrification in Islington.* London: Bransbury Peoples Forum.

Pooley, C. 1977. The residential segregation of migrant communities in mid-Victorian Liverpool. *Transactions, Institute of British Geographers,* New ser. 2.3:364-382.

———. 1979. Residential mobility in the Victorian City. *Transactions, Institute of British Geographers,* New ser. 4.2:258-77.

Power, A. 1972. *A battle lost, Barnsbury, 1972.* Islington, London: Friends House.

———. 1973. David and Goliath, Barnsbury 1973. Islington, London: Holloway Neighborhood Law Centre.

Raban, J. 1974. *Soft city.* London: Fontana.

Rex, J., and Moore, R. 1967. *Race, community and conflict.* London, Oxford University Press.

Romanos, M., ed. 1979. *Western European cities in crisis.* Lexington, Mass: Lexington Books.

Rose, D. 1981. Accumulation versus reproduction in the inner city: The recurrent crisis of London revisited. In *Urbanization and urban planning in capitalist society,* ed. M. Dear and A. Scott. London: Methuen.

Royal Town Planning Institute. 1981. Renewal of older housing areas in the 1980s. Policy paper prepared by the Housing Working Party, London: RTPI.

Saunders, P. 1981. *Social theory and the urban question,* London, Hutchinson.

Shaw, M. 1977. The ecology of social change: Wolverhampton 1851-1871. *Transactions, Institute of British Geographers,* New Ser. 2.3:332-48.

———. 1979. Reconciling social and physical space: Wolverhampton 1871. *Transactions, Institute of British Geographers,* New Ser. 4.2:192-213.

Simpson, R. 1972. Housing in an inner London borough. Unpublished M.Phil Thesis, Univeristy of Oxford.

Social Science Research Council. 1980. The inner city in context. A series of eleven reports commissioned by the SSRC Inner Cities Working Party, London: SSRC.

Stedman Jones, G. 1972. *Outcast London.* Oxford: Clarendon Press.

Ungerson, C. 1971. *Moving home: A study of the redevelopment process in two London boroughs.* London: Bell.

University of Amsterdam. 1967. *Urban core and inner city.* Proceedings of the International Study Week. Amsterdam, Leiden: E.J. Brill.

Vance, J. E. 1967. Housing the worker: determinative and contingent ties in nineteenth century Birmingham. *Economic Geography* 43.2: 95-127.

Vining, D. R., and Kontuly, T. 1978. Population dispersal from major metropolitan regions: An international comparison. *International Regional Science Review* 3.1: 49-73.

Ward, D. 1980. Environs and neighbors in the 'Two Nations', residential differentiation in mid-nineteen century Leeds. *Journal of Historical Geography* 6: 133-62.

Weclawowicz, G. 1979. The structure of socio-economic space in Warsaw in 1931 and 1970: A study in factorial ecology. In *The Socialist City*, ed. R. French and I. Hamilton. Chichester: Wiley.

White, J. 1979. Campbell Bunk, A lumpen community in London between the wars. *History Workshop Journal* 8: 1-49.

Williams, P. 1976a. The role of institutions in Inner London housing market, the case of Islington. *Transactions, Institute of British Geographers*, New ser. 1.1:72-82.

——. 1976b. Change in an urban area: the role of institutions in the process of gentrification in the London Borough of Islington. Ph.D. diss. University of Reading, U.K.

——. 1978. Building societies and the inner city. *Transactions, Institute of British Geographers* 3.1: 23-34.

Willmott, P., and Young, M. 1973. Social class and geography. In *London: Urban Patterns, Problems and Policies*, ed. D. Donnison and D. Eversley. London: Heinemann.

Zunz, O. 1980. Residential segregation in the American metropolis. *Urban History Yearbook 1980*: 23-33. Leicester: Leicester University Press.

CHAPTER TWELVE

Gentrification in Australia

HAL L. KENDIG

In marked contrast to the American experience, the inner areas in Australian cities have demonstrated substantial and sustained development since the Second World War. Suburbanization has certainly diminished the relative importance of the central areas, but the old nineteenth century city has nonetheless captured a substantial share of the growth: employment has increased, and most of the housing stock has been upgraded or renewed. Although Australia shared with the U.S. a postwar concern for housing obsolescence, the residential rejuvenation was unexpected and amounted to a substantial success story. It was not brought about by any public action, however, and the rising property values and middle-class invasion are now viewed as major threats to the availability of low-cost housing. In the Australian inner areas, gentrification has become the problem rather than the solution.

This chapter considers gentrification to be the movement of the

Hal L. Kendig is Research Fellow, Urban Research Unit, Research School of Social Sciences, The Australian National University.

This chapter is based in part on H.L. Kendig, *New Life for Old Suburbs* (Sydney, London, and Boston: George Allen and Unwin, 1979), and readers interested in further information should consult this source. I am grateful for assistance from Susan Sheridan, and advice and comments from my colleagues, Peter Harrison, Max Neutze, and Peter Williams.

middle classes into areas previously occupied by the working classes and the poor. Gentrification takes many different forms and it is but one of many forces behind displacement. In understanding the complex process and explaining international differences, it is necessary to consider broader questions about the interrelationship between housing and land use in metropolitan areas, and basic structural changes in the economy and population as well as in spatial patterns. This chapter ventures into these larger issues in order to put the Australian experiences into context. It begins by outlining in a comparative way the distinctive features of Australian urban areas that make inner-city housing particularly attractive, proceeds to describe and explain the stages of gentrification, and then moves on to discuss the implications for the poor and possible policy responses.

Contrary to the popular bucolic image, Australia is highly urbanized with two-thirds of its population in the five capitals of the mainland states (Neutze 1977). More than 40 percent live in Sydney or Melbourne (nearly 3 million in each). Both cities have experienced intense pressures on inner-area housing. This chapter focuses on these two cities but some comparisons are made with Adelaide, a state capital of 800,000, in order to show how the process has been influenced by city size.[1] The definitions of the inner areas of these cities embrace the local government areas around the central city, covering only about 6 percent of the metropolitan urban area, much smaller than the American central city. In 1976 they housed only about 10 percent of the urban population but provided about 40 percent of the jobs.

STRUCTURAL PRECONDITIONS

Unlike the capitals of the United States, the Australian mainland state capitals are the principal ports and commercial and manufacturing centers, and the focus of state rail and road systems. Their hegemony arises from a combination of commercial, financial, and political power, the ability to direct public investment (notably the rail systems, highways, and port facilities), and to attract private investment. All have at least doubled their populations in the last 30 years and have consistently increased their share of their state populations, to 63 percent for Sydney, 71 percent for Melbourne, and 72 percent for Adelaide.

Although the three cities have all experienced a suburbanization of employment and other activities, the inner areas have retained more than 40 percent of all jobs and nearly two-thirds of clerical jobs. Jobs in manufacturing and warehousing, lost to the suburbs, have been more than replaced by the increase in office employment. The jobs in Sydney's inner areas, for example, have increased by a third in the postwar years. The CBDs have retained and expanded most of the attractions that established them as the principal employment centers and continue to provide the highest levels of service in commerce, and arts, and entertainment.

While adding to the demand for inner-area housing, nonresidential development has seriously depleted the supply. From 1947 to 1976, redevelopment and conversion had removed more than one-fifth of housing accommodation, displacing more than 60,000 people in inner Sydney (Kendig 1979, pp. 104, 155). Offices and other kinds of commercial development were the single most important cause of housing losses (44 percent of the total), but industrial expansion was also significant (35 percent), as was the development of roads and railways (12 percent) and public institutions— universities, schools, and hospitals (9 percent). The losses were primarily of poor-quality dwellings in mixed-use areas, thus reducing the supply of low-cost accommodation and displacing relatively poor residents.

An additional attraction of the inner areas for middle-class resettlement in Sydney and Melbourne is the quality of the housing stock, much of it in the form of two-story, terraced (attached) single-family dwellings in solid brick, with,occasionally, more stately villas; in Adelaide there are many stone and brick cottages. Even after decades of neglect, the basic fabric of these dwellings is usually sound and capable of rehabilitation. Although most were orginally rental properties, each terrace and semi-detached house has its own plot of land and a separate title, which facilitated purchase and upgrading by individual owners.

The other characteristic conducive to middle-class occupation is the residential quality of many inner-area localities. In Melbourne and Adelaide generous tree-lined streets, and in Sydney picturesque harborside environments, more than compensate for some of the disadvantages arising from mixed land uses.

Fortunately, the organization of local government in Australia has not disadvantaged inner areas in any way comparable to the fiscal crisis of major American cities. In Australia, there are many small local government areas, but the property tax supports only a narrow range of property-related services. The important and expensive services—education, health, law enforcement, and welfare—are provided and financed by state and national government.

RISING OWNER OCCUPANCY

Prospects for the inner areas did not look very bright immediately after the Second World War. At the time of a severe national housing shortage, the inner area housing was overcrowded and run-down after middle-class flight during the 1920s and disinvestment during the Depression and the Second World War. Each of the older captial cities established commissions to study the problem of deteriorated housing and recommended radical public redevelopment (Spearritt 1974; Jones 1972). In 1947, the Sydney metropolitan planning authority, the Cumberland Council, determined that a third of the housing in inner Sydney required immediate replacement and three-quarters of the housing required replacement within 25 years (Cumberland County Council 1948). Fortunately, funds were not available to embark on any major redevelopment of dwellings that spontaneoulsy improved as a result of market forces within the next decade.

Ironically, the rent control that had contributed to earlier disinvestment became the major force in the first stage of residential rejuvenation. Since landlords could neither charge a market rent nor evict sitting tenants, they had a considerable incentive to sell to sitting tenants on very favorable terms (Vandermark and Harrison 1972). The working-class occupants, whose incomes were rising with growing postwar affluence, frequently bought with vendor financing that involved little or no down payment. By the mid-1950s, houses in run-down parts of inner Sydney and Melbourne were being sold for an average of little more than a year's average earnings (Neutze 1972; Johnson 1972). Owner-occupancy rose rapidly, from less than 10 percent to over 70 percent in some suburbs; the overall increase in inner Sydney was from 27 percent in 1947 to almost 40 percent in 1954.

The change from depressed rental housing to upgraded owner-occupancies was stimulated in the 1950s and 1960s by the influx of tens of thousands of migrants. Displaced persons from central and northern Europe in the immediate postwar years were later followed by assisted migrants, particularly from southern Europe. Like their counterparts entering the U.S. at the turn of the century, many of them were attracted to the jobs and the chance of home ownership in the inner areas. By 1961, nearly a third of the residents in innermost Sydney and Melbourne were from Italy, Greece, or other non-British countries (Kendig 1979, p. 114). Most purchases were financed by vendors, finance companies, or pooled family savings; banks were still reluctant to make loans on inner-city homes, despite the rising property values. The migrant invasion, unlike the American experience, enhanced rather than depressed property values and did not lead to an exodus of the Australian-born; nearly all neighborhoods continued to have a majority of native-born Australians.

Rent control and tenant protection on the one hand, and migrant demand, on the other, in a period of sustained economic expansion, transformed most of the inner suburbs. By the early 1960s nearly two-thirds of the dwellings in the inner areas of Sydney and Melbourne were owner-occupied, half of them by migrants. Major reconstructions and additions increased markedly and even lower-income owners did a considerable amount of cleaning up, repainting, repairing, and plumbing (Kendig 1979, p. 115). The inner areas of all three cities experienced sharp increases in prices and rents which exceeded those for established homes elsewhere in the metropolis.

This resettlement of the inner areas was nicely balanced by massive suburbanization driven by the baby boom, economic improvement, and rising car ownership. The movement outward by some inner-city households was sufficient to relieve the postwar overcrowding and free housing for migrants but was not so extensive as to cause any problems of abandonment or high vacancy rates. Nor was there any increase of social segregation: the moves outward were explained more by life cycle (young families) than by class, and the manufacturing workers who left (at the same rate as higher status workers) were replaced by migrants having similar kinds of jobs. Overall, the improvement of inner-area housing brought substantial benefits to the working classes: tenants usually had the choice of purchasing their home at moderate cost or receiving financial inducements to vacate that made a suburban home attainable. The housing stock in inner areas improved substantially without any significant increase in the social status of the areas. These developments provided the groundwork for the further improvement and gentrification that followed in the 1970s.

PRIVATE INFILL AND REDEVELOPMENT

By the mid 1960s, important structural changes began to apply new pressures on inner-area housing. The rapid increases in white-collar jobs in the city center, combined with massive household formation by the postwar generation, considerably increased the demand for small inner-area housing. At the same time, the stock of rental accommodation had been reduced by conversions to owner occupancy. From 1954 to 1961, the number of tenanted dwellings in inner Sydney and Melbourne had almost halved, while average rents in inner Sydney rose by 27 percent in real terms. During the late 1950s, the first tentative response to these changes was the conversion of some larger houses, boarding houses, and hotels into inexpensive flats. The relatively small number of new flats built during the 1950s generally were sold under "company title" to owner occupants. By the early 1960s, fears of rent control had receded and the private market responded fully to the strong demand: the construction of new flats, mostly inexpensive walk-up structures, was almost totally responsible for the net increase of dwellings in inner Sydney, from 120,000 to 144,000 during the 1960s. Initially built in higher status areas near the harbor, they later spread out along rail routes to the city center and eventually to almost any area where enough land accessible to public transport could be assembled. Melbourne had a flat boom of comparable scale, while in Adelaide low land costs and good accessibility to jobs moderated the demand for flats.

To a surprising degree, this massive development took very little housing and displaced relatively few residents. It was estimated that only one inner-city dwelling was taken for every seventeen new flats—a total of less than 1 percent of the 1947 housing stock in inner Sydney (Kendig 1979, p. 133). One explanation is that regulations were permissive and sites could be used intensively (Vandermark and Harrison 1972, p. 36; Urban Research Unit 1973, p. 36). Another explanation is the availability of vacant or underutilized land: industrial land with minimal structures in residential areas (Neutze 1971, p. 33; 1972, p. 119), single houses on large awkward sites, or single houses combined with the backyards of other houses (Kendig 1979, p. 133). The private market proved very sensitive to the value of existing housing—especially dense terrace houses on small blocks—and the planning hopes of the 1940s for redevelopment of older homes was never realized on a large scale.

The boom in flat development effectively compensated for inner-area population loss resulting from falling occupancy rates and nonresidential incursion in all three cities. The young white-collar workers who occupied the flats were the first and largest wave of the middle classes moving to the inner city from the suburbs. However, many of the new flats were let at relatively low rents, which meant that they also increased housing opportunities for less affluent households. Of the relatively few people displaced by flat development, most were owners who made profitable and voluntary sales.

During the 1970s the flat boom waned as a result of high interest rates and perhaps satisfaction of demand; the reductions in building were especially sharp in the inner areas because little suitable land was left, home values were too high to redevelop them, and local government limited their density and location. Many old flats were upgraded and converted to condominiums for sale to owner-occupants, in some cases displacing low-income tenants (Centre for Urban Research and Action, p. 141). Flat building has fallen less in inner Adelaide, where suitable land is still available, and in the innermost areas of Sydney, where expensive high-rise condominiums continue in demand.

GENTRIFICATION

In the later part of the 1960s, the settlement of migrants in most of inner Sydney's terrace housing areas tapered off sharply as immigration fell and established migrants moved outward (Burnley and Walker 1977). Increasingly they were replaced by the Australian-born middle classes: blue-collar workers as a proportion of the resident labor force in these areas fell dramatically, by up to 15 percent compared with 5 percent for the whole metropolis; equally the percentage of professionals and managers rose by 5 percent or more compared to only 0.5 percent metropolitan-wide. Innermost areas also had sizable losses of children, large gains of young adults between the ages of 16 and 25, and small losses of the aged (Roseth 1969, p. 124).

This "filtering up" of the old houses, radiating from the innermost areas outwards, resulted from the complicated inter-relationship of a variety of developments. Household formation by the baby boom and the growth of white-collar jobs certainly were major determinants. Households with two income-earners also increased as participation by women (aged 15 to 64) in the labor force rose rapidly in Sydney, from 40 percent in 1961 to 48 percent in 1971. There was a considerable minority of young adults—more than in earlier generations—who were postponing childbearing and leading the career- and consumer-oriented lifestyles well-suited for city living. Many openly rejected the image and lifestyles of outer-suburban living.

The childless young adults had less need for large houses and gardens in the outer suburbs. They also were less able to pay for them as interest rates rose and the number of years of average earnings needed to buy an average house in Sydney rose from 3.4 in 1960 and 1965 to 3.9 in 1970 and 1978. Although car-ownership rates had climbed to one per household by 1971, new houses were increasingly distant from the jobs and attractions of the city center. For all of these reasons, inexpensive old houses in the inner suburbs became increasingly attractive for some middle-income households. The affluent young adults in the inner suburbs found that old houses had considerable advantages over new flats. Terraces offered some outdoor space and were usually more commodious. Migrants had already reversed much of the slum image, and terraces had become fashionable symbols of urbane lifestyles, community diversity, architectural charm, and historical significance —a rejection of the suburban stereotype and an acceptance of cosmopolitan values and Australia's colonial history. Renovating an old terrace house presented a different image from buying a condominium, and one with opportunities for self-expression.

Paddington exemplifies gentrification thoughout Australia; a detailed case study is available of its postwar development (Roseth 1969). Located only three kilometers east of the city center in Sydney, Paddington has many outstanding residential features, acknowledged even by the postwar planners who declared it a slum. The terrain slopes down from a central ridge, providing many harbor views. It is located near high-status areas to the east and has little intrusive industry. Unlike many of the terraces in other areas, those in Paddington were designed for rental by middle-class businessmen and professionals. Built in the 1880s, they have two, three, and sometimes even four stories, fairly wide (five-meter) frontages, and elaborate cast-iron balconies and other attractive ornamentation. It is hardly surprising that Paddington was the first inner area to undergo gentrification.

The trend-setters—the first of the middle-class arrivals—were a few artists, journalists, and other white-collar workers during the early 1950s. The movement became more widespread in the late 1950s and accelerated in the mid-1960s. White-collar workers were 14 percent of the buyers from 1959 to 1962, but 40 percent from 1963 to 1966. They were almost entirely young and Australian-born, mostly married couples but some single people. In sharp contrast to the migrant buyers, only a few had school-age children. Their individual incomes were about the metropolitan average but households' incomes were well above average because many had two incomes.

Later in the 1960s middle-class buyers began to move into less attractive housing in other inner area suburbs as the trend strengthened and prices rose in Paddington. While the middle classes were re-establishing themselves in Paddington after a fifty year absence, the other areas previously had always been occupied by tradesman and other blue-collar workers. They were, however, generally free of industrial intrusion and most had some striking locational advantage: Balmain has a village atmosphere, spectacular harbor views, and a short ferry ride to the city center; Glebe is next to Sydney University; and Surry Hills has handsome, wide, tree-lined streets within walking distance of thousands of office jobs. By the early 1970s, the old slum stigma had been nearly entirely removed and the middle-classes were buying in all the innermost areas.

To label this process as a "back to the city" movement would be a misnomer on two counts. Very few of the new residents had moved directly from the suburbs: most of them came from inner-city flats, deciding to buy an inner-area home rather than one in the outer areas as they moved ahead in their housing careers. Moreover, the population of gentrified areas dropped sharply as one- and two-person households replaced families with children, and inner houses were kept unoccupied during major renovations or while awaiting sale or rent. The influx did, however, slightly reduce the growing imbalance of white-collar jobs over resident workers.

The inner-area housing stock proved to be very adaptable to shifts of demand. During the 1960s nearly 5,000 buildings (mainly terraces) in inner Sydney were converted from rooms in shared houses or boarding houses back to single occupancy. The small, low-cost end of the market was increasingly being met by newer flats, and the large, previously subdivided homes were very attractive to middle-class purchasers. This further decreased occupancy rates, providing additional evidence that "filtering down" is by no means irreversible.

The terrace housing also underwent considerable "filtering up" in terms of housing quality. Unlike the migrant and sitting-tenant buyers of the 1950s, the young "trendies" were able to pay, soon after moving in, for major alterations and additions. These usually made the houses even more attractive than the original dwellings. Of the Paddington owner-occupants who bought during the early 1960s, 43 percent had, by 1966, made some structural changes and rebuilt both bathroom and kitchen; 70 percent had rebuilt the bathroom; 3 percent only painted and cleaned; but only 5 percent had done nothing (Roseth 1969, p. 216). Typical renovations cost about a third of the purchase price of the dwellings.

The number of major alterations and additions throughout the inner suburbs started to increase sharply from the late 1960s onwards; by 1970 they were as extensive in other areas as they were in Paddington in the mid-1960s (Ogilvie 1969, pp. 55-56). From 1970 to 1976 there was a further increase by 50 percent in the annual number of approved alterations and additions (Kendig 1979, p. 133). Although improvement was most intense in areas of middle-class invasion, established migrants and working-class families in other areas were also making substantial, if less visible, improvements.

In Paddington, and probably elsewhere in the inner city, the renovations were made almost entirely by owner-occupants during the early years. The market was too uncertain for renovation by investors for either sale or rent. Banks were reluctant to give loans in former slum areas and many renovators used their own funds, or borrowed at high interest rates. Despite doubts about future market values, owners nonetheless were conscious of investment values. Roseth (1969) reported that four-fifths of the renovators in Paddington expected property-value increases by at least as much as was spent on improvements. By the mid-1960s, steadily rising property values made it easier to borrow for renovations, and renovation by landlords and speculative purchasers increased.

During the 1960s the areas of middle-class invasion had increases of sale prices up to three times greater than those in nearby areas (Kendig 1979, p. 128). Even in areas of continued working-class occupancy, the value of buildings rose more rapidly than that of the sites. House rents continued to rise more rapidly in inner Sydney than elsewhere in the metropolis. In 1976, house prices in inner Sydney were still 25 percent below the metropolitan average, but the gap had narrowed appreciably and it probably has narrowed further since then.

Unlike the rejuvenation during the 1950s, owner-occupancy rates were no longer rising. In fact, there is some evidence that owner occupancy has dropped slightly in recent years. Most middle-class purchasers were buying from owner occupants wishing to move outward (especially migrants), older people, or deceased states. Equally, many investors found it profitable to rehabilitate houses and rent them to young students and white-collar workers; these tenants increasingly preferred to form groups sharing houses rather than live alone or in pairs in flats. While working-class owners often made profitable sales, some tenants were dislocated and the poor among them were hard pressed by increasing rents.

Gentrification also wrought major changes during the 1960s in inner Melbourne (Logan 1980; Maher 1978). The first areas were generally near the middle-class employment of the city center, the university, and hospitals. Nodes of better housing in elevated areas, built for the middle classes and subsequently "filtered down," have also been at the fore of gentrification in Melbourne. More than in Sydney, the rejuvenation started from particularly attractive streets and then spread outward. During the late 1960s, almost all suburbs in the City of Melbourne had increases in the number of middle-class residents in old houses (Victorian Council of Social Services

1975, pp. 45-46). In some areas, the proportion of professionals and managers among house buyers rose from approximately 5 to 50 percent (Logan 1980, p. 199).

A study of house sales in two inner areas in Melbourne found that, in the early 1970s, white-collar workers comprised almost two-thirds of the owner-occupant buyers but less than half the owner-occupant sellers (Centre for Urban Research and Action 1977, p. 12). Moreover, these ownership changes have been accelerating rapidly and, in 1975, nearly two-thirds of sales were from blue-collar to white-collar households. Similarly, sales from immigrants to Australians rose from a quarter to over one-half. Unlike the earlier years, when established migrants sold to more recently arrived compatriots, the migrant working classes were being replaced by the Australian-born middle class. The explanation lies in both the strong middle-class demand and the reduced inflow and moves outward of immigrants.

The study shows that the invasion by white-collar workers was accompanied by price inflation. From 1970 to 1975, median prices in inner Melbourne rose at twice the rate of the next ring of suburbs to the northwest, and by more than they rose in the more affluent southeast. By 1975, the location of Melbourne's cheapest houses had shifted from the inner suburbs to the next ring of suburbs in the inner northwest. The population change consequent to these sales was accentuated by the high turnover rates in the buoyant market: up to 16 percent a year during the 1972 boom. In just six years, two out of every five houses in the study areas had been sold at least once.

Investors, who comprised a quarter of the buyers, have played an important role in the transition from the working classes to the middle classes. In one area they bought almost half of those properties sold by blue-collar workers, widows, or retired persons; those that they resold to owner-occupants went mainly to middle-class purchasers. Investors often resold at much higher prices, within six months of buying, after only superficial renovations. The heavy involvement of investors seeking capital gains provides further evidence that owner-occupancy rates may have fallen. In fact, owner-occupants accounted for two-thirds of the sellers but only half of the buyers. No figures are available on subsequent house rents but they probably rose (although perhaps more slowly than prices), and most were probably leased to middle-class occupants. Investors have not caused gentrification but they almost certainly have contributed to the accelerated turnover and large increases of prices and rents.

In inner Adelaide, the number of renovations also increased (Pugh

1976, p. 374) and house prices rose considerably faster than in the rest of the metropolis. However, there were considerable differences among inner Adelaide and inner Melbourne and inner Sydney. Because the quality of the inner-area housing in Adelaide is far better, owner-occupancy rates had always been higher, and the prices in 1976 were about equal to the metropolitan averages. During the 1970s there were increases of white-collar workers but, unlike the other inner areas, inner Adelaide also had net increases of skilled blue-collar workers and relatively small losses of migrants; the main losses were of pensioners and nonskilled workers.

Since the demise of rent control in the late 1950s, the rejuvenation of the inner areas of the three cities has not been influenced very directly by public policy. Although zoning limited incursion by nonresidential uses, market pressures explain the small amount of intrusion by flats into existing residential areas. Indeed, policies designed to preserve and improve these areas generally came after the gentrification process had been firmly established. For example, Paddington was zoned as a conservation area in 1968, ten years after the middle class started to move in.

The new middle classes did, however, have a major influence on local and state policy. Inner city councils, long dominated by the right wing of the Labor party, were taken over by young representatives of the left wing. Amenities and property values were enhanced by a wide variety of improvements, such as street closures, tree planting schemes, the provision of small parks, and the establishment of "historic zoning" for residential areas (Logan 1980; Jager 1976). The middle classes were active in mobilizing opposition to flat development, commercial intrusion, and inner city freeways (Center for Urban Research and Action 1977; City of Sydney Resident Action Group Committee 1977; and Sandercock 1975). While these improvements undoubtedly had major benefits for the residents on lower incomes, they proved to be a mixed blessing for those tenants who faced higher rents and further risk of displacement.

CONSEQUENCES AND IMPLICATIONS

The postwar developments of inner Sydney, Melbourne, and Adelaide resulted in substantial and widespread gains in the housing stock. From 1947 to 1967, the number of dwellings increased in all inner areas as flat development more than compensated for losses caused by nonresidential incursion and amalgamations. Owner occupancy jumped from one-quarter to almost two-thirds in inner Sydney and Melbourne, and from one-half to three-quarters in inner Adelaide. Rents and property values rose relative to the rest of the metropolis. By almost any available measure the postwar slums have been largely transformed into solid residential areas.

Ironically, the housing improvement was directly responsible for dramatic drops of population—by 35 percent in inner Melbourne, 30 percent in Adelaide, and 28 percent in Sydney. Detailed analysis of inner Sydney attributes a quarter of the net losses to lower occupancy rates in houses, and fully half to the redevelopment and conversion of rooming houses and other kinds of nonprivate housing (Kendig 1979, p. 73). If it were not for flat development, there would have been a further loss of nearly 20 percent in inner Sydney and Melbourne. It is clear that housing improvement in inner areas has done little to overcome the problems of increasing suburban sprawl.

The changes in the occupational status of the residents demonstrate that middle-class invasion was one of the dominant features of postwar change. During the 1950s, the inner areas shared equally with the rest of the metropolis in a shift away from blue-collar employment. But during the flat development and gentrification of the late 1960s, white-collar workers (as a proportion of the resident workforce) rose by 9 percent in inner Sydney and 10 percent in inner Melbourne—twice the increases of the rest of the metropolitan areas. With the process continuing during the early 1970s, the occupational profile of inner-Sydney residents in 1976 was very close to that of the rest of the metropolis.

The rising status of inner areas in recent years results largely from the replacement of postwar migrant families with the young Australian-born. From a postwar high of about 30 percent in 1971, the non-British born populations in inner Sydney and Melbourne had fallen slightly by 1976 as the overall immigration rate fell (Australian Population and Immigration Council 1976) and previous immigrants moved outward. While this process worked toward equalizing social-class and ethnic distributions, it increased the long-term tendency for fewer children to live in inner areas.

The effect of these changes on disadvantaged groups has depended mainly on the overall state of the housing market. During the 1950s and 1960s, tenants of modest means suffered from the burden of making forced moves, but many became owners and others usually could find comparable housing at a modest price elsewhere in the inner suburbs. Except for cases of public resumption, most notably the renewal activities of housing commissions, as discussed below, owner-occupants could choose not to move or else make profitable sales that would re-establish them elsewhere.

The position of poor tenants has proved to be much more precarious during the 1970s. In recent years the number of the poor throughout Australia has risen considerably as a result of rapid increases of the unemployed, single parents, and the aged. At the same time, housing costs have risen rapidly throughout the metropolis, high interest rates have made home ownership unattainable for modest earners, and expenditures on public housing have been halved in the last few years. Losses of low-cost housing in inner areas have not been offset by increases elsewhere; rents in middle areas have risen relatively slowly, but with few exceptions they still exceed those of inner areas.

Thus, many of the poor remain in inner areas: 16 percent of inner Sydney households in 1976 were on annual incomes under $3,000, compared to 7 percent elsewhere in the metropolis. Only one-quarter of the inner area poor were owners, 6 percent were public tenants, and average private rents amounted to more than half of the income of the poor (Kendig 1979, p. 166). The strong demand has also enabled landlords to require large bonds of up to several hundred dollars, to avoid making repairs, and to discriminate against single parents and others whose ability to pay high rents is suspect. The poorest tenants can often adjust only by overcrowding or living in poorly maintained dwellings. A continuation of these trends would mean that the inner suburbs would be increasingly segregated into some areas of high-quality housing, with pockets of overcrowding, undermaintenance, poor amenities, and yet high rents.

A 1976 survey provides more information on moderate-and low-income households that had recently moved in Melbourne (Centre for Urban Research and Action 1977, pp. 70-85). Tenants forced to move by evictions, houses being sold, or increased rents, all accounted for 15 percent of the moves from inner and middle suburbs but only 4 percent of those from outer areas. The displaced had considerable difficulty finding other accommodations. Among private renters, almost two-thirds reported problems of high rents and high bonds, of finding housing in desired localities, or of discrimination against families with children. The costs of moving averaged more than two weeks' earnings. Rents for their new dwellings averaged 50 percent more than their previous rents, and half of those earning under $100 weekly reported repair problems in their new dwellings.

POLICY RESPONSES

Land-use controls in Australia can potentially play a more

constructive role in urban development than in the U.S.. A single planning agency in each state establishes an overall structure plan for the entire metropolis. The plans are prescriptive as well as proscriptive: in addition to minimizing negative externalities, the goals include coordinating development in ways that minimize journeys-to-work and efficiently use public investment on infrastructure. In application, mainly by small, local government authorities, there has been little restraint on centralized development of nonresidential lands. While incursion has been limited in some inner areas, planners were unable to restrain the powerful forces behind the central growth of jobs. In many respects the worst offenders were powerful state agencies that added jobs and took land in central areas with scant regard for planning goals.

Public housing authorities have had a mixed record in responding to the problems of inner areas. In all three of the major capital cities, there was very little clearance and redevelopment by these agencies during the 1950s. Scarce funds were used for supplying suburban housing, which was less expensive and more in demand, and the improvement of the existing housing in inner areas made redevelopment even more expensive. By 1970, the Housing Commission in Sydney had cleared less than 1 percent of the inner land (1,430 dwellings) originally considered in need of redevelopment. Very poor housing was taken, and displaced residents were offered alternative accommodations. Replacement housing was increasingly provided by high-density flat building in order to limit land costs and provide more accommodation for those on modest incomes.

While the authorities in Sydney recognized the decreasing need for slum clearance, the Victorian Housing Commission in Melbourne pressed ahead with massive redevelopment without much regard for the improvement that had already occurred. By 1970, nearly 4,000 dwellings, most of which had become owner-occupied, were compulsorily acquired at below-market prices and replaced with nearly 7,000 high-rise flats for which there is now little demand (Jones 1972, p. 72; Brady 1976). The displaced owners suffered substantial financial losses, tenants were relocated far from their previous dwellings (Holdsworth and Brooks 1971), and rejuvenation of many neighborhoods was retarded by the threat of public redevelopment. Although public redevelopment was also fought by residents in inner Sydney (New South Wales Housing Commission 1976) and Adelaide (Sandercock 1975), the disputes were particularly bitter in Melbourne (Hargreaves 1975; Brady 1976). A series of court battles, union bans, street demonstrations, and other direct action have virtually halted high-rise public redevelopment in the inner areas of all three cities.

In contrast to the public redevelopment in inner Sydney and Melbourne, the Housing Trust in Adelaide pioneered a program of purchasing and rehabilitating old homes for rental to public tenants (South Australian Housing Trust 1977). Low land costs made this program no more expensive than the construction of a new home in less accessible outer areas. With the Adelaide example in mind, the Commonwealth government purchased the Glebe estate of 720 dwellings in inner Sydney (Department of Housing and Construction 1980; Wagner 1977) and 134 dwellings in Emerald Hill in inner Melbourne, in order to preserve the housing for tenants on low incomes. A joint program of the city, the state Housing Commission, and the Commonwealth rebuilt or rehabilitated an additional 720 dwellings in the inner Sydney suburb of Woolloomooloo.

There has been a major controversy about whether redevelopment or rehabilitation are the best ways for public authorities to provide housing for tenants of modest means. While purchase and rehabilitation is very expensive and provides no additional housing capacity, it does preserve accommodations for the poor in dwellings that are more desirable than high-rise developments and in locations preferable to outer-area estates. Few residents are displaced and neighborhoods are enhanced rather than destroyed. A detailed cost-benefit analysis of the Glebe project (Beattie 1978) found that the costs of rehabilitation were comparable to redevelopment and far greater than that of new housing in outer areas. However, if the social costs of moving and long journeys-to-work are taken into account, the cost differences between inner-area rehabilitation and outer-area construction were about eliminated.

In recent years the housing authorities have been attempting to meet the inner-area demand by providing a mixture of medium-density infill housing and rehabilitation of the existing stock. However, land costs and waiting lists have been increasing while budgets have been cut sharply. There is little indication that public housing will compensate for much of the erosion of low-cost housing resulting from gentrification.

SUMMARY

Over the postwar period, development in the inner suburbs of Australia's major cities contrasts sharply with both the predictions of the invasion/incursion model and the American experience. Indeed, it is remarkable how the old zonal model, which was roughly reflected in Australian inner-area development during the first half of the century, has been turned inside out. The explanation is the strong demand from a succession of groups—the Australian working-class tenants, migrants, and then the young middle classes—combined with the natural and historical advantages of the areas themselves. Public policy played relatively little part in bringing about these changes, and it is difficult to envisage how it could ever generate improvement on such a massive scale; the major policy success was the absence of any actions that would have inhibited the improvements.

It seems that major urban change usually exacts the highest costs of those who are least able to afford them. There was a major exception when the inner areas were improved by and for the working classes during the economic expansion of the early postwar years. However, history has more recently reverted to form: just as the poor were left in a deteriorating inner city during the early days of suburbanization, they are now experiencing considerable hardship as the middle classes outbid them for newly fashionable housing near jobs and amenities. Public policy can limit the excesses of the private market in two ways. First, land-use controls that direct economic activity to outer areas would lessen the forces behind gentrification in inner areas and reduce the journey-to-work in outer areas. Second, direct public acquisition of existing housing in inner areas would preserve a share of accommodation for poor tenants. While some helpful action in these directions is being taken, the economic and political obstacles are substantial and there is little prospect for policies that would fully ameliorate the problems for those on modest incomes.

NOTES

1. There is little literature specifically on gentrification in other Australian cities. Among the few available studies are examinations of Brisbane (Cities Commission 1975), Newcastle (Crooks Michell Peacock Stewart Pty Ltd. 1976), Freemantle (Newman 1977), and Hobart (Graham 1977). There is also a series of atlases that show population distributions and changes in Sydney (Poulsen and Spearritt 1981), Melbourne (Cities Commission and Davis 1975), Adelaide (Babcock, Jaensch, and Williams 1977), Brisbane (McDonald and Guilfoyle 1981), and Perth (Houghton 1979).

REFERENCES

Australian Population and Immigration Council. 1976. *A decade of migrant settlement: Report on the 1973 immigration survey.* Canberra: Australian Government Printing Office.

Babcock, B., Jaensch, D., and Williams, M. 1977.*Adelaide at the census: A social atlas*. Adelaide: Australasian Political Studies Association.

Beattie, D. 1978. Economic evaluation of the propsal to acquire and rehabilitate residential property in Glebe. In *Australian project evaluation; Selected Readings*, ed. J. C. McMaster and G. R. Webb. Sydney: Australia & New Zealand Book Company.

Brady, R. H. 1976. Urban renewal: the Melbourne experience. In *Australian urban economics: A reader*, ed. J. C. McMaster and G. R. Webb. Sydney: Australia & New Zealand Book Company.

Burnley, I. H. , and Walker, S. R. 1977. *Population and social change in the inner city of Sydney*. Sydney: School of Geography, University of New South Wales.

Centre for Urban Research and Action. 1977. *The displaced: A study of housing conflict in Melbourne's inner city*. Melbourne.

Cities Commission. 1975. *Moreton region growth strategy investigations: Inner urban redevelopment potential*. Canberra: Cities Commission.

Cities Commission and Davis, J. R. 1975. *Melbourne at the census, 1971: A social atlas*. Canberra: Cities Commission.

City of Sydney Resident Action Group Committee. 1977. *Planning for residential living in the City of Sydney*. The Council of the City of Sydney.

Crooks Mitchell Peacock Stewart Pty. Ltd. 1976. *Inner city residential study: Newcastle city council*. Sydney.

Cumberland County Council. 1948. *Report on the planning scheme for the County of Cumberland, New South Wales*. Sydney.

Department of Housing and Construction. 1980. *Glebe Project*. Canberra: Australian Government Publishing Service.

Graham, R. J. 1977. Battery Point: social action and planning for human scale development. Paper presented to the 48th Australia and New Zealand Academy for the Advancement of Science Congress, Melbourne.

Hargreaves, K. 1975. This house not for sale: Conflicts between the housing commission and residents of slum reclamation areas. Report by the Centre for Urban Research and Action, Melbourne.

Holdsworth, J., and Brooks, G. 1971. Pilot study into displacement through slum reclamation. *Architecture in Australia* (April): 186-90.

Houghton, D. C. 1979. *Perth at the 1976 census: a social atlas*. Perth: Department of Geography, University of Western Australia.

Jager, M. 1976. Urban conservation and social change in the inner areas of Melbourne. MA (preliminary) diss. Department of Sociology, La Trobe University, Melbourne.

Johnson, K. M. 1972. *People and property in North Melbourne*. Canberra: Urban Research Unit, Australian National University.

Jones, M. A. 1972. *Housing and poverty in Australia*. Melbourne: Melbourne University Press.

Kendig, H. L. 1979. *New life for old suburbs*. Sydney, London, and Boston: George Allen & Unwin.

Logan, W. S. 1980. Gentrification in Inner Melbourne: Pattern, process and meaning: A political geography responding to the politicization of the social sciences. Ph.D. diss. Department of Geography, Monash University, Melbourne.

Maher, C. 1978. The changing residential role in the inner city: The example of inner Melbourne. *Australian Geographer* 148: 112-22.

McDonald, G. T., and Guilfoyle, M. J. 1981. *Urban social atlas of Brisbane: 1976.* Brisbane: Institute of Applied Social Research, Griffith University.

Newman, P. 1977. Freemantle: a case study in inner city population decline: Policy and planning implications. Paper presented to the 48th Australia and New Zealand Academy for the Advancement of Science Congress, Melbourne.

New South Wales Housing Commission. 1976. *Waterloo Development Proposals; Analysis of options and environmental impact statement.* Sydney.

Neutze, Max. 1971. *People and property in Randwick.* Canberra: Urban Research Unit, Australian National University.

―――. 1972. *People and property in Redfern.* Canberra: Urban Research Unit, Australian National University.

―――. 1977. *Urban development in Australia.* Sydney: George Allen & Unwin.

Ogilvie, D. 1969. *The rehabilitation of decayed urban residential areas.* Sydney: Department of Town and Country Planning, University of Sydney.

Poulsen, M., and Spearritt, P. 1981. *Sydney: A social and political atlas.* Sydney: George Allen and Unwin.

Pugh, C. 1976. Older urban residential areas and the development of economic analysis: A comparative study. In *Australian urban economics: A reader,* ed. J. C. McMaster and G. R. Webb. Sydney: Australian & New Zealand Book Company.

Roseth, J. 1969. Revival of an old residential area. Ph.D. diss. Faculty of Architecture, University of Sydney, Sydney.

Sandercock, L. K. 1975. *Cities for sale.* Melbourne: Melbourne University Press.

South Australian Housing Trust. 1977. South Australian Housing Trust Annual Report, submitted to the Minister for Planning, Adelaide.

Spearritt, P. 1974. Sydney's "slums" :Middle-class reformers and the labor response. *Labour History* 26:65-81.

Urban Research Unit. 1973. *Urban development in Melbourne.* Canberra: Australian Institute of Urban Development.

Vandermark, E., and Harrison, P. F. 1972. *Development activities in four Sydney suburban areas.* Canberra: Urban Research Unit, Australian National University.

Victorian Council of Social Services. 1975. *Towards an inner urban strategy.* Melbourne.

Wagner, C. 1977. Sydney's Glebe project: An essay in urban rehabilitation. *Royal Australian Planning Institute Journal* 15(1):1-24.

IV

Concluding Remarks

CHAPTER THIRTEEN

Through the Glass Darkly: Gentrification, Revitalization, and the Neighborhood

J. JOHN PALEN AND BRUCE LONDON

Ideally, the concluding remarks for an anthology such as this should integrate the diverse findings of the works represented by highlighting new insights into the subject gained through the collected evidence presented in the volume. Presumably, this knowledge may then be used to predict future developments and guide the formulation of policy. Such an ideal, however, assumes that more agreement than disagreement will be found. This is not necessarily so with the present study of gentrification and revitalization. Our knowledge of the causal processes involved is still imperfect and our ability to make reasoned judgements about future developments and trends is thus limited.

EXTENT OF REVITALIZATION

Our final comments properly begin therefore with some caveats. For example, the popular press has a tendency to discuss gentrification as if it is an irresistable new wave that will wash over neighborhood after neighborhood (see, for example, and article by David Blum, in *Newsweek,* January 3 1983). This will not necessarily occur. Middle- and upper-class revitalization is still a risk-taking enterprise involving substantial investment. This investment includes large amounts of time and energy as well as money. Only a limited proportion of the population is able to make such an investment and, of course, not all who are able are so inclined. Not everyone is attracted to the idea of restoring inner-city housing. Recent migration data indicate that the majority of home-buying adults still prefer suburban homes (U.S. Department of Housing and Urban Development 1979).

Such popular magazine statements as "We are driving out the poor and middle class, making cities the exclusive domain of the young and affluent" (*Newsweek* 3 January 1983) profoundly over-estimate the extent of gentrification. To spur such massive gentrification the city would again have to become the place of choice for middle-class residence. As noted in the introduction, a substantial "back to the city" movement has yet to occur. As of the mid-1980s the counter-movement toward central-city residences remains more symbolic than substantive.

Moreover, the number of neighborhoods in any city that have advantageous location, access to amenities, and housing of historic or architectural appeal are distinctly in the minority. The major question for the 1980s, thus, is whether revitalization will spread beyond neighborhoods meeting the architectural, construction, and accessibility criteria found in the gentrifying areas of the 1970s. Urban revitalization will not seriously affect the physical structure, economic health, or social diversity of the city per se if its effects are restricted to one or two neighborhoods of young professionals.

Historically, prognostications regarding American cities have a disturbing tendency to prove highly inaccurate. (The classic example is the fascinating 1937 National Resource Committee report, *Our Cities: Their Role in the National Economy*). However, while soothsaying may be of limited utility, there is real value in discussing the possible role in the city's future to be played by differing factors, particularly the demographic, economic, and lifestyle variables.

DEMOGRAPHIC CHANGES

Probably the most predictable indicators are the demographic variables. The last census clearly documented the continuing decline in the number of young children per family while the young adult and elderly populations increased rapidly (Current Population Report 1981). The changing population composition of urban households, with more of both the young adults and the elderly living in separate households, means increasing demand for housing. This demand is compounded by the fact that the baby boom generation is now of the home-buying age.

Housing construction, however, has clearly not kept pace with demand. The year 1982, for example, witnessed the lowest number of new housing starts in two decades. The slowdown in new suburban housing starts, in turn, has meant greater interest in existing residences. Some of the increased demand for existing city housing would thus have occurred even without any changes in lifestyle favoring city residence. Since there is generally an inverse relationship between the level of new housing construction and the rate of investment in older city housing (U.S. Department of Housing and Urban Development 1981, p. 14), existing areas thus should profit from the gap between new housing starts and households seeking housing.

ECONOMIC CHANGES

There are also economic factors favoring increased gentrification. Economic considerations, particularly for single persons, or two-income households, are now likely to encourage central-city location more than in the past. This is a major change. For most of the years following the Second World War, both the cost of purchasing new housing and the availability of mortgage money clearly favored the suburbs. It was easiest for new homeowners to obtain minimum down-payment, low-interest loans on suburban housing. And, in spite of critics of suburbia, suburban housing met the needs of families with young children (Gans 1967). And, if a suburban move necessitated a long commute to work, the cost of gasoline was cheap.

Today the situation is altered: Commuting costs, which were judged prior to 1973 almost solely in terms of time, have soared. Suburban-home heating and cooling expenses can also be a problem. Couples are rediscovering what their grandparents knew: heating and/or cooling a two-story townhouse with buildings on either side is usually far more efficient than heating/cooling a single-story, free-standing ranch style home. Higher energy and maintenance costs are particularly onerous when both partners work, leaving the home empty during large portions of the work week.

Revitalizing existing city housing is often less expensive than new construction on the suburban periphery. This is especially so if the new urban homeowners are willing to put in sweat equity by doing rehabilitation and upgrading work themselves. Equally important, mortgage funds for city properties are also available as a result of changes in government loan policies. Lending institutions are also increasingly realizing that revitalizing areas are good investment risks.

LIFESTYLE CHANGES

Changes in living patterns, as well as increasing numbers of people of home-buying age and fewer new housing starts, have increased pressure on the available housing stock. Compared to earlier decades, young adults now more often live independently, and there are rising rates of separation and divorce. Where in the past there would have been one household of several people, today there is often a fragmentation into several households, each containing fewer people. During the 1970s these and other factors resulted in a 9 percent increase in persons but a 25 percent increase in number of households (Current Population Reports 1980, p.1).

As noted previously, many of these new households are not two-children families. Young couples are postponing, and sometimes side-stepping, matrimony. Childbearing, likewise, is being postponed in favor of dual incomes and freer lifestyles. Inner-city living tends to have a disproportionate appeal to such nontraditional households. The potential quality of the housing units, the greater convenience to central-city work, and the availability of adult amenities associated with the central city all dovetail well with the needs of the increasingly numerous, smaller adult-oriented households. At the same time, one of the most serious liabilities of central-city neighborhoods, the quality of the public schools, is of no direct significance to childless households.

The post-Second World War American ideal of a suburban home, your own backyard, good schools, and so on, neatly met the needs of that era's many new families with children. However, this option has far less appeal for contemporary two-career childfree or single-child couples. Lesser availability of parks for children and low-quality city schools do not weigh as heavily on such urbanites. The availability of cultural and social activities and shorter commuter time are more important. Establishments and activities that low-density suburban areas tend to ban, such as late-night bars, restaurants, and grocery stores, are just the things that give high-density urban areas their vitality. A growing number of middle-class urbanites are in effect voting for sticking with their image of good city life. As discussed in the introduction, these new urbanites are not returning from the suburbs: they are simply staying in the city.

There also seems to be a change in esthetic values. After several decades in which newer homes were more or less automatically judged better, there appears to be a reversal of values among some buyers. Older, restorable houses are in demand. Residences in regenerating neighborhoods frequently have design and construction features that appeal to young, upwardly mobile adults—a group whose tastes often outrun their pocketbooks. Where else but in older neighborhoods can one obtain a first home possessing hardwood floors and trim, fireplaces built with tile and/or marble, lath and plaster walls, leaded glass windows, and oak doors with solid brass trim? True, much of this charm may be under several coats of paint at the time the house is purchased, but the basic quality is present. To central-city afficionados, the ones to be pitied are those suburbanites who remain trapped in outlying postwar suburban housing developments.

THE NONGENTRY

So far, our discussion has focused largely on the urban middle- and upper-middle-class population, which is popularly glamorized by the terms "urban pioneers" and "urban gentry." We have said little about groups traditionally associated with central-city residence who do not have the above characteristics: minorities, the poor, ethnic groups, the working class, and the elderly. What is happening with these populations? What will happen to their neighborhoods? What are likely to be the consequences of neighborhood revitalization for these groups? Will any or all of these groups benefit from neighborhood upgrading? Or will they be the victim of urban displacement, pushed out by more affluent newcomers?

Discussion of the impact and consequences of neighborhood regeneration for these less affluent, central-city residents should begin by distinguishing between the physical changes in the neighborhood and their social consequences for the residents. The physical consequences of neighborhood reinvestment and regeneration are generally quite positive. Homes are refurbished, housing code violations decrease, and property values rise. There is little dispute that upgraded areas are better maintained physically, more prosperous, and even cleaner than they were prior to undergoing change. The tax base—and resulting city revenues—increase. In short, this is the warp and woof of which city mayors' dreams are woven.

In some instances the transformation of an area from decaying slum to upgrading community has been dramatic. In other neighborhoods the major development has been continuity: the absence of obvious change while surrounding areas have gone through deterioration and abandonment. The continued vitality of such areas as Boston's North End or Chicago's Hyde Park sharply set them apart from their less successful urban brethren.

DISPLACEMENT

However, physical regeneration can have social costs. While there is widespread agreement that it is desirable for neighborhoods to improve and upgrade themselves, there is less agreement as to how to evaluate this change if it also causes some displacement of incumbent residents. While in the abstract, almost everyone favors the idea of the city's being composed of all social classes, some spokespersons for the poor and/or minorities are far less favorable to the concept if it means middle-class newcomers moving into "their" central-city neighborhoods. They are concerned—and rightly—that middle-class revitalization will result in lower-class displacement (Hartman 1979; National Urban Coalition 1981).

There are very real problems of displacement. However, they need to be placed in perspective (Cybriwsky 1978). The impression is sometimes given that prior to the onset of revitalization, both a neighborhood and its population were stable and secure. The implied suggestion is that, were it not for revitalization, the area would again return to stability. Both these assumptions are usually inaccurate. While displacement of long-term residents does occur (see chaps. 3, 4, 8, and 9), the media portrait as for example, *Sixty Minutes* (CBS 29 November 1981) of typical potential displacees having lived in the area for years is usually inaccurate. Actually potential displacees are most often poorer renters: and poorer renters as a group have high mobility. For example, national data document that nearly 40 percent of all renters move at least once a year (Palen 1979). For the poor who rent from month to month rather than under long-term leases, the moves are far more frequent. Areas undergoing revitalization are thus likely to have had high levels of residential mobility prior to renewal activity. Such areas frequently also have high levels of displacement through eviction and building abandonment. The trick is to determine how much additional displacement in upgrading areas is the result of renovation. Displacement due to revitalization is a relatively recent concern; for most inner-city neighborhoods, displacement is still more likely to come from the more common problem of decline and disinvestment.

As Ernest Burgess noted over half a century ago, neighborhood stability has never been a characteristic of the American city (Burgess 1924). More affluent populations have long occupied the areas they considered most prestigious. Within inner-city neighborhoods the poor were at first displaced by industrial plants and the commercial expansion of the Central Business District (CBD) and, following the Second World War, by urban renewal and expressways. These processes have often been undesirable, but it is impossible to deny their impact on changing central-city neighborhoods (Greer 1965).

What is new is not that the poor and other vulnerable groups (such as female-headed households and minorities) are being displaced, but that they are now sometimes being replaced by middle-class newcomers living in the same—albeit upgraded— homes. What is unique is that the old neighborhoods are not being torn down and replaced with something else, be it office, high rise, expressway, or public housing. Also, change today does not automatically mean that everything and everyone existing in the area must go.

Change may be a long-standing central-city pattern, but some of these changes are definitely not going to benefit existing residents. The difficult task is determining what should be done about displacement. Some see the only response as "resisting forced displacement, in whatever form it takes" (Hartman 1981, p. 6). The problem is that, while righteous stances offer emotional benefits to external protagonists, they provide less usable aid to those faced with displacement.

Fortunately, the increasing body of data on displacement indicates that the phenomenon is not as pervasive as first feared (see the introduction); nor are its consequences always negative (U.S. Department of Housing and Urban Development 1981). While displacement has high emotional costs for some displacees, others find moving has long term benefits. Research findings (as opposed to public statements) usually indicate that, as expressed by HUD, "the majority of displacees move to nearby housing of comparable or better quality, but they pay more after moving" (1981, p. 57). Displacees are also generally more satisfied with their new homes and neighborhoods after moving (Schill and Nathan forthcoming).

None of the above, however, changes the fact that some families and individuals who do not want to move are forced to do so, and that some of these people will be worse off because of the move. A central problem of the theory of "the common good" is that there is often a minority that does not benefit. If the goal is the good of the majority, and if the city as a whole profits from refurbished housing, increased tax base, and maintaining a middle-class population, then it is inevitable that in this process some poorer householders are going to be displaced. The question is not whether this will occur, but rather whether the costs are too high using the criterion of the common good. Of course, there is also the question of whose good is the common good. This is a matter where judgments differ, often sharply. (see for example, chap. 3).

Some places have enacted legislation designed directly to encourage rapid rates of gentrification. In a number of cities, for example, tax incentives have been provided to people willing to purchase and renovate older homes in designated areas. Similar legislation designed to encourage historic preservation has also stimulated some gentrification.

On the other hand, legislation ostensibly designed to stop forced, involuntary displacement has also been enacted in some areas, but with mixed results. Zeitz (1979, pp. 80-83) discusses the situation in Washington, D.C., in the middle and late 1970s. Groups opposed to gentrification lobbied with the District of Columbia City Council, in 1975, to introduce a bill that would limit housing speculation. "The bill pertains to houses that have been sold more than once within a certain time period. Therefore the shorter the time a house is owned the higher the tax ... on profit" (Zeitz 1979, p. 81). The bill was designed to prevent the speculative phenomenon known as "flipping" (or purchase and rapid resale of homes) and, in so doing, to prevent eviction and displacement of incumbent residents.

Opponents of the bill, representing almost all facets of the local real estate industry, formed the Washington Residential Development Coalition (WRDC) to fight passage of the bill. After a long delay, a revised bill was passed in the summer of 1978. In the process, "the entire displacement issue was either lost or avoided. Under the revised bill ... the builder would merely warrantee the basic heating, electrical, and plumbing systems on his newly remodeled house and thus would be entirely exempt from this tax" (p. 83). In reality, then, legislation ostensibly designed to ameliorate displacement actually helped to accelerate the process.

NEIGHBORHOOD UPGRADING

As indicated in chapter 7, the long-term future of the city as a place of residence lies more with what happens in the numerous so-called grey areas of the city. The projection of most city neighborhoods as potential targets for gentrification is as unrealistic as it would be undesirable. Most central-city neighborhoods were originally constructed to house working class populations. Housing in such areas may be solid but it is not especially physically attractive or architecturally unique. Nonetheless, unless revitalization and upgrading occurs in such ordinary neighborhoods, the revitalization movement will be of limited impact.

Implied in the above are the suppositions that the bulk of the changes will come from internal or incumbent upgrading, and that as a consequence the neighborhood will not change in social-class composition. How realistic is it to assume increasing vitality in ordinary central-city neighborhoods? Is there any real possibility that the post-Second World War pattern of disinvestment will be arrested, or reversed?

As chapter 7 indicates, because attention has been focused elsewhere the comparative data are thin. However, based on a limited number of studies and Palen's research findings, we would like to hazard a few hypotheses as to likely future patterns. The reader is warned that we are largely projecting from Palen's Milwaukee findings, which may or may not apply nationally.

In comparison with gentrifying neighborhoods, the housing in adjacent communities is usually not architecturally distinctive, but neither is it as severely deteriorated. Structures often need cosmetic work but are basically sound. Property values generally tend to be low with housing usually undervalued, particularly in comparison with nearby revitalizing neighborhoods. It is the undervalued nature of this housing that may well spark upgrading and revitalization in grey areas.

The rapid appreciation of property values has placed gentrifying neighborhoods beyond the price range of most middle-class homebuyers while newer suburban housing also remains expensive. Exisiting city neighborhoods near gentrifying areas are by contrast still affordable.

The literature, by implicitly dividing the neighborhood residents either into old-timer incumbents or newcomer gentrifiers, overlooks the fact that newcomers need not be gentrifiers. Central-city neighborhoods—particularly ethnic neighborhoods—have retained their character over time, not through lack of population turnover, but through the social and ethnic compatibility of those moving out and those moving in. It is not lack of household change that distinguishes such areas, but the type of household change.

Young couples moving into older working-class neighborhoods are more likely to be employed in white-collar jobs than were their parents, but their white-collar jobs are lower paying white-collar jobs. Also they enter the neighborhood individually rather than as a block by block reinvasion as is often the pattern in gentrifying areas. Therefore their entry does not significantly change the socioeconomic status of the neighborhood. Newcomers of moderate income may be younger and more white-collar than incumbent residents, but the newcomers are not gentrifiers. Equally important the new inmovers are not perceived as being different or a threat. This, plus the gradual nature of the process, suggests that displacement is usually not a problem.

Residential change is less visible to a casual passerby in an established neighborhood than in a gentrified one. Because those moving into existing neighborhoods are of moderate income they are far less likely to engage in visible restoration work. They are more likely to work on their homes than old-timers, but the work is more likely to be repairs and maintenance. Signs of upgrading are real but often gradual and undramatic. Rather than gas lights and major external restoration, improvements are more likely to run toward new paint, gutter replacement, or a flower bed. To save costs, most of the work is likely to be done by the owner or a local handyman. Building permits, which raise assessments, are rarely obtained.

Because of its comparatively slow and unspectacular character, the revitalization of ordinary central-city neighborhoods has thus far escaped widespread attention. They can perhaps best be thought of not as stable traditional neighborhoods but as areas in transition. While they are undergoing some of the same reinvestment phenomena as gentrifying areas, the pace is slower and the change less visible. If this continues, there is a possibility that cities will not further evolve toward the residence only of those with wealth or on welfare, but rather could be developing into a new, more complex form where residents are indeed socially, racially, and economically diverse. As noted earlier, predictions as to urban change have always been risky.

CONCLUSION

Ultimately, our reading of these most recent contributions reaffirms the notion that gentrification, like so many other aspects of social change, is in large measure a political-economic issue. Wherever inner-city neighborhood change occurs—be it Manhattan or Milwaukee, Sydney or Vancouver—vested interests are threatened and dispute and disagreement become the norm. As inner-city space again becomes a scarce resource and the object of competition, policies will be developed that shape the competitive process.

In the study of phenomena such as gentrification, our best effort can only be directed toward understanding who decides what these policies will be and who does, and does not, benefit from the policies implemented. Inevitably, where class interests become so salient, ideology enters into the analysis and the achievement of true understanding of the causal processes involved becomes no mean task.

REFERENCES

Blum, D. 1979. The evils of gentrification. *Newsweek*, 3 January 1983.
Burgess, E. W. 1924. The growth of the city: An introduction to a research project. *Publications of the American Sociological Society*. 18: 85-97.

Current Population Reports. 1980. *Household and family characteristics,* P-20 (March). Washington, D.C.: U.S. Government Printing Office.

Current Population Reports. 1981. *Population profile of the United States: 1980,* P-20. Washington, D.C.: U.S. Government Printing Office.

Cybriwsky, R. 1978. Social aspects of neighborhood change. *Annals of Associaton of American Geographers* 48 (March):17-33.

Gans, H. J. 1967. *The Levittowners.* New York: Vintage.

Greer, S. 1965. *Urban renewal in American Cities.* Indianapolis, Ind.: Bobbs-Merrill.

Hartman, C. 1979. Comment on neighborhood revitalization and displacement: A review of the evidence. *Journal of the American Planning Association* 45 (October).

———. 1981. Commentary. *Urbanism Past and Present* 6 (Summer/Fall): 28.

National Resource Committee. 1937. *Our cities: Their role in the national economy.* Washington, D.C.: U.S. Government Printing Office.

National Urban Coalition. 1981. *Displacement: City neighborhoods in transition* (October). Washington, D.C.

Palen, J. J. 1979. The urban nexus: Toward the year 2000. In *Societal Growth,* ed. Amos Hawley, pp. 141-56. New York: Free Press.

Schill, M. H., and Nathan, R. P. Forthcoming. *Neighborhood reinvestment and displacement.* Albany, N.Y.: State University of New York.

U.S. Department of Housing and Urban Development. 1979. Signs of urban vitality and of distress: Citizen views on the quality of urban life. *Occasional Papers in Housing and Community Affairs* 4 (July): 21-49.

U.S. Department of Housing and Urban Development. 1981. *Residential displacement: An update* (October), Office of Policy Development and Research. Washington, D.C.: U.S. Government Printing Office.

Zeitz, E. 1979. *Private urban renewal.* Lexington, Mass.: Lexington Books.

Index

DATE DUE

JUN 01 2011		
JUN 01 2011		
FEB 15 2012		
FEB 18 2013		
FEB 16 2015		
FEB 15 2019		
GAYLORD		PRINTED IN U.S.A.